From Iron Rice Bowl to Informalization

Frank W. Pierce Memorial Lectureship and Conference Series

Number 14

From Iron Rice Bowl to Informalization

Markets, Workers, and the State in a Changing China

Sarosh Kuruvilla, Ching Kwan Lee, and Mary E. Gallagher

ILR Press
an imprint of Cornell University Press
Ithaca and London

We thank the ILR school and Jay Waks for funding to hold the international conference that formed the basis for this book.

First published 2011 by Cornell University Press

Printed in the United States of America

Library of Congress Cataloging-in-Publication Data

From iron rice bowl to informalization : markets, workers, and the state in a changing China / [edited by] Sarosh Kuruvilla, Ching Kwan Lee, and Mary E. Gallagher.
p. cm.
Includes bibliographical references and index.
ISBN 978-0-8014-5024-2 (cloth : alk. paper)
1. Industrial relations—China. 2. Labor policy—China. 3. Labor market—China. 4. Informal sector (Economics)—China. I. Kuruvilla, Sarosh. II. Lee, Ching Kwan. III. Gallagher, Mary Elizabeth, 1969– IV. Title.

HD8736.5.F76 2011
331.10951—dc22 2011007723

Cornell University Press strives to use environmentally responsible suppliers and materials to the fullest extent possible in the publishing of its books. Such materials include vegetable-based, low-VOC inks and acid-free papers that are recycled, totally chlorine-free, or partly composed of nonwood fibers. For further information, visit our website at www.cornellpress.cornell.edu.

Cloth printing 10 9 8 7 6 5 4 3 2 1

Contents

1. Introduction and Argument 1
Mary E. Gallagher, Ching Kwan Lee, and Sarosh Kuruvilla

Part I. Informalization and the State

2. The Informalization of the Chinese Labor Market 17
Albert Park and Fang Cai

3. Legislating Harmony: Labor Law Reform in Contemporary China 36
Mary E. Gallagher and Baohua Dong

4. Social Policy and Public Opinion in an Age of Insecurity 61
Mark W. Frazier

Part II. Transformation of Employment Relations in Industries

5. Enterprise Reform and Wage Movements in Chinese Oil Fields and Refineries 83
Kun-Chin Lin

6. The Paradox of Labor Force Dualism and State-Labor-Capital Relations in the Chinese Automobile Industry 107
Lu Zhang

7. Permanent Temporariness in the Chinese Construction Industry 138
Sarah Swider

Part III: Unions, Nongovernmental Organizations, and Workers

8. "Where There Are Workers, There Should Be Trade Unions": Union Organizing in the Era of Growing Informal Employment 157
Mingwei Liu

9. The Anti-Solidarity Machine?: Labor Nongovernmental Organizations in China 173
Ching Kwan Lee and Yuan Shen

10. Conclusion 188
Mary E. Gallagher, Sarosh Kuruvilla, and Ching Kwan Lee

Notes 193

References 205

Notes on Contributors 223

Index 227

From Iron Rice Bowl to Informalization

Chapter 1

Introduction and Argument

Mary E. Gallagher, Ching Kwan Lee, and Sarosh Kuruvilla

Thirty years of economic reform in China have produced economic growth unparalleled in terms of its speed, longevity, and geographical spread (Brandt and Rawski 2008); has lifted millions out of poverty; and has increased GDP per capita from $224 in 1978 to $3,180 in 2008. It has also transformed China from one of the most egalitarian societies in the world to one of the most unequal societies in Asia (Lee and Selden 2008). The accumulated result of economic liberalization has been a drastic shift in the structure of employment. The following stylized statistics sum up the extent of transformation. In the thirty years since reform, the urban workforce increased from 95.1 million to 293.5 million, employment in the state sector decreased from 78.3 to 21.9 percent of the total urban employment, and employment in the foreign-invested sector (including Hong Kong-, Macao-, and Taiwan-invested enterprises) grew from zero to 15.8 million. Agriculture, which accounted for the largest share of employment in 1978 (69.9 percent), now accounts for only 40.8 percent of total employment, whereas industry and services have seen gains (employment in industry increased from 17.1 to 26.8 percent, and service sector employment rose from 12.2 to 32.4 percent during the same period; National Bureau of Statistics of China 2008). Perhaps the most dramatic instance of change in the structure of employment has been the rapid increase in the number of migrant workers. Although precise numbers are difficult to obtain, the National Bureau of Statistics estimated the number of migrant workers to be 225 million by the end of 2008.

The transformation in the Chinese employment structure is broadly consistent (migrant worker numbers excepted) with similar transformations in fast developing Asian countries (Kuruvilla 1996) What concerns us in this volume is the changed nature of employment security, in particular the recent and marked trend toward the informalization of employment. By *informal,* we mean employment that is not stable or secure, that lacks a written agreement or contract, and that does not provide social insurance or benefits. A plethora of terms are used in the available literature to characterize these workers, such as *casual workers, contingent workers, temporary workers,* and *agency/dispatch workers.* The last category, agency/dispatch workers (*laowu paiqian*), which is also referred to in some industries as labor leasing or co-employment, is a typical triangular employment relationship in which workers employed by a contractor are sent to work at client firms on a contingent basis. A recent estimate finds that the use of agency workers in China has become widespread (they now number more than 75 million), accounting for a hefty 15 percent of the employed population in the industry and service sectors (Wong 2009). The growth of these employment arrangements that reduce employment security, divide workers into core formal workers and peripheral subcontracted agents, and reduce the provision of welfare benefits has been significant over the past two decades.

Although precise estimates of the degree of informal employment in China is difficult to obtain, Albert Park and Fang Cai (chap. 2 in this volume), who have carefully and comprehensively mined a variety of official data sources, suggest that an astounding 39 percent of urban employment is informal! This estimate roughly accords with other studies that have tried to determine the degree of informalization. Variation among the studies is often related to different definitions of *informal work.* Cai Fang, Du Yang, and Wang Meiyan (2008) use the China Urban Labor Survey data to estimate the number of informal workers. The survey is unusual because it surveys migrant workers as well. These data show that 18.5 percent of local residents (belonging to urban areas) were informally employed in 2001 and that this number grew to 32.6 percent by 2005. For migrants, 72.5 percent were employed informally in 2001, increasing to 84.3 percent in 2005. Of those surveyed, 54 percent of local urban residents had access to pension benefits in 2005, but only 2.1 percent of migrants had similar access. Till Barninghausen, Yuenli Liu, Zhiping Zhang, and Rainer Sauerborn (2007) suggest that there are 140 million informal workers, whereas Fang Lee Cooke (2008) opines that informal employment accounts for more than 50 percent of urban workers. It is beyond the scope of this chapter to reconcile these disparate estimates on the number of informal workers; nevertheless, it is clear that the number of workers in informal employment is large and growing. A conservative estimate of 107 million informally employed workers means that approximately 35 percent of the urban workforce is working without employment contracts, a figure close to the estimate here by Park and Cai.

Our analysis in this volume also bolsters the argument that efforts by the state to protect labor through legal reform over the last ten years, culminating in the new laws of 2007, may have had the unintended consequence of driving even more employment "underground" into the informal arena. There is, in fact, some early evidence that the number of "dispatched workers" (agency workers) increased sharply after the enactment of the Labor Contract Law (Chung 2010), and Lu Zhang (chap. 6 in this volume) provides some case evidence of this phenomenon in the auto industry.

The sectoral distribution of informal employment is also alarming. Rather than being relegated to the margins of the economy and the secondary labor market, informal employment is increasingly a permanent part of corporate strategy both in state-owned monopolies and in large private and state-owned companies, as demonstrated by Kun-Chin Lin (chap. 5 in this volume) for the state-owned oil industry and Lu Zhang (chap. 6) for the automobile industry. The prevalence of informal labor has a longer history in secondary competitive industries such as construction, as shown by Sarah Swider (chap. 7). Although the proportion of informal employment may be lower in the state and collectively owned sectors, it abounds in the private sector, where it now exceeds 80 percent of all workers. Women, the very young, the very old, migrants, and unskilled workers tend to be highly represented in informal employment.

The chapters in this volume allow us to explore this new and unfolding dynamic in the China labor scene at the end of the first decade of the new millennium, thirty years after reforms were initiated. The focus here is understanding the strategies and responses of the Chinese state, workers, and civil society to informalization. The timing is crucial. In 2007, the state enacted far-reaching changes in labor law designed to improve employment security and alleviate labor discontent. This was done against a background of state efforts to educate workers about their rights and to channel labor discontent into the legal realm. These political and legal reforms were predicated on the assumption that Chinese labor markets were becoming tighter as migrant flows from the inland provinces slowed and the population of young workers declined due to the effects of the one-child policy. As the Chinese economy recovers from the global financial crisis of 2008, these trends have reappeared. Labor activism by workers and civil society organizations is building as workers take advantage of the changed policy environment and the growing perception of labor shortages in coastal manufacturing centers.

Argument

Within a generation, urban China has moved from a highly protected "iron rice bowl" system that guaranteed workers in state-owned enterprises (SOEs) and collectively owned enterprises permanent employment, cradle-to-grave benefits, and a relatively high degree of equality to a market-determined employment system characterized by considerable variation in wages, welfare provision, labor law enforcement, and job security. The growing field of China labor studies offers rich documentation of this change in working conditions, enterprise and managerial reforms, systems of remuneration, patterns of labor disputes and unrest, class and gender relations, unemployment, and labor law reforms (Chan 2001; Gallagher 2002, 2005a, 2005b; Lee 1998a, 1998b, 1999, 2007; Ngai 2005; O'Leary 1998; Sheehan 1998; Solinger 2002; Taylor, Chang, and Li 2003; Warner 2000).

In our view, the transition from a socialist system to a contract-based employment system is now largely complete, even though some SOEs are still mired in restructuring, bankruptcy disputes still trigger workers' mobilization, and large numbers of migrant workers are still battling for their rights to get paid or compensated for industrial injuries. Chinese workers and the Chinese state, like their counterparts elsewhere in the world, now have to confront the challenges of movable capital and its continuing demands for labor flexibility. In our view, the growth of informal employment is but the latest step in a downward slide of workers' employment security since the introduction of the labor contract system in 1986. The transition from state socialism meant the unraveling of permanent employment to create a system of contractual employment; the current period, however, is witnessing an accelerated transition into precarious informal employment, despite a legislative efforts by the Chinese government to provide some degree of formal employment security.

Precarious labor, as many sociological and labor studies have maintained, has spread like wildfire in an age of neoliberalism and flexible accumulation, afflicting the advanced industrialized world no less than the underdeveloped economies (Barley and Kunda 2004; Houseman 2001; Kalleberg 2000; Lautsch 2002; Mangan 2000; Vosko 2006). Although the competitive pressure of global capitalism may be commonly felt, we argue that national circumstances and institutions dictate the extent and effects of increased flexibility and informalization. It is to these national circumstances and institutions that we turn to next.

What explains the dramatic increase in informal employment in China? The journey from an employment system characterized by the iron rice bowl to one of extreme insecurity and informalization unfolded in three phases. In the early stages of reform, the process of denationalization—the withdrawal of the state from the management of SOEs and the consequent increase in managerial autonomy, diversity of ownership (the advent of private and foreign ownership), and joint ventures that are a "recombination of ownership" (Gallagher 2004, 20)—spawned the increasing variation in employment practices and increasing insecurity of employment, particularly as SOEs sought increased labor flexibility to be more competitive. Regional and local government responses to the flexibility strategies pursued by employers were quite varied. To attract foreign investment, local governments emphasized firm autonomy and labor flexibility at the expense of workers' jobs, rights, safety, and health. In contrast, political and social pressures led several local governments to attempt to protect employment by preventing SOEs from laying off workers. Thus, the initial movement toward informalization was uneven. Many foreign-invested enterprises whose competitive advantage stemmed from low costs and labor-intensive production made use of the growing pool of migrant laborers who were willing to work without formal contracts, whereas SOEs began to lay off workers as part of their restructuring efforts.

The second phase commenced with the 1995 National Labor Law, seen by many as a decisive step by the state to the "smash the iron rice bowl" to accelerate the restructuring process. The labor law, which permits short-term contracts, was seen as a solution to two different problems. First, formal labor contracts would improve the efficiency of SOEs by ending the practice of lifetime employment. Second, the legalization of labor relations through a written employment contract would reduce the potential for labor exploitation, particularly in the nonstate sectors, by enshrining "certain rights and responsibilities." But, as many have noted, the formalization of the labor contract system had two consequences. First, it helped facilitate and legitimize the massive layoffs that began in 1997 in the SOE sector (Gallagher 2005b) because termination of employment at the end of the contract was done using the language of the law. By the end of the restructuring period, over 30 million SOE workers had lost their jobs. Second, the inability of the state legal system to adequately enforce the law, coupled with the growing number of migrant workers, produced a decisive increase in informalization. Eli Friedman and Ching Kwan Lee (2010, 509) cite a report stating that by 2007 only 50 percent of all enterprises had signed contracts with their employees (the rate among nonstate firms was as little as 20 percent) and only 12.5 percent of migrant workers had signed contracts. Notably, fully 60–70 percent of those written contracts were for a period of one year or less. The large percentage of workers outside the formal system has critical implications for the social insurance system. As Friedman and Lee (2010) suggest, workers not only lost their right to employment but also lost key social insurance benefits tied to employment, such as pensions and medical insurance.

If the intention of the 1995 labor law was to smash the iron rice bowl system, it succeeded beyond the wildest dreams of the state. The law has intensified the process of "commodification and casualization of labor" (Friedman and Lee 2010, 510), in which the labor flexibility strategies of employers interact with the lack of effective regulation and result in plummeting labor standards. The remarkable growth in the variety of labor standards violations and declining working conditions (long hours, low pay, lack of social insurance, wage arrears, poor safety and health, illegal firings, and so forth) during the 1995–2007 period has been well documented by a new generation of China labor scholars. A recent story in the Chinese media is particularly illustrative of informalization. A migrant worker cut his chest in front of the government occupational disease protection agency to prove that he had silicosis, in response to the refusal by the agency to provide treatment because he could not show that he had a formal labor contract with his employer (Ke 2009; Dan 2009). The lack of a formal contract therefore, not only meets employers need for flexibility but also permits them to employ workers without contributing toward social insurance and labor protection, which have become only gradually institutionalized since 2000.

In this context, it is important to note that many of these informal jobs are rather permanent (e.g., workers in mines or call centers), as documented by Lu Zhang, who writes about the growing class of "temporary workers in permanent jobs" (2008, 28). There is also a surprising degree of "formalization of informalization" as seen through the thriving labor dispatch agencies and vocational schools throughout China that serve as large subcontracting organizations for the delivery of informal workers to Chinese manufacturing and service industries. These subcontracted workers are linked to an employment agency but are often denied key benefits. Student workers linked to vocational schools are often paid less than the minimum wage and subject to harsh conditions. Although the 2008 Labor Contract Law increased protections for subcontracted workers, firms continue to invent new informal arrangements to evade the new, more onerous protections of the new laws.

The third phase is the current period in which the Chinese government has attempted to rein in the rampant use of extremely short-term contracts, labor subcontracting, and disregard for the legal restrictions on informal labor. In 2007, growing concern about these issues led to the passage of three new major labor laws. The most consequential is the new Labor Contract Law, which came into effect in 2008 and was intended to shore up labor protections against the trend of diminishing employment security through new restrictions on short-term contracts and labor subcontracting, much to the consternation of employers (Mary Gallagher and Dong Baohua, chap. 3 in this volume). Globally, many countries (from France and Australia to Argentina and nations in South Africa and southern Africa) have in recent years reformed their labor laws to accommodate or fight against the labor market effects of global competition (Cook 2007; Cooper and Ellem 2008; Hall 2006; Howell 2009; Theron 2004), but the response of China has been more drastic (at least on paper). Implementation of such a sensitive and conflict-ridden law is bound to be uneven, but the law signals the severity of the challenge of informalization as well as the palpable desire of the Chinese government to preserve social stability at a time when employment has become increasingly insecure for the vast working public. In a similar vein, Mark Frazier (chap. 4) suggests that pension reform is another instance of a counter-countermovement initiated by the state to mitigate the socially destabilizing effects of employment insecurity.

Aside from central and local government actions, there is also evidence of a countermovement from below. Workers in many parts of China are beginning to take the initiative, as demonstrated in June 2010 by a wave of wildcat strikes at foreign-invested enterprises in the Chinese coastal development zones. New grassroots organizations have emerged in response to workers' new vulnerability and needs. Labor-oriented nongovernmental organizations (NGOs) operate in a semi-legal zone under the watchful eyes of the Chinese state. Their activities, of varying scope, nature, and effects, have created pressures on the official unions to innovate. Mingwei Liu (chap. 8 in this volume) shows how some local and regional unions are experimenting with new forms of union organizing and bargaining in localities where small and medium-size enterprises concentrate. But, as Ching Kwan Lee and Yuan Shen (chap. 9) suggest, these unofficial NGOs face inherent structural limitations in defending workers' interests, as do the local unions and the official All-China Federation of Trade Unions (ACFTU). Whereas grassroots unions are often hamstrung by the ACFTU political dependence on the Chinese Communist Party (CCP) and beholden to the pro-investment inclination of the local governments, labor NGOs are subjected to the twin pressures of political cooptation and commercialization.

In a nutshell, this volume elucidates the evolving tensions among these three forces—the market (exemplified by the strategies of SOE and private employers), the state (the central government and the CCP, as well as local governments), and the Chinese working class (including workers, unions, and NGOs)—as these are reconfigured by the rising tide of informalization, a global phenomenon from which China is not exempt. Whether informalization will increase or decrease depends on the interplay both within and among these three actors. Each of three sections of this volume focuses on one of these three actors, their interests, and strategies.

State Imperatives

Part I begins with Albert Park and Fang Cai's (chap. 2) careful estimation of the extent of informalization among Chinese workers. This is followed by two chapters that focus on the response of the state to the changes in employment structures and the decline in employment security. We interpret the Chinese central government response as an effort to balance the competing logics of economic competitiveness, social justice and protection, and continued political control. These chapters illustrate the state response in two critical issues for labor: the introduction of the new Labor Contract Law and the reform of the pension system, both of which are likely to have far-reaching consequences for the future of employment security in China.

State interests are heterogeneous everywhere, and the Chinese state is no exception. Particularly germane to our argument regarding the future of informalization is the differential interests of the central government and party, on the one hand, and the provincial and local governments, on the other. Economic reform provided the basis for a divergence of interests and objectives at different levels within the Chinese state. As Eli Friedman and Ching-Kwan Lee note, "by allowing revenue retention at the provincial and local levels, fiscal decentralization has generated vested interests amongst local officials to nurture a pro-capital climate favorable to foreign investors to privatize previously collectively owned or state owned enterprises, and to allow a weak regulatory regime for labor" (2010, 515). On the other hand, the central government also benefits from this decentralization because of the increased taxation and revenue remission from the localities and provinces back to the center. Thus, in a roundabout way the central government is complicit in the weak regulation of labor.

The plethora of labor legislation passed since 1994 was never uniformly implemented in the provinces and localities. Furthermore, when workers responded to the urgings of the central state to use the law to redress their grievances rather than turning to the streets, the workers often found the local judiciary and administrative institutions unresponsive. Dependent on the local state for funding and appointments, these institutions were vested in the continued economic growth of the locality and protected capital from the full effects of the strict enforcement of labor standards. It is the discontent fostered by the violation of labor rights, the rising informalization of employment, and the widespread dissatisfaction with existing dispute resolution machinery that drove the state toward greater protections.

Mary Gallagher and Baohua Dong (chap. 3) elucidate the varying interests within the Chinese state on the legislative process that produced in 2007 three major new employment laws in China: the Employment Promotion Law, the Labor Dispute Mediation and Arbitration Law, and the Labor Contract Law. Focusing on the most important of these laws, the Labor Contract Law, Gallagher and Dong demonstrate that intragovernment disagreement about how much protection the law should bestow to workers led to widely divergent draft laws and much internal and public discussion about the direction of Chinese labor relations. Whereas there was strong support from the central CCP leadership for enhanced workers' rights and security, other government ministries and actors opposed action that would reduce economic growth, raise employers' costs, and potentially reduce overall employment. These internal conflicts were brought out into the open during the period of public comment on the law in March 2006. The National People's Congress received more than 191,000 comments on the draft law, far exceeding the commentary on any other recent law. In particular, the detailed comments by foreign business associations operating in China received extensive media attention domestically and abroad. The final version of the draft law reflected these internal disagreements as well as the broader public concerns articulated during the period of public comment. The version of the law that was passed contained significantly watered-down provisions that were designed to strengthen the role of the trade union in determining workplace rules. Internal disagreements within the state therefore ensured that the law has enough strategic ambiguities that allow for flexible implementation.

Gallagher and Dong suggest that, despite the significant increase in workers' protections offered by the law, the implementation and enforcement of the Labor Contract Law are weakening its overall impact. This brings to light internal disagreements between the central and local governments. That its adoption coincided, unfortunately, with the onset of the global financial crisis (the law took effect in January 2008) has meant less central government support for legislation that threatens economic growth and increases employers' operating costs. Local governments in coastal manufacturing centers have already taken their own regulatory measures that aim to dilute the impact of the law on their local economies. In addition, as firms attempted to cut costs to survive, local governments looked the other way at a time when they were expected to do more to implement the law. On the other hand, the very rapid rise in labor disputes since the passage of the law indicate that Chinese workers are taking these new protections seriously and invoking these newly bestowed rights in the courts and on the streets.

The effect of the law on curbing informalization is therefore uncertain, especially given the lack of local government support for laws that may slow growth, reduce employment, and potentially drive investors to other localities that are less vigilant in enforcement of laws and regulations. Although the law did increase the obligations of employers that rely on labor subcontracting (agency workers), the use of subcontracted laborers has increased since its passage as employers look for ways to evade the new restrictions and heavier obligations of formal employment (CECC 2009). Recent evidence suggests a significant expansion in informal employment after 2007, close to almost 20 million jobs as Lu Zhang notes in chapter 6 in this volume.

The division and tension between the interests of the central and local governments has been an enduring feature of the Chinese political system since the pre-reform era. Even if top leaders prioritize the pursuit of social justice and protections, local officials often develop their own imperatives shaped by local interests and pressures. Mark Frazier (chap. 4) discusses changes in pension policy in China and also reflects on the tensions and gaps among central government policy, local government countermeasures, and the increasing societal pressure from below to close those gaps. In the wake of declining employment security, Chinese workers now place the burden of social insurance on the state as a citizenship right. He shows that pension reform in China, although linked to SOE restructuring and its consequent retrenchment, did not lead to the scaling back of pension commitments. On the contrary, the Chinese state embarked on an ambitious program to offer pension benefits to all urban workers. More recently, these welfare initiatives have even begun to cover migrant workers in cities and some rural residents as well. The central state initiative, however, was left to the local municipal governments to implement. Moving from a system that based pension entitlements at the state-owned workplace to a system that pooled and centralized pension benefits at the city level has empowered and enriched many municipal governments. Resistant to calls for further centralization at the provincial level, these governments have used increased pension payments to expand pension programs to more workers. This new system has also increased incentives for local governments to enforce labor laws that require firms to pay into pension pooling funds. Frazier notes that workers too are highly cognizant of their pension rights, with an increasing proportion of labor disputes stemming from the nonpayment or underpayment of social insurance benefits. Through survey research and focus groups interviews, Frazier links the expansion of the pension program to the correct state assessment that Chinese workers feel that they have a citizenship right to pensions. For older workers in particular, there is a strong expectation that this right is a responsibility of the state to ensure.

As with Gallagher and Dong, Frazier's analysis of the competing interests of labor policy reform demonstrates interesting dynamics among central government policymakers, local government implementers, and the Chinese workers who are the recipients and subjects of changing policy. Local government officials are often at odds with the central government over the nature and direction of a guiding policy. With ample advantages in local knowledge and expert ability to manipulate information, these local agents of the central state are, however, increasingly responsive to the bottom-up demands, challenges, and the rising expectations of urban citizens.

Employer Strategies

Part II presents industry-focused studies of the growth in the informal labor force and the contradictory effects of this labor force in the workplace. Together these studies show that, for both state and private employers, the introduction of temporary, casual, and informal workers is an essential aspect of their business strategy to cut costs and subordinate workers by creating a hierarchy of rewards and by fragmenting the collective interests of workers. For workers, this movement aggravates their class vulnerability to employers while also occasionally prompting collective rebellion.

Kun-Chin Lin (chap. 5) focuses on the oil and natural gas industry, highlighting the growing variation in wages within the industry. This is a nationally important industry whose employees have hitherto been protected from market vicissitudes and have traditionally enjoyed higher wages and benefits than average in China. A state-sponsored restructuring brought about a formal split in the industry, dividing it into a core of highly profitable companies and a slew of noncore service companies. The noncore companies work under semi-feudal relationships to the core companies, and a duality of increased wages and job security at the core firms versus a high degree of employment uncertainty in the noncore firms was formed. State-owned capital is the original driving force behind this transformation, although it has since been fueled by international capital, which has invested in the core, publicly listed firms.

The story is broadly similar in the automobile industry studied by Lu Zhang (chap. 6), who argues that informalization induces both fragmentation and resistance by workers. On the one hand, Zhang notes how intensive competition among foreign auto manufacturers in the 1990 has driven Chinese automobile assemblers to reduce costs and increase flexibility by replacing permanent workers with informal labor (both temporary and agency workers) on very short-term contracts, creating a core-periphery distinction within the firms by engaging large numbers of casual workers. One the other hand, Zhang uncovers increased resistance to these management strategies from both formal contract workers and temporary workers. Whereas formal workers exercise their limited bargaining power on the shop floor through the politics of noncooperation, informal workers resort to disruptive forms of everyday resistance, such as sabotage, slowdown, absenteeism, and, in some cases, wildcat strikes. Invoking Karl Polanyi's famous double movement thesis, Zhang writes about how the effect of the current deregulation of the labor market in China is provoking a corresponding "countermovement." The resistance highlighted by Zhang in the automobile industry is quite common among migrant workers and has compelled grassroots unions to innovate lest their disgruntlement gets out of control.

No industry epitomizes the precarious nature of employment security more than the construction industry, investigated here by Sarah Swider (chap. 7). Like the auto and oil industries, the Chinese construction industry (a large contributor to employment) also underwent a shift from the iron rice bowl system to a more segmented one through successive waves of regulation and deregulation. The current industry is characterized by differing modes of employment, varying from formalized contract employment to completely informal part-time hiring. The mode of mediated employment analyzed in by Swider highlights the peculiar working conditions of a segment of Chinese migrant workers in the construction industry. On the one hand, this mode of employment prevents migrants from becoming integrated into the cities where they work, thus denying them the basic rights of citizenship in China. One the other hand, their long engagement on city job sites gradually weakens their ties to their home and family, impacting the one source of permanence in their lives. Thus, they remain suspended, without rights, without citizenship, in permanent temporariness. In many ways, the construction industry is the one place (apart from household labor) that appears completely outside the labor law in terms of enforcement.

Thus, these studies of three diverse industries show a remarkable uniformity in the business and employment strategies of state, domestic, and foreign capital. But they also hint at a discernible growing activism among workers.

Informal Worker Organizations and Incorporation

Growing insecurity of employment is spawning new modes of formal and informal worker organizations and incorporation by the local states. Part III presents empirical studies of two institutions with the potential to protect workers from informalization. These are labor NGOs and new grassroots unions formed in response to the needs and demands of workers whose precarious worlds no longer conform to those assumed by conventional unions. This development in China is parallel to the rise and growth of worker centers in the United States and elsewhere (Fine 2006; Gordon 2007; Milkman 2006), catering to the needs of immigrant and day laborers, as traditional bureaucratic and workplace-based unions decline in membership and leverage.

Ching Kwan Lee and Yuan Shen (chap. 9) analyze Chinese labor NGOs and find that these nonprofit grassroots organizations are usually founded by former workers or professionals, such as academics and journalists, and that they are funded by international foundations and civil society groups. Under Chinese labor laws, which recognize the official ACFTU as the sole trade union representing Chinese workers, these NGOs cannot recruit members and cannot be registered as unions. Even registration as nonprofit social organizations is extremely difficult due to the stringent financial and official sponsorship requirements imposed by the Ministry of Civil Affairs.

Thanks to the pivotal political and economic significance of labor compliance, the Chinese government has a keen interest in controlling, if not outright suppressing, these organizations. Local governments, however, are eager to take advantage of the services of labor NGOs—recreation, education, health care, counseling, and legal aid—to the migrant population and often tolerate their existence while the national security apparatus keeps a watchful eye over them. Professing the goals of pursuing "solidarity," "cooperation," "rights protection," and "integration of migrant workers," these NGOs are nevertheless subjected to twin structural pressures coming from the state and the market. First, through cooptation and state patronage, some labor NGOs have grown in size and reputation, providing services needed by workers and endorsed by the state. Second, some NGOs have become an industry, tapping into the global market to fund their independent research, monitoring of factories, or promotion of human rights. When their organizational goals are displaced from promoting workers' solidarity and rights to the survival and expansion of the NGOs and organizers' careers, market demands rather than workers needs dictate what NGOs do. NGOs that have so far avoided the twin traps of cooptation and commercialization are struggling to find the political space and the financial wherewithal to survive.

The growth of informal worker organizations has spurred some grassroots branches of the official ACFTU to innovate. Mingwei Liu (chap. 8) depicts institutional innovations by regional unions that have organized community unions (*shequ gonghui*), market unions (*shichang gonghui*), office building unions (*bangonglou gonghui*), and union associations covering multiple workplaces in areas with high concentration of small enterprises and individually owned businesses. Notwithstanding the weak bargaining power of these union associations, they are often active in other functions, including organizing migrant workers, providing welfare and entertainment, and representing workers in labor dispute mediation. Liu is cautiously optimistic that the relative independence of these unions from employers, in contrast to the employer-dominated enterprise unions, suggests some potential for a more independent role in representing labor in the future.

Even more progressive are regional unions that choose to organize union associations by trade (*hangye gonghui lianhehui*) and engage in local trade-level negotiations of wages and other employment conditions. This type of unions emerges only when several favorable conditions are found: a high concentration of enterprises in one industry in the locality, tight labor market conditions, government support for more aggressive unions, and energetic unionists. In a small town in Zhejiang where the water pump industry dominates, the Zeguo Water Pump Industry Union Association (ZWPIU) was established under the regional unions and included all twenty-two enterprise unions as its branches. With the strong support of the local party and local government, this union association successfully bargained for an industrywide wage agreement that raised workers' wages and reduced labor conflicts and mobility, to the satisfaction of all the parties concerned.

That local governments acquiesce to the existence of labor NGOs and encourage grassroots unions to form union associations indicates these authorities desire that stability be maintained under the aggravated employment insecurity and uneven effectiveness of the labor laws. Hence, many local governments have even been making efforts to gradually extend their welfare provisions to migrant workers.

Conclusion

In many ways, China is not unique in the transformations of the employment system that it is experiencing. Consistent with the experiences of both European and Asian nations under the effects of globalization (see Kuruvilla and Erickson 2002), employer strategies have spawned increased informalization and inequality in all countries. And consistent with the experience of those countries, the state is responding in a variety of ways to the growing instability created by declining employment security. Uniquely, however, the response of the Chinese state has been typified by an aggressive legislative effort, with a vast and ongoing rewriting of the major labor laws and social welfare laws. This aggressive effort, however, has been partially undermined by the inability and unwillingness of city and local governments (particularly during the current financial crisis) to implement these laws. Thus, the state finds itself caught between the competing logics of economic competitiveness and social justice and protection, while attempting to maintain its political control. Chinese workers, unions, and civil society, although subject to state attempts at direct control or incorporation, have responded with experimental strategies, organizational innovation, and more recently direct action (at this time, a wave of wildcat strikes have occurred in southern China, where workers in Honda parts factories are demanding the right to elect independent trade union leaders). They have found, in both the state responses and the employer strategies, some limited opportunities for a countermovement. In the short term, however, the evidence from this volume and our evaluation of these dynamics point to the continued growth of informalization of the Chinese workforce until there are enough incentives to alter the behavior of the national and local governments, the employers, and the workers and their advocates.

Part I

Informalization and the State

Chapter 2

The Informalization of the Chinese Labor Market

Albert Park and Fang Cai

The Puzzle of the "Missing" Workers of China

The Chinese urban labor market has experienced a substantial diversification of ownership types. The most striking change was the rapid decline of the state and collective sectors. According to official employment statistics published in the *China Statistical Yearbooks,* employment in the state-owned enterprise (SOE) sector, which had actually grown in absolute number from 1990 to 1994, fell at a mean annual rate of 6.4 percent from 1995 to 2000, a total loss of 31.5 million jobs or 15 percent of the urban labor force. The collective sector, which had begun declining earlier, had already shed over 10 percent of the 1990 workforce by 1995 and shrank by another 13.8 percent per year from 1995 to 2000, losing 16.5 million jobs over the period. As a share of all urban employment, jobs in the state and collective sectors fell from 76 percent in 1995 to 41 percent in 2000 to only 27 percent in 2005 (fig. 2.1 and table 2.1). The employment shares of other enterprise ownership forms, especially private ownership and limited liability corporations, increased significantly.

Remarkably, the category of workers that witnessed the fastest rate of increase was "other" workers (see fig. 2.1 and table 2.1). Starting from a low base in 1995, "other" workers increased by 24 percent per year and accounted for 39 percent of all workers in 2002 and 2003, before declining to 36 percent in 2005. These workers can be described as "missing" workers because they reflect differences in the numbers of workers reported using different statistical reporting systems. It is our estimate that *all* of these workers are working informally.

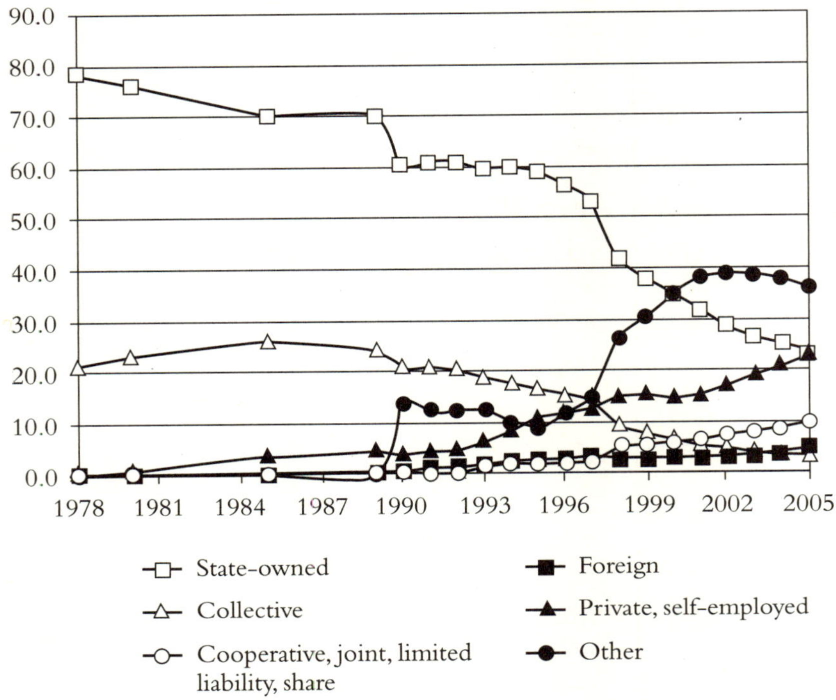

Figure 2.1 Employment by employer type, 1978–2005.
Source: National Bureau of Statistics of China ([NBSS] 1979–2006).

Total urban employment comes from the annual labor force surveys conducted by the National Bureau of Statistics (NBS), which are sample surveys of the entire population. The number of workers employed by different ownership types comes from the Comprehensive Labor Statistics Reporting System (CLSRS), which is based on direct reporting by all independent accounting units to the NBS each year. Estimates of self-employed workers are based on the number of such individuals registered with the Industrial and Commercial Bureau. The difference between the larger number calculated from the labor force surveys and the smaller number of workers reported by the CLSRS is precisely the "other" category reported in table 2.1. In principle, this category should include unreported urban workers and unregistered informal employment, including undocumented work by migrants in urban areas. The large increase in the number of such workers thus suggests that informal urban employment may have increased significantly in recent years.

The Chinese annual population and labor force surveys also are likely to undercount migrants working in urban areas. According to the 2000 census,

TABLE 2.1
Urban employment by employer type, 1978–2005

Year	State-owned	Collective	Cooperative	Joint ownership	Limited liability corporation	Share-holding corporation	Private enterprise	Foreign and joint venture	Self-employed	Other
1978	78%	22%	—	—	—	—	—	—	—	—
1980	76	23	—	—	—	—	—	—	1%	—
1985	70	26	—	—	—	—	—	—	4	—
1989	70	24	—	1%	—	—	—	—	5	—
1990	61	21	—	1	—	—	—	—	4	14%
1991	61	21	—	—	—	—	—	1%	4	13
1992	61	20	—	—	—	—	1%	1	4	13
1993	60	19	—	—	—	1%	1	2	5	13
1994	60	18	—	—	—	2	2	2	7	10
1995	59	17	—	—	—	2	3	3	8	9
1996	56	15	—	—	—	2	3	3	9	12
1997	53	14	—	—	—	2	4	3	9	15
1998	42	9	1%	—	2%	2	5	3	10	26
1999	38	8	1	—	3	2	5	3	11	31
2000	35	6	1	—	3	2	5	3	9	35
2001	32	5	1	—	4	2	6	3	9	38
2002	29	5	1	—	4	2	8	3	9	39
2003	27	4	1	—	5	2	10	3	9	39
2004	25	3	1	—	5	2	11	4	10	38
2005	24	3	1	—	6	3	13	5	10	36

which did a better job counting long-term migrants, 10.8 percent of the Chinese population did not have a resident permit for the location in which they resided (authors' calculations from 0.95 percent census sample). This compares to just 4.8 percent of the population estimated to be long-term migrants in 1999 and 7.7 percent in 2003, based on the annual population change surveys, which use the same sampling system as the labor force surveys (see National Bureau of Statistics of China [NBS], 2000 and 2004). To the extent that migrants are undercounted in estimates of the total workforce and are likely to work in the informal sector, our estimates of informal employment are likely to be underestimates of actual informal employment.

But what is the precise definition of *informal*? The International Labour Organization (ILO) emphasizes that informal employment is characterized by a lack of stability or security. Although there is no universally agreed-on definition, such employment is often temporary, lacks a formal contract, and does not provide social insurance benefits or other worker protections. Based on this definition, the very fact that workers are not registered by their employers itself is *prima facia* evidence that such work is informal because it means that the workers lack formal contracts and that there is little if any monitoring of how such workers are treated by their employers (e.g., job termination, social insurance, and working conditions). If "missing" workers and self-employed workers are counted as informal workers, the share of the urban workforce that was employed informally reached 46 percent in 2005.

In this chapter, we employ different definitions of *informal employment,* depending on the data being examined. In most cases, the focus is on workers who lack formal labor contracts and on explaining the "missing" workers already described. It should be recognized, however, that such simple definitions of *informality* aggregate many different types of workers. Some of these workers could be employed full-time on a relatively long-term basis with high job security but have limited participation in social insurance programs. Some may work part-time or for very short periods of time with no security or sense of control. Some are self-employed.

The rise of informal employment represents a fundamental change in the Chinese labor market that brings new policy challenges; to date, however, the phenomenon has received remarkably scant attention. Here we examine multiple sources of evidence to quantify and characterize the extent of informal employment in urban China. We then discuss its potential policy implications. The increase in "missing" workers raises two immediate questions: (1) Why are these workers not being reported by their employers? (2) Who are these workers, and what kinds of work are they performing? If economic activity can be hidden from authorities, then taxes can be avoided. This is especially true for the self-employed or for small private enterprises. But even large registered work units may have strong incentives to avoid signing labor contracts with workers and not report such employees. First, by hiring informally enterprises can avoid paying the required payroll taxes for pensions, unemployment insurance, medical insurance, and work injuries, which can be quite costly. For example, in Shanghai in 2004, the regular employer contribution rate for these types of insurance totaled 36.5 percent of wages.[1] Hiring workers on an informal basis also gives employers greater flexibility to adjust the size of the labor force to respond to changes in economic conditions.

Who are the "missing" workers? We offer four complementary explanations for which types of individuals may be "missing" workers. First, many "missing" workers may be working in the rapidly growing but very imperfectly monitored private sector, including unregistered self-employed workers. Second, many of the "missing" workers could be rural migrant workers, who are often hired on an informal basis or are self-employed and anxious to evade taxes. Third, laid-off or retired workers are likely to be hired on an informal temporary basis, even if they are employed by government departments or SOEs. Fourth, recent adjustments by China to its GDP statistics suggest that many of the "missing" workers may work in the tertiary sector, where economic output has been significantly underestimated.

The Size of the Private Sector

One reason for the confusion about who employs "missing" workers is that little summary information on employer characteristics is available from the labor force surveys. If these surveys contained more detailed information about employers and if the NBS released the tabulated results, then the nature of underreporting might be clearer. Starting in 2001, the *China Labor Statistical Yearbooks* did begin reporting limited information on the share of labor engaged in different types of employment (table 2.2). In 2004, 40 percent of urban laborers worked in "urban units," which appears to include all categories of workers reported in table 2.1 except for private enterprises, the self-employed, and "other." Multiplying this share by the total number of urban workers (265 million) yields an estimated 106 million workers in urban units. This turns out to be fairly close to the 111 million reported for "unit employment" by the CLSRS.

What is interesting about table 2.2 is that, in contrast to table 2.1, in which 38 percent of workers are "missing," it accounts for nearly all labor not working in urban units. Nearly all these individuals turn out to be working in the private sector! In 2004, 3.7 percent of urban workers worked in township and village enterprises (TVEs), 14.0 percent worked in agriculture, 18.8 percent were

TABLE 2.2
Urban employment by employer type, 2001–2004 (%)

Year	Urban units	TVEs	Agriculture	Private-sector employee	Private employer (*Geti*)	Self-employed	Others	Total
2001	49.2	3.7	12.6	12.0	6.1	13.6	2.8	100.0
2002	44.1	3.7	17.2	14.1	6.2	12.8	1.8	100.0
2003	44.0	3.8	15.0	15.5	6.5	13.3	2.0	100.0
2004	40.2	3.7	14.0	18.8	7.1	13.4	2.9	100.0

Sources: NBS and MOLSS (2002, 2003, 2004, 2005).

private sector employees, 7.1 percent were private employers, and 13.4 percent were self-employed. Only 2.9 percent were described as "other." By 2004, nearly all TVEs had been privatized. If we categorize agriculture as a type of self-employment, then 53 percent of employment was in the private sector, which is much higher than the 21 percent of workers reported in the private sector or self-employed categories in table 2.1.[2] Some categories of urban workers captured in the labor force survey appear to have been missed completely by the CLSRS. For instance, although TVEs and agriculture, which accounted for 17.7 percent of urban workers in 2004, may not even seem like urban employment categories, in fact many suburban-urban districts do have substantial populations with rural residence permits (*hukou*). Even if these two rural categories are excluded, however, according to table 2.2 the private sector would still account for 48 percent of employment. If we subtract the 11 percent of workers reported to be working in private enterprises by the CLSRS in 2004, who are presumably formally employed, then 37–42 percent of the labor force worked informally in the private sector. Thus, one major source of increasing informalization is the rapid growth of the unregulated private sector (Cook 2008; Du, Cai, and Wang 2007).

Migrant Workers

To get a better sense of the extent to which unreported migrant workers might explain the large "other" category, we used the 2000 census data to examine the correlation between the share of unreported workers and the share of migrant workers in different sectors (table 2.3). The census data document all individuals living in their current place of residence for at least six months in the past year and provides information on the type and place of each individual's residence permit (*hukou*), as well as each person's occupation and sector of employment (but not ownership type). The first column of table 2.3 presents

TABLE 2.3
Employment comparison: CLSRS and census by sector, 2000

	CLSRS total (thousands)	Census sample total (thousands)	"Missing" workers (%)	Urban residents (thousands)	R-U migrants (thousands)	Census sample migrants (%)
Total	144,594	171,734	18.8	118,660	29,319	17.1
Mining and quarrying	5,975	4,060	−32.0	3,416	316	7.8
Manufacturing	39,334	56,739	44.2	36,745	13,774	24.3
Electricity, gas, and water	2,838	3,398	19.7	2,610	153	4.5
Construction	8,598	10,680	24.2	6,777	2,674	25.0
Geological prospecting	1,102	695	−36.9	553	32	4.6
Transport and telecommunications	8,588	12,220	42.3	9,506	1,096	9.0
Trade and catering services	29,338	35,271	20.2	23,561	7,091	20.1
Finance and insurance	3,268	3,450	5.6	2,389	147	4.3
Real estate trade	1,004	1,533	52.7	1,014	143	9.3
Social services	9,220	11,680	26.7	7,653	2,132	18.3
Health and social welfare	4,881	5,530	13.3	4,201	311	5.6
Education, culture, and broadcasting	15,658	11,189	−28.5	8,446	719	6.4
Science and polytechnical services	1,745	1,379	−21.0	1,025	35	2.5
Government and social organizations	11,038	12,483	13.1	9,676	587	4.7
Others	2,007	1,427	−28.9	1,088	109	7.6

Sources: National Bureau of Statistics [NBS] and Ministry of Labor and Social Security [MOLSS] (2001); 0.95% Sample Data of 5th National Census Long Form.

Notes: In the census data, *employment* denotes those who are 15 years old and above. Employment in agricultural sector is not included. CLSRS, Comprehensive Labor Statistics Reporting System; R-U, rural-urban.

estimates of urban total employment and its distribution among sectors based on the CLSRS. The second column contains corresponding figures from the 0.95 percent sample of the 2000 Census Long Form, which is consistent with the labor force surveys in terms of definition, and shows 18.8 percent more employment than that reported by the CLSRS. The last column is the proportion of migrant workers in various sectors based on the census sample data. Migrants account for 17.1 percent of all workers.

Although the overall share of migrants is similar to the overall share of "missing" workers, this does not necessarily mean that most of the "missing" workers are migrants; for instance, employers could be reporting migrants in the CLSRS but not reporting urban residents. Nevertheless, the correlation between "missing" and migrant shares across sectors is approximately 0.5, suggesting that unreported migrants account for a significant share of the missing workers or that migrants and urban unreported workers are concentrated in the same informal sectors.

More recently, the *China Labor Statistical Yearbook* began providing statistics on the number of rural workers, presumably primarily rural migrants, reported by urban units.[3] In 2004, rural workers accounted for 11.9 percent of workers reported by urban units (6.4 percent of all workers), an increase from 10.4 percent in 2003. The share was smallest in state-owned units (4.5 percent) and larger in collective and other ownership units (17.8 and 24.6 percent). It is likely to have been still larger in the private sector. These data do suggest that some migrants are, in fact, being reported by their employers but that most migrants are undocumented or "missing." As noted earlier, it is also likely that the annual labor force surveys undercount migrants in their total employment estimates.

Informal Employment of Urban Permanent Residents

Another source of information on the ownership types of employers is the urban household survey data collected annually by NBS. Table 2.4 presents the employment shares for state (including government), collective, and nonpublic enterprises from 1988 to 2001 for six provinces. The share of individuals employed in the state and collective sectors falls from 93 percent in 1995 to 81 percent in 2001. In figure 2.2, we present a more detailed breakdown for 2003 using the entire national urban household survey sample. As we see in the figure, 71 percent of workers are employed in the state and collective sectors, with 39.2 percent working in state-owned enterprises, 25.6 in government organizations, and 7.0 in collective enterprises. Overall, these numbers suggest much higher levels of state and collective sector employment and a slower

TABLE 2.4
Urban employment by employer type from NBS survey of urban households in six provinces, 1988–2001

Year	*N*	State-owned unit (%)	Urban collective (%)	Nonpublic enterprises (%)
1988	6,087	74.5	24.8	0.7
1989	5,615	75.2	23.8	1.0
1990	6,194	76.0	22.9	1.1
1991	6,225	77.2	21.8	1.1
1992	7,853	76.5	20.7	2.8
1993	7,017	76.1	20.4	3.5
1994	6,752	76.8	17.8	5.4
1995	6,830	78.0	15.4	6.6
1996	6,651	78.5	15.2	6.4
1997	6,641	77.4	14.9	7.7
1998	6,331	76.8	14.4	8.8
1999	6,094	74.0	14.0	12.0
2000	6,197	72.6	11.3	16.1
2001	5,404	70.2	10.9	19.0

Source: Authors calculations using NBS urban household survey data.
Notes: The six provinces surveyed were Beijing, Liaoning, Zhejiang, Guangdong, Shaanxi, and Sichuan. NBS, National Bureau of Statistics of China.

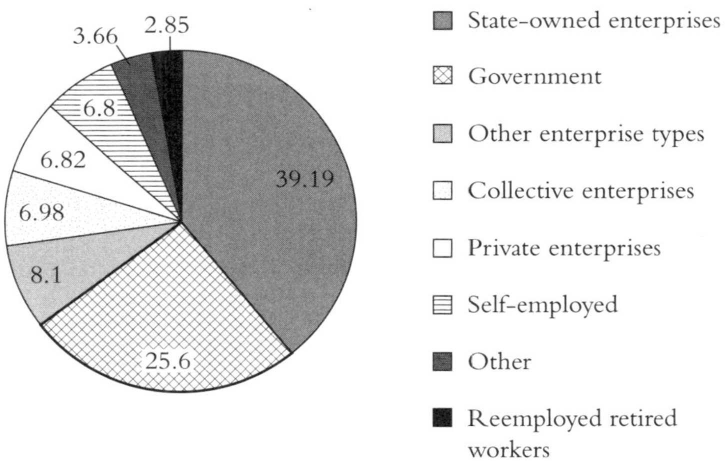

Figure 2.2 Employer ownership types, 2003 (%)
Source: NBS Urban Household Survey, 2003.

rate of decline in such employment than the statistics reported in tables 2.1 and 2.2.

Of course, the main reason for the discrepancy between the structure of ownership calculated from the urban household survey data and other sources is that the urban household survey excludes nearly all migrants from its sample.[4]

But this alone is insufficient to explain the difference. Even if we assume that migrants make up 20 percent of urban employment, that no migrants work in the state or collective sector, and that the NBS urban household survey is a representative sample of urban permanent residents, this would imply that 56 percent of urban laborers worked in the state and collective sectors in 2003, much higher than the 31 percent in table 2.1, based on the numbers reported by the CLSRS. A 2002 Ministry of Labor survey of 75,000 households in sixty-six cities focusing on urban permanent residents also found that 60 percent of workers were employed in the state or collective sectors.

Part of the difference could be that the NBS urban household survey is not fully representative due to refusal bias. For example, highly mobile workers who change jobs frequently may be less likely to stay in the NBS survey sample, which requires that self-recorded diaries be kept year-round. In a much larger urban household survey conducted by NBS in 2004 using a brief survey instrument, information on 340,000 employed workers was obtained; of these, 57 percent worked in the state or collective sectors, which is considerably lower than the 71 percent calculated using the 2003 urban household survey.[5] Adjusting for the lack of data on migrants as before produces a revised estimate that at least 46 percent of urban workers are employed in the state or collective sectors.

One way of reconciling the remaining gap between the survey-based and unit reporting–based estimates of the share of the urban labor force in the state and collective sectors is to allow for the possibility that the state and collective sectors hired urban permanent residents informally and did not register them as employees when reporting to the CLSRS. This explanation accords well with field interviews that found that many laid-off workers were hired by government agencies or SOEs informally, for example on a part-time basis with wages paid per hour worked and no labor contract or social insurance provided. To avoid the payroll charges for social insurance programs, many enterprises have a natural incentive to hire as many workers as possible on an informal basis. Shanghai pioneered a type of retiree employment called *xiebao* in which laid-off workers could take new jobs in other firms without formal contracts while their former SOE employer continued to pay social insurance contributions until retirement (Gallagher 2009). This model spread to other cities in China.

Another common way in which enterprises and other formal work units hire workers informally is by contracting with labor service companies to provide temporary workers for specialized labor services (e.g., security and janitorial services) for a contracted period of time. In most instances, the labor service company takes responsibility for the social insurance coverage of such workers, but relatively little is known about the extent to which such companies actually provide such coverage or the number of workers employed in this way.

How common is the informal employment of workers who are urban permanent residents? Yaowu Wu and Fang Cai (2006) examine this question by analyzing survey data collected by the Ministry of Labor and Social Security (MOLSS) in sixty-six cities nationwide at the end of 2002.[6] The survey collected data on over 75,000 households and 189,000 individuals older than sixteen years of age. The MOLSS sixty-six-city survey asked detailed questions about employers, whether there was a labor contract, work conditions, and social insurance coverage. The survey concentrated nearly exclusively on urban permanent residents. The authors applied multiple criteria to determine whether an individual worker was employed informally. The most important categories are those who were self-employed workers, those who worked on a temporary or hourly basis, and those who lacked a labor contract and were not considered officially registered workers.[7] A rich description of the extent of informal employment among different subgroups of the population is provided in table 2.5, taken from Wu and Cai (2006). The authors find that 45 percent of employment was informal in nature. In the state and collective sectors, 22 percent of employment was informal, and in other sectors informal employment was the rule rather than the exception, accounting for 84 percent of workers. Informal employment also was more prevalent among women, among the youngest and oldest workers, and among less educated workers (table 2.5).

If we assume that state- and collective-sector employees reported to the CLSRS were all employed formally (31 percent of all urban labor in 2003) and that 22 percent of total state- and collective-sector employment was informal (which excludes informally employed migrants), then the share of all urban workers employed in the state and collective sectors was 40 percent. We have now made considerable progress in reconciling the different estimates of state- and collective-sector employment from our different sources. These calculations also imply that workers employed informally in the state and collective sectors account for 9 percent of the urban labor force.

In table 2.6, we provide further evidence about the extent of formal and informal employment among different types of employers, drawing on survey data from the China Urban Labor Survey (CULS), conducted in five large and five smaller cities in different regions of China.[8] An advantage of the CULS data is that the survey included migrants in the same cities. The weaknesses of the survey are that it covered only a small number of cities and that it undersamples migrant workers living in dormitories or on worksites, so that it overrepresents self-employed workers. We report the proportion of workers with formal labor contracts, broken down by type of employer. Lacking a labor contract is, of course, only one indicator of informal employment, and it is even possible that

TABLE 2.5
Share of informal and formal employment in urban China, 2002 (%)

	Informal employment	Formal employment
All	45.25	54.75
By sector:		
State and collective	22.87	77.13
New	83.99	16.01
By sex:		
Male	42.16	57.84
Female	49.52	50.48
By age:		
16–24	57.24	42.77
25–34	44.57	55.44
35–44	42.23	57.77
45–54	42.17	57.83
55–64	55.63	44.37
> 65	83.88	16.12
By education level:		
Primary school and below	78.41	21.6
Middle school	62.59	37.41
High school	48.63	51.37
Junior technical school	35.85	64.15
Specialized college	24.55	75.45
College and above	14.75	85.25

Source: Wu and Cai (2006), calculated from the Ministry of Labor and Social Security (MOLSS) sixty-six-city survey.

some permanent workers might not recall signing an official document and so might report not having a labor contract even though they are permanently employed. We find that 62 percent of urban permanent residents had labor contracts, whereas only 13 percent of migrants had labor contracts. As expected, the share of those with labor contracts was highest in the government and state sectors. It was very low in the private sector, with 27 percent of urban permanent residents and only 7 percent of migrants having labor contracts. Across all ownership categories, the share of workers with labor contracts was lower for migrants than for urban permanent residents. And, because over 85 percent of migrants were in the private sector, where the prevalence of labor contracts was lowest, the rate of informal employment among all migrants was extremely high. This also suggests that "missing" migrants and "missing" private-sector workers are likely to have a large overlap.

We can compare the CULS findings with results of analysis of the 2005 population mini-census, which has more complete coverage of cities and migrants and which conveniently includes a question on whether workers have labor contracts (table 2.7). Compared to the CULS, the proportion of workers with contracts is lower for local residents (49.9 vs. 62 percent) and much higher for migrants (31.2 percent for rural migrants and 61.9 percent for urban

TABLE 2.6
Workers with formal labor contracts, 2005 (%)

	Urban permanent residents		Migrants	
	Has labor contract	Employment share	Has labor contract	Employment share
All	61.8		12.9	
Government	76.2	0.236	43.2	0.030
State-owned	88.5	0.306	55.6	0.032
Collective	71.7	0.052	47.4	0.016
Private	26.5	0.281	7.0	0.847
Foreign and joint ventures	74.9	0.057	57.8	0.023
Other	28.4	0.068	18.0	0.054

Source: Wave 2 of the China Urban Labor Survey, conducted by the Chinese Academy of Social Sciences in 2005.
Note: City samples for five large and five small cities given equal weight.

TABLE 2.7
Composition of urban informal workforce, 2005 (%)

	Local residents	Rural migrants	Urban migrants	All
Cities	56.3	31.9	64.2	51.8
Townships	39.6	29.2	49.9	38.4
All urban	49.9	31.2	61.9	47.4

Source: Institute of Population and Labor Economics (IPLE) Project Group (2007), analyzing the 2005 1% mini-census data.
Note: Informal employment includes the self-employed and those without formal contracts.

migrants, compared to 13 percent overall in the CULS). These differences probably reflect the fact that the CULS oversamples large cities and self-employed migrants.

The Service Sector

In January 2006, the NBS announced revised GDP estimates based on the results of the economic census undertaken in 2005. The main adjustment was a significant increase by nearly 50 percent of the tertiary, or service, sector in the 2004 GDP. Adjustments for previous years were made back to 1994. As seen in figure 2.3, as a result of the revisions, the share of the tertiary sector in overall GDP increased from 31.9 to 40.7 percent while the shares of the primary and secondary sectors decreased from 15.2 and 52.9 percent to 13.1 and 46.2 percent.

The changes reflect the discovery of previously unrecorded economic activity reported by work units, but they do not necessarily imply that similar adjustments are required for the number of workers in the tertiary sector because the

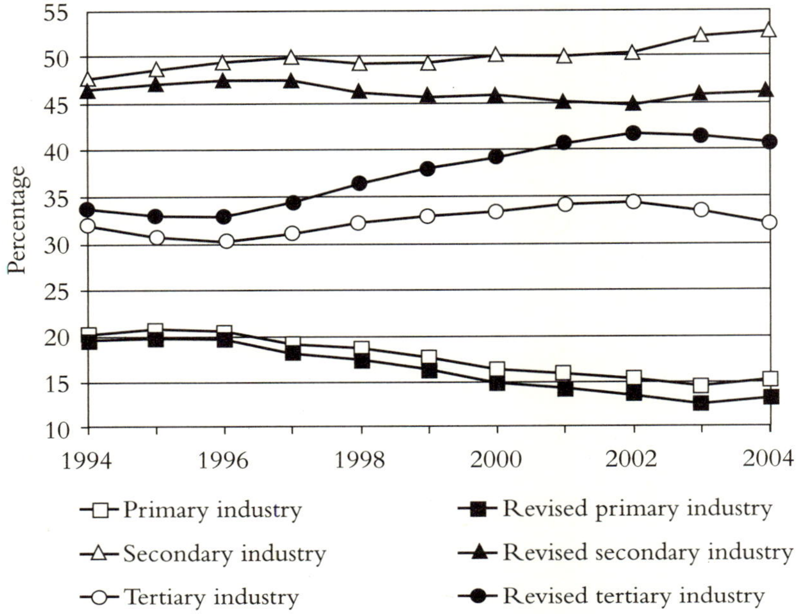

Figure 2.3 Revised GDP statistics, 1994–2004. Revised January 2006.

employment data are based on the labor force surveys, which in principle cover the entire population. Assuming that the adjusted tertiary sector GDP is accurate, then in 2004 33 percent of tertiary-sector activity was not recorded under the previous statistical system (table 2.8). If the output-to-labor ratio of recorded and unrecorded activity is roughly the same, then the same percentage of employees (33 percent) in the tertiary sector was engaged in activity not recorded by the CLSRS. That implies that 76 million workers were involved in tertiary-sector activity in 2004 without the output being recorded, or 19 percent of all those employed in the secondary and tertiary sectors (table 2.8). These calculations do not distinguish between activity in rural areas; however, if most secondary and tertiary activity is in urban areas, it does provide an indication of how many "missing" workers may have been engaged in undocumented tertiary-sector activity.

The 2008 Labor Contract Law

China implemented a new Labor Contract Law on January 1, 2008 (see Mary Gallagher and Baohua Dong, chap. 3 of this volume). The new law strengthened worker protections, building on the earlier labor law passed in 1994, which

TABLE 2.8
Employment implications of 2006 GDP revisions in China

	(1) Unrevised tertiary-sector GDP (billions of yuan)	(2) Revised tertiary-sector GDP[a] (billions of yuan)	(3) "Missing" share of tertiary GDP (%) [(2) − (1)]/(2)	(4) Secondary-sector employment (millions of people)	(5) Tertiary-sector employment (millions of people)	(6) Imputed "missing" share of secondary- and tertiary-sector employment (%) (3) × (5)/[(4) + (5)]
1996	2,043	2,346	0.13	162	179	0.07
1997	2,303	2,717	0.15	165	184	0.08
1998	2,517	3,078	0.18	166	189	0.10
1999	2,704	3,410	0.21	164	192	0.11
2000	2,990	3,894	0.23	162	198	0.13
2001	3,315	4,463	0.26	163	202	0.14
2002	3,607	5,020	0.28	158	211	0.16
2003	3,919	5,632	0.30	161	218	0.18
2004	4,372	6,502	0.33	169	230	0.19

[a] Revised January 2006.

formalized the system of labor contracting (Cai, Du, and Wang 2009). The new law reaffirms the requirement that all workers sign formal contracts and participate in social insurance programs, strengthens rights to collective bargaining, requires severance payments be paid when contracts are not renewed, and, most controversially, requires that workers with ten consecutive years of service, or having signed two consecutive fixed-term contracts with a company, be given a contract without a fixed end date. In recent years, China also has implemented other reforms affecting the treatment of labor, including a comprehensive document to protect the rights of migrant workers (2006), new rules to improve labor dispute resolution, and new social insurance programs to make migrants benefits more portable and to extend health insurance and pension coverage to the self-employed and nonemployed.

Enforcement of the new law could have a large impact on the prevalence of informal employment, but because the change is so recent, there is little empirical evidence on its actual impact. In principle, the requirements of the law for formal labor contracts should increase the share of workers formally employed, but it also could lead firms to be more cautious in hiring workers if it makes firing workers more difficult. Many employers have complained that the new law has increased labor costs and limited employment flexibility. Interviews by the authors of Labor Bureau officials and enterprise managers in 2009 in Shenyang and Shanghai confirm that the new labor law is being enforced and that some workers have filed complaints and lawsuits to protect their rights under the new law. The impact of the global financial crisis in 2008–2009 may have weakened enforcement, however, at least temporarily, as many local governments sought to help firms cope with the crisis.

A small-scale survey directed by the authors of approximately four hundred urban residents in two Chinese cities, Shenyang in the northeast and Shenzhen across the border from Hong Kong, provides some evidence on the enforcement of the new labor law.[9] Results of the survey are summarized in table 2.9. Despite the new law, a surprisingly low percentage of urban resident workers had signed labor contracts in Shenyang (~34 percent) and even fewer migrants had (~19 percent).[10] In Shenzhen, which is famous for its open labor markets, a much higher percentage of both local residents and migrants had signed contracts (~61 and 67 percent, respectively). These results suggest that despite the new labor law a significant proportion of workers are informal, including the self-employed and those working for others without formal contracts, and that enforcement of the new law varies across regions. When asked whether employers were abiding by the new law, respondents were mostly satisfied but with different levels of enthusiasm. The vast majority of respondents felt that enforcement had been satisfactory or very good. Just 16 and 18 percent of local and migrant workers in Shenyang expressed ambivalence or dissatisfaction, and

TABLE 2.9
Compliance with the labor contract law of 2008 (%)

	Local residents		Migrants	
	Shenyang	Shenzhen	Shenyang	Shenzhen
Have you signed labor contract with your working unit or employer for your current job?				
Yes	34.3	60.9	18.8	66.7
No	53.4	14.1	40.6	21.7
Self employment	12.3	25.0	40.6	11.6
Before August of 2008, how well did your employer abide by the labor contract law?				
Very well	46.8	13.0	42.4	26.6
Satisfactory	40.3	68.8	36.4	31.7
Just so-so	10.4	16.9	19.7	35.4
Very poorly	2.6	1.3	1.5	6.3
Currently, how well does your employer abide by the labor contract law?				
Very well	47.5	8.2	46.9	26.7
Satisfactory	34.4	69.9	37.5	30.7
Just so-so	14.8	20.6	15.6	37.3
Very poorly	3.3	1.4	0.0	5.3

Source: Based on surveys of a random sample of fifty local residents and fifty migrant households in each city, conducted by the Institute of Population and Labor Economics, Chinese Academy of Social Sciences (CASS), in March 2009.

22 percent of local workers in Shenzhen. The one group that reported a rather high share of ambivalence or dissatisfaction was migrant workers in Shenzhen (42 percent). Still, the results overall provide some optimism that the new law is being taken seriously. The survey also found no evidence that adherence to the labor law was undermined by the onset of the economic crisis, with assessments of compliance changing little between August 2008 and March 2009, the time of the survey.

Conclusion

Drawing on multiple data sources, we have documented a rapid, unprecedented rise in informal employment in urban China since the mid-1990s. By 2005, 10 percent of urban workers were registered as self-employed and another 36 percent were undocumented—neither reported by employers nor self-registered. We have shown that many of these "missing" workers were probably employed in the private sector and in the service sector. Most migrant workers were employed informally, but a large number of urban permanent residents were also employed informally.

Is informalization of the Chinese labor market a positive or negative development? On the positive side, the informal sector creates jobs and allocates labor based on market principles, thus furthering the development of the labor market. On the negative side, informalization creates new policy challenges because the government is poorly informed about informal economic activities and has difficulty regulating such activity. This makes it hard to enforce protective regulations for workers to ensure safe working environments and fair treatment of workers. It also makes it difficult to develop sustainable social insurance systems that cover most of the population and are adequately financed. Tables 2.10 and 2.11 show that informal workers have very low rates of social insurance coverage compared to formal workers. According to the 2002 MOLSS sixty-six-city survey, the share of informal workers with pension, unemployment, and health insurance were 37, 21, and 14 percent compared to 85, 73, and 62 percent for formal workers (table 2.10). According to the 2005 mini-census, in both cities and towns in China, the majority of citizens lack pensions, health insurance, and unemployment insurance (table 2.11); this is consistent with findings made by Mark Frazier (chap. 4 in this volume). For hired workers with labor contracts, the percentages with pensions, health insurance, and unemployment insurance were 74, 78, and 55, compared to the percentages for hired workers without labor contracts of 20, 27, and 8 percent. Coverage rates for the self-employed and household workers were much lower. These findings suggest that the informalization of the Chinese labor market is exposing urban workers to considerably more uncertainty and risk, creating new vulnerability in the lives of Chinese urban citizens.

Through its new Labor Contract Law and other reforms, the Chinese government has signaled its commitment to improving the security and quality of employment for Chinese workers and to reducing discriminatory policies toward migrants. In addition to enforcing the new labor law, the government has sought to strengthen social insurance and protection systems, for example, by making benefits more available and portable for migrant workers, expanding health insurance and pension programs to urban residents who are not working, and expanding subsidies for the poor through its minimum living standards guarantee (*dibao*) program. In addition, as labor becomes increasingly scarce in

TABLE 2.10
Social insurance coverage under informal and formal employment, 2002 (%)

	Informal workers	Formal workers
Pensions	37.0	84.5
Unemployment	20.7	72.5
Health	14.1	61.5

Source: MOLSS sixty-six-city survey.

TABLE 2.11
Social insurance coverage rates, by location type and formality of employment, 2005 (%)

	Pensions	Health insurance	Unemployment
All	17.9	32.9	13.6
By location:			
Cities	42.4	47.1	23.1
Towns	19.7	32.8	10.2
Rural areas	3.9	25.3	2.7
By employment formality (urban):			
Formal employment			
Hired	73.8	78.0	54.7
Employer	26.6	30.5	10.2
Informal employment			
Hired	19.5	26.6	7.9
Self-employed	11.8	21.2	2.6
Household labor	11.5	19.9	2.4

Source: Institute of Population and Labor Economics Project Group (2007), analyzing 2005 1% mini-census data.

Note: Informal employment includes the self-employed and those without formal contracts.

the years to come, which is inevitable given the rapid growth and changing demographics of China, workers themselves will demand more benefits and security. All these trends point to an attenuation or reversal of the trend toward increasing informalization of the labor force that occurred from the late 1990s to the early 2000s. In fact, the share of "missing" workers in the urban labor force started to decline after 2003.

Although such a change is, of course, appropriate given the higher level of economic development in China, such a reversal is not without its potential challenges and costs. Greater worker protections could increase labor costs and reduce employment, especially of marginal workers, who are most vulnerable. Reducing the incentives for firms to evade the high levels of required social insurance contributions will be difficult and could require that the government lower those requirements and pay a greater share of such costs out of government budgets. Chinese policymakers will undoubtedly continue to pragmatically balance these competing concerns as the economy and labor market continue to develop and mature.

Chapter 3

Legislating Harmony

Labor Law Reform in Contemporary China

Mary E. Gallagher and Baohua Dong

In March 2006, the NPC opened a thirty-day period of public comment on the then-draft Labor Contract Law (passed in June 29, 2007). The increasingly frequent process of public comment on draft laws is touted as part of the NPC "mass line" in legislation, part of its new commitment to public participation and social voice in the legislative drafting process ("Mass Line for Legislation" 2006). In recent years, at least a dozen laws have had a period of public comment during drafting. In the thirty-day period of public comment, the NPC received over 191,000 comments regarding the draft Labor Contract Law. This number far exceeded the comments received about other important and controversial laws. For example, the Property Law, passed in March 2007, received only a little over 11,000 comments. The degree of public attention to the Labor Contract Law is unprecedented in the reform era. The drafting and implementation processes of this new important law are windows into the Chinese rule of law development and its transformation through greater social participation and transparency. They are indications of the increasing contentious state of labor relations in China today as that state attempts to improve working conditions and employment security in the wake of increased public attention to labor abuses, sweatshop conditions, and growing informalization of employment.

By following the process of legislative drafting and subsequent implementation of this new law, we can gain insights into the structural dimensions of Chinese politics that affect labor legislation, including which social actors are formal participants in the legislative process and which are excluded. We also gain greater understanding of the dynamic forces of change that are putting pressure on the institutions of a political system that has remained far more static than the Chinese economy, especially with its rapid integration with global production networks through foreign direct investment and the creation of a domestic private sector. Perhaps because Law (writ large) is one of the critical institutions that connects politics to the economy, it is exactly in this lawmaking process that we see the internal contradictions of the Chinese political system most clearly.

This chapter examines the evolution of Chinese labor and employment legislation, from the initial drafting of the first National Labor Law in 1994 to the drafting and implementation of the Labor Contract Law. We first compare the social contexts of the 1994 National Labor Law and the 2007 draft of the Labor Contract Law. The National Labor Law (passed July 1, 1994) was part of a top-down strategy to rework Chinese labor relations from the "iron rice bowl" of the Maoist era to more flexible and efficient "contract labor relations." It was also a response to the rapidly growing, but largely unregulated, foreign and private sectors on China's coastal provinces. By 2007, the Hu-Wen administration had new concerns, some of which were directly related to the successes of the earlier attacks on lifetime employment and job security. Abusive working conditions, lack of employment security, widespread use of temporary and informal workers, and annual increases in labor conflict were all indicative of the radically changed social context of Chinese labor legislation. Whereas the 1994 legislation was a premeditated move to "smash" the "iron rice bowl," 2007 was touted as the "year of social legislation," the belated government attempt to catch up with and mitigate some of the adverse effects of the rapid transformation of China (Zhu 2007). The Labor Contract Law was the key law amid several new labor laws that were passed or were drafted during this period.

Next, we examine the drafting process itself, with particular attention to the effects of increased transparency and public participation. The draft labor contract law became one of the touchstones for a growing debate between the continued pursuit of economic reform, flexibility, and globalization and a switch to increased social protection, stability, and decreased reliance on foreign investment. The public comment period further emphasized divergent interests, in particular a clash between the interests of foreign companies and the rights of Chinese workers. This chapter questions whether this clash is really the most salient issue surrounding this law; nevertheless, the fact that public discourse focused on it made it the central issue for the media and many other public commentators. We examine why certain voices become more engaged in this period of public comment while other actors choose either to not participate or to make their voices heard through nonpublic mechanisms, both formal and informal.

Third, we focus on policy output—the competing versions of different drafts as the labor contract law moved through the legislative process. By examining the different drafts of the law, we can follow the competing interests, articulated both formally and informally during the process, as they had impact on subsequent drafts. We argue that the Chinese legislative process remains chaotic and unsystematic. Legislating harmony is not achieved; instead, the legislative process draws greater attention to the internal contradictions and inconsistencies of the Chinese legal and political system. For a regime that aspires to a rule of law in the absence of political liberalism, these conclusions are not optimistic. If the "authoritarian resilience" of China is built on the successful adoption of new institutions to manage social change, the debate over the labor contract law highlights that the rule of law demands institutional complementarity.

Fourth, we highlight these problems of institutional capacity through an examination of the initial implementation period of the new laws. Although the law was hotly debated and much publicized in the media, the initial implementation period in 2008–2009 was simultaneous with the global financial crisis and deep declines in Chinese export sectors. Many of the new standards and worker protections in the final law were weakened by local governments responsible for its implementation. With the increased pressure on the Chinese economy and employment during the crisis, local governments moved to weaken key aspects of the law through local implementing regulations that favored employers and labor market flexibility. We also note, however, that workers themselves have pushed back against the lax implementation and enforcement through bottom-up attempts to enforce the law. This bottom-up mobilization includes a huge increase in the filings of labor arbitrations by workers since the law went into effect and also increased collective action through strikes, demonstrations, and work stoppages. Two institutional problems are revealed: the gap between central and local governments in implementation and the lack of legitimate bargaining bodies.

From 1994 National Labor Law to 2007: The Year of Social Legislation

In 1994, the Standing Committee of the NPC passed the first national labor law of the People's Republic of China (PRC). Drafting of the labor law had begun early in the reform period but was delayed for several years as different competing interests in the bureaucracy argued for different provisions. The nature and direction of Chinese labor law was naturally tied up in other issues of economic reform, including state enterprise reform and the formation of new firms in the private and foreign sectors. As Murray Scot Tanner notes in his study of lawmaking in China, labor law was affected by the vagaries of central leadership struggles over the path and speed of economic reform (Tanner 1999).

Prior to the 1994 passage of this first national law, Chinese employers and workers had been regulated by a wide array of administrative regulations, State Council directives, and laws passed by the NPC. These regulations, laws, and directives were not, however, unified or comprehensive. In many cases, the rules covered one type of enterprise but not another. Workers in different types of enterprises had very different levels of rights and entitlements; for example, workers in foreign-invested enterprises had higher mandated pay than workers in state firms, and workers in the public sector had many more mandated benefits delivered through the workplace. The chaotic nature of employment law and the unequal standards among different enterprises based on ownership type became increasingly untenable as economic reform deepened in the 1990s.

By the time the labor law was passed in 1994, many controversial issues of economic reform in the 1980s had been resolved, clearly in favor of the reformist camp. Therefore, despite the many protections offered by the law, its general principles leaned toward greater employment flexibility and enterprise autonomy from state intervention. Two examples make this point clearly. First, the labor law made a radical break with the past by regulating employment relations across ownership sectors that previously had been treated separately and differently. We could say that state-sector employees saw their workplace rights reduced through the law, whereas employees in the foreign and private sectors saw their rights clarified and expanded. Second, the law heralded the end of the "iron rice bowl" system of lifetime employment by legislating into law the labor contract system as the basic mode of employment relations in the PRC. An experiment that had begun in 1986 with the Temporary Regulations on the Labor Contract System now had the force of law.

The social context of the legislative journey of the labor law was very different from the current environment. The promulgation of the labor law in 1994 was motivated by two different concerns of the government. The first was how to increase managerial autonomy and efficiency of state-owned enterprises (SOEs) and urban collective enterprises. (The majority of the urban workforce was still employed in these sectors.) The second concern was how to increase oversight and regulation of the still small, but rapidly growing, foreign-invested and private sectors that were then concentrated in development zones along the coast. High-profile strikes had already occurred in development zones in the south, mainly in Korean- and Japanese-invested factories, and the regime had grown concerned about the lack of institutional capacity to address labor problems in the nonstate sector generally. The major changes in the law reflect these divergent goals.

In addition to the comprehensive nature of the law and its coverage of all ownership sectors, key aspects of the law included much increased labor flexibility through the extension of the labor contract system, basic standards of labor protection and social insurance, and new mechanisms to resolve employment disputes outside the firm (Gallagher and Jiang 2002). The National Labor Law codified the use of the labor contract system to manage the labor relationship. All workers in China should have a written labor contract with one employer that establishes the basis for rights and responsibilities at the workplace: the labor relationship. The 1994 Labor Law allowed either fixed-term or non-fixed-term (open-ended) contracts between employer and employee. The law stated that employees with over ten years tenure at one employer have the right to request a non-fixed-term contract, but this clause has been difficult to enforce because the language seems to indicate joint agreement, which is often difficult to achieve. After the 1994 law, labor contracts in China tended overwhelmingly to be fixed-term contracts with the length of the contracts becoming shorter and shorter, especially for entry-level and unskilled workers. Whereas labor contracts of three to five years were more common in the mid-1990s, by the early 2000s most companies in China signed one-year contracts with their regular employees, offering to longer-term contracts to their more highly valued and scarce-skilled technicians and managers. Although the early termination of contracts requires showing cause and the payment of severance compensation, until the passage of the Labor Contract Law in 2007, an employer could freely decide to end employment on expiration of the labor contract with no severance compensation. Given that the switch to labor contracts was originally aimed at ending the lifetime employment guarantee of the system of public ownership under the planned economy, the current situation shows how successful this reform has been. Indeed, some NPC officials and labor specialists have argued that this reform has been too successful, leading to widespread employment insecurity and seriously reducing the bargaining power of workers, given that any worker can be let go on the expiration of his or her contract (Xu 2007). The problems presented by the labor contract system are indicative of the difficulty legislating employment laws that have two different, even opposing, functions. The 1994 Labor Law was designed to both end the entitlements of socialism and ensure increased workers' protection and rights under the market economy. Combined with the realities of a large labor surplus, these legal developments were more effective in ending socialist employment than in protecting workers in the new market economy.

The 1994 Labor Law also sets out basic standards and benefits. In some cases, these standards and benefits exceed or at least match the employment standards and benefits of Organization for Economic Cooperation and Development (OECD) countries. The law sets out a standard eight-hour day; forty-four-hour workweek; overtime limitations; and social insurance for retirement, illness, occupational illness or disease, maternity leave, and unemployment. The labor law also instructs that lower-level governments institute a minimum wage system. The law prohibits the termination of labor contracts of pregnant or breast-feeding employees as well as employees with occupational injuries or illness. Some of the standards in the labor law were largely aspirational at the time because local governments did not have the financial and institutional capacity or the political will to implement extensive social insurance programs and to monitor firms aggressively for labor violations. Outside observers are often struck by the vague clauses of the labor law and the lack of legal penalties for nonenforcement.

The law also reiterates some of the basic responsibilities of the enterprise trade union, always a branch of the state-sanctioned All-China Federation of Trade Unions (ACFTU) that were first set out in the Trade Union Law (passed in 1992 and revised in October 2001). These responsibilities include helping workers sign labor contracts and file labor disputes. The responsibilities of the trade union in both the Labor Law and Trade Union Law reflect the political position of the ACFTU and its related unions at lower levels.

The ACFTU is the umbrella organization for all legal trade unions in China. Operating in a state-corporatist fashion, with strong ties to the Chinese Communist Party (CCP) and guaranteed monopoly representation of Chinese workers, the ACFTU is an important actor in the national level debates on worker issues and employment legislation. Its legal responsibilities within firms, however, reflect its subordinate position to the CCP. It is instructed to:

> [O]bserve and safeguard the Constitution, take it as the fundamental criterion for their activities, take economic development as the central task, uphold the socialist road, the people's democratic dictatorship, leadership by the Communist Party of China, and Marxist-Leninism, Mao Zedong Thought and Deng Xiaoping Theory, persevere in reform and the open policy ... (Trade Union Law 2001)

The difficult position of the ACFTU at the national level is mirrored at the lower levels of local administration and within firms. Local-level trade union organizations must take their orders from the local party and government, which are usually more focused on boosting economic growth than on protecting the rights of workers. The trade union organization within a firm is usually closely tied to management and must balance any concerns over worker issues with the concerns of management. Trade union officials within firms are also hired and paid by the firm directly, further constricting their ability to act on the behalf of the workforce. For these reasons, the legal responsibilities of the trade union in protecting and helping workers are often ignored.

In 1993 the Ministry of Labor put out new regulations setting out the procedures for the resolution of labor disputes in all firms (Harper-Ho 2005). Prior to reform, formal workplace disputes were handled internally by the enterprise with input from the enterprise trade union and CCP leadership. Large disputes were handled administratively by higher levels of government. Regulations passed in 1987 to resolve labor disputes set out new processes of resolution, but these regulations applied only to SOEs. With the gradual enlargement of the foreign and private sectors in the 1980s and early 1990s, the need for new institutional mechanisms became much more pressing. In particular, past reliance on internal firm procedures to resolve workplace disputes, most often through formal mediation by the trade union, became untenable. Most nonstate firms did not have the institutional capacity to resolve disputes (in most cases, lacking both a trade union and the related mediation committee). In addition, the more marketized and "capitalistic" proclivities of the managers of these firms also reduced workers' desire to resolve disputes internally.

The 1994 Labor Law formalized the 1993 Regulations into law, setting out a three-tier system of labor dispute resolution. This system relies on voluntary internal firm mediation, compulsory labor arbitration through labor arbitration committees overseen by local labor bureaus, and finally, civil court litigation in the event of an appeal of an arbitrated decision. This system allows workers in the nonstate sectors to head directly to labor arbitration, bypassing firm mediation, and also gives them the opportunity to appeal the arbitration decision at court. In the twelve years since its inception, this system of dispute resolution has drawn workplace disputes out of the firm and into the local political and legal arenas.

Several characteristics of this system are important in understanding the current state of labor relations in China. First, this system relies on mediation as a main channel for resolution despite the rapid decline of firm-based mediation after the 1994 law. Even though most workers reject firm-based mediation as too closely associated with firm management to be fair, local labor arbitrators and civil court judges are encouraged through salary and career incentives to push mediated resolutions at every level. Therefore, arbitration cases can result in an arbitrated mediation or an arbitral award. Judges may also resolve their cases through judicial mediation. Second, the important and compulsory arbitration stage has been beset by a number of problems, including weak institutional capacity, lack of professionalism and training, political interference from powerful local actors, lack of legitimacy due to the strong dependence of committees on local labor bureaus, and lack of finality given the court appeal option. Most arbitral awards are now appealed in civil court, making the arbitration process simply a stepping-stone to final resolution in court. This has added to the burden of the civil court system, undermined the authority

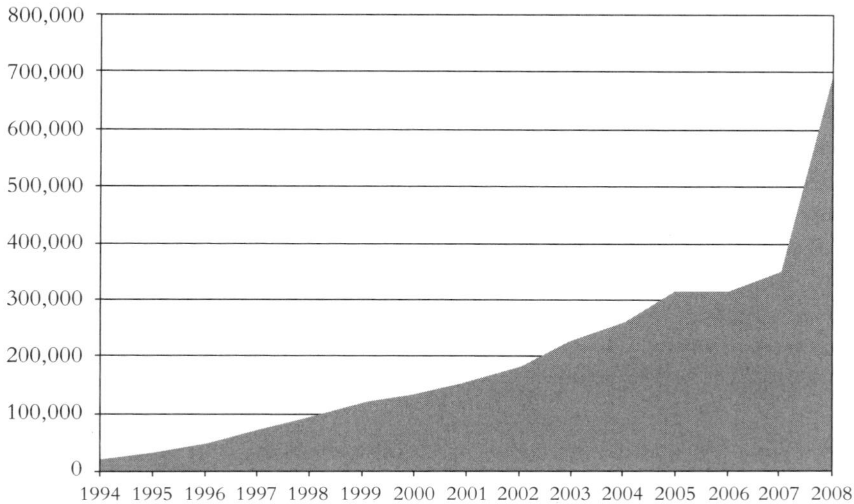

Figure 3.1 Arbitrated labor disputes, 1994–2008.

and legitimacy of labor arbitration, and complicated and lengthened an already difficult and expensive process for workers.[1] Third, despite the problems and frustrations of the formal resolution system, workers continue to make use of these institutions in increasing number. In 1995, the number of arbitrated labor disputes reached 33,000; in 2006, this number had increased to 447,000, with an annual average increase of over 25 percent (Ministry of Labor and Social Security and National Statistical Bureau 2007). In 2008, with the financial crisis and the onset of these new laws, the number of disputes climbed even more rapidly, reaching 693,000 arbitrated claims (see fig. 3.1). These large increases reflect the growing awareness among Chinese workers of their legal rights and the continuing problem of rampant violations of labor laws and regulations by many firms.

Although the 1994 Labor Law is an impressive symbol of the labor rights newly bequeathed by the state to urban workers, rights and entitlements of socialism were also taken away by this law. Workers are now subject to an employment system that depends on fixed-term labor contracts. Socialist benefits beyond the five legal provisions (pensions, medical insurance, unemployment insurance, occupational injury, and maternity insurance) are not required. Provisions regarding trade union participation in management decisions and employment issues also circumscribe the powers of worker organizations while enhancing managerial authority compared to the previous system under the planned economy. These changes indicate that the driving concern of the Chinese government at that time was to rework the employment relationship entirely. This concern was largely related to the government focus on state-sector inefficiencies and the growing financial problems caused by state-sector losses. The new flexibility accorded to firms through the labor law and other changes in the economy (expanding labor markets and large-scale rural-to-urban migration) was well-timed as the state moved to privatize and restructure the state sector more radically in 1997. The legal changes in the 1994 law made it easier for firms to lay off workers and to sign new short-term contracts with new entrants in the later 1990s. It is estimated that at least 30 million urban workers were laid-off during the restructuring, and many more millions of workers saw their employment relations transformed as the "iron rice bowl" was replaced by contract relations.

Since the heyday of SOE reform and restructuring in the late 1990s and the first few years of the twenty-first century, much has changed in the landscape of employment relations. First, most Chinese workers are now employed in private companies (Yusuf, Nabeshima, and Perkins 2006). Second, rural-to-urban migration has continued unabated and many labor-intensive industrial sectors rely almost totally on migrant labor for production-level workers. Third, because many millions of laid-off and unemployed workers from the public sectors are not employable in the new labor markets, which value skills, education, and youth, large numbers of urban workers have found unstable and temporary work in the informal sectors of the economy, as Albert Park and Fang Cai (chap. 2 in this volume) show. Fourth, the rates of labor disputes and labor conflict continue to increase annually despite repeated attempts by the government to reduce conflict, mediate tensions, and channel disputes more effectively toward quick resolution. Fifth, given the much increased participation of China in the global economy and, in particular, global production networks, Chinese labor conditions are important to and monitored by many groups and actors outside China.

Although the goals of the 1994 law were to both increase the flexibility of the public sectors and increase the protection of the other sectors, the labor law was far more successful in increasing flexibility than in increasing protection and reducing conflict. Moreover, given the large expansion of the migrant and informal workforces in the 1990s, large swaths of the Chinese workforce found the law almost completely irrelevant to their working lives. Even though in many cases the law should cover them, enterprises ignored the law with impunity because of the lack of effective implementation and enforcement by local regulatory or supervisory organizations, including the trade union, the local labor bureau, and the courts.

The social context of the drafting, passage, and implementation of the new Labor Contract Law, then, is quite different from the period before the promulgation of the national labor law in 1994. These trends of increased flexibility, marketization, privatization, and informalization were extremely disturbing to most legislators and government officials in charge of shepherding the law to its eventual passage by the NPC. The yearly increases in mass incidents and signals of rising social instability were at least partly attributed to the lack of legal protections afforded most Chinese workers.[2] As one academic expert involved in the legislation publicly noted, "China's recent economic growth and success has been at the expense of its workers. They have been sacrificed" ("Chang Kai Explains" 2007). These voices strengthened and found greater reception because the political context also changed with the consolidation of political power by the Hu Jintao and Wen Jiabao administration. The new commitment of the central leadership to reducing inequality, protecting the weak members of society, and cultivating social harmony gave the voices that advocated large and fairly radical changes in employment relations in China much greater confidence and influence. The labor contract law reflected this newfound interest in reducing inequality and enhancing social justice.

Drafting the Labor Contract Law: The Mass Line in Legislation

The labor contract law is one of many supplementary laws to the 1994 National Labor Law, and its drafting went on for several years. The Ministry of Labor and Social Security (MOLSS; now renamed the Ministry of Human Resources and Social Security, MOHRSS[3]) aspired to draft and pass on to the NPC many of these laws much more quickly than had been the case. Legislative drafting became more difficult, more contentious, and therefore much slower than the MOHRSS anticipated. Other important laws include the Employment Promotion Law (passed in August 30, 2007), the Labor Dispute Mediation and Arbitration Law (passed December 29, 2007), the Social Insurance Law (passed October 28, 2010), and the Law on Collective Contracts. Based on the texts of the three labor laws promulgated in 2007, these new laws are in a model of greater social protection, less mobility, and decreased flexibility. Many observers expected that the Chinese labor markets and employment situation would change markedly as these news laws came into effect. But, because the implementation period of these laws coincided with the onset of the global economic crisis in 2008 and new government concerns about unemployment, the implementation of these new laws has been more contentious and fraught with the competing concerns of the state, capital, and labor.[4]

The drafting process of the labor contract law began in the MOLSS. The MOLSS was responsible for drafting numerous versions for comments by and discussion with academic experts, other government ministries and institutions, and (to less extent) local labor bureaus and officials. A limited number of academics participated formally in the legislative drafting process. In 2005, the draft Labor Contract Law was passed to the State Council and a more extensive period of consultation and negotiation began. Formal participants at this stage include the MOLSS, the ACFTU, and members of the legislative drafting committee of the State Council. For this law, three groups of academic and professional experts were also consulted. Professor Chang Kai, of Renmin University, led one group of academics; the Labor Law section of the China Bar Association led a second; and labor law professors at the University of Politics and Law University directed a study group. One notable aspect of this drafting process is the important position of the ACFTU in the legislative drafting process. The trade union had far more influence and voice in the process than any other nongovernmental organization (NGO) and especially far more influence than organizations that represented the interests of employers or business more generally. The Chinese Enterprise Directors Association (CEDA), which could be considered the counterpart of the trade union for employers, issued comments during the period of public comment and did so only after strict instructions from the government that it must issue comments.[5] So, while the ACFTU was directly involved in the drafting process, the CEDA played a more marginal role as an outside commentator.

The imbalance of influence in the legislative process between labor and capital was quite striking and affected the trajectory of the legislation in many interesting ways. This structural characteristic of the Chinese legislative process is related to the high position of the ACFTU within the party-state more generally. The chairman of the ACFTU is a member of the politburo of the CCP, and the close relationship of the ACFTU with the CCP is reflected in its important role in legislation and national debates on labor issues. Although the ACFTU branches at the local and firm levels are generally considered to be quite feeble (beholden to local government priorities and the imperatives of enterprise management, respectively), the centralized body of the Chinese trade union is well-connected through its structure and personnel to powerful institutions in the party-state. Given the orientation of the current leadership and even perhaps Hu Jintao's close connections to another mass organization, the Communist Youth League, it is perhaps not surprising that the ACFTU was influential in the drafting process. The rights and responsibilities of the trade union expanded in later drafts (see later discussion); the final version of the law granted the trade union new powers at both the firm and local levels.

After deliberation in the State Council, the draft law was passed to the NPC for further discussion, revision, and comment. A draft of the Labor Contract Law was made public for a thirty-day period in March 2006. Interested parties could write letters or post messages to the NPC to register their comments on the draft law. As already mentioned, the draft law received over 191,000 comments, far exceeding the number of public comments on previous laws and causing a media furor. Detailed information about the nature of these comments is hard to come by. The NPC reported that 65 percent of the comments came from ordinary workers, but others involved in the drafting discussions reported that many "worker" comments were from grassroots trade union organizations, mobilized by the trade union apparatus to support a draft that proposed expanding the power and influence of the trade union. If the majority of these comments were from trade union members, they might have been representative of trade union interests and concerns, but not perhaps of the broader workforce, given that the ACFTU is not well represented in the nonstate sectors and tends to count few migrant or temporary workers as members. Because the government has not released any aggregate or detailed information about the comments, it is difficult to analyze public opinion on the March 2006 law, although it is clear that the law sparked a great deal of debate and commentary.[6]

Some of the comments submitted to the NPC, however, were publicly released and did attract significant attention in China and abroad.[7] These comments were submitted by organizations representing large European and U.S. foreign investors. Three groups, the American Chamber of Commerce in Shanghai, the US-China Business Council, and the European Union Chamber of Commerce (EU-Cham) all offered formal comments that were made public and circulated widely; the US-China Business Council comments were posted on their website. The comments submitted by these organizations were quite detailed, but they also addressed larger, more philosophical issues related to the development of Chinese labor laws and the larger social context of the pervasive lack of implementation and enforcement.

The American Chamber of Commerce (Am-Cham) is the largest U.S. business association in China, representing "2,600 individuals from over 1,200 companies" (American Chamber of Commerce 2011). It has a long history of paying attention to human resource issues in China and regularly convenes special subgroups to discuss labor issues at foreign ventures in China. It released thirty-three pages of bilingual commentary on the draft law, which included very specific criticisms and recommendations on nearly the entire draft law. The comments began and ended, however, with some attention to the larger issues of legal development and the desire of China for a "harmonious society" (the comments invoked this politically charged term). As the comments stated in length in the conclusion, Am-Cham placed its mostly critical stance on the law as part of the general "reformist" camp emphasis on economic development (and employment growth):

> China is still a developing country and its main focus at this stage is still economic development, as correctly pointed out by Premier Wen Jiabao. In making and

> revising laws, the starting point should be the specific circumstances of China, not good intentions and hastily-set goals.... In the highly competitive global economy of today, the welfare of Chinese workers depends not only on protections afforded by labor law, but also depends on the survival and steady growth of the enterprises in which they work. It is not wise to kill the chicken to get the egg. The serious flaws in the Draft, if left uncured, would not help to resolve the problems in enforcement of the current Labor Law. On the contrary, they will bring chaos to the labor market, weaken the competitiveness of Chinese enterprises, and bring adverse consequences to the national economy. (Zimmerman 2006)

The EU-Cham similarly focused its criticisms on the folly of raising standards even higher while continuing to ignore the pernicious problems of lack of implementation and enforcement. Noting that much of Chinese labor law borrows from the European experience, the EU-Cham remarked that "unlike in Europe, the key challenge in China to improving labor conditions on the ground is the compliance by employers and the enforcement by authorities of existing Chinese laws rather than legislative deficiencies" (European Union Chamber of Commerce 2006). The EU-Cham warned that:

> Indeed raising the bar before focusing on the root cause of the problem—the lack of implementation of existing labor laws—may actually worsen the current situation as the gap between law and reality will increase and may further discourage enforcement. The European Chamber therefore encourages the Chinese government to focus its efforts on improving the implementation of existing regulations and, if necessary adopting new implementing regulations, before passing additional laws. (European Union Chamber of Commerce 2006)

These foreign business associations also had specific, detailed concerns regarding the new draft law. Some of the concerns focused on issues that relate to higher-end employees, including managerial and technical staff. Chinese labor laws interpret the definitions of *worker* and *employee* quite broadly, which means that very high-level managers in firms are afforded the protections of the labor law in addition to other benefits that they may have as senior managers and top executives. Compensation packages for skilled employees in the Chinese foreign sector have been improving dramatically in recent years as continued economic growth and the localization policies of firms have increased the demand for their skills. New rules on hiring, firing, training, and probationary periods apply to workers across the board and therefore have made disputes with higher-end workers even more costly.[8] Many of the concerns raised in these comments on the draft, for example, on noncompete agreements (restrictions on subsequent employment to protect trade/industrial secrets), focused on how these laws would affect a smaller subset of the workforce. Although the organizations were roundly criticized by labor activists for adding their objections to various restrictions on noncompete clauses and probationary periods, these clauses are less relevant for the vast majority of Chinese workers.

The comments issued by the foreign business associations did not mark the beginning of the controversy over the draft Labor Contract Law. Academics, labor officials, trade union officials, and practicing lawyers had been privately debating the law since drafting began within the MOLSS. Among academic experts on labor law and industrial relations, a debate between the Southern and Northern Schools of labor relations sharpened and heightened as the drafting process moved toward the third reading (Chinese laws should be passed after the third reading of the law) (Xu 2007). This academic debate on the nature of Chinese labor law focused on the basic question of whether Chinese labor standards are, in effect, too high. Proponents of this position, in the Southern School, argued that Chinese labor markets were not yet fully developed and that, moreover, the government did not have the will or the capacity to implement standards of the 1994 law. They argued that the Chinese government should focus on regulating minimum labor standards; on extending these standards more broadly to include migrant workers, temporary workers, and workers in the informal sectors; and on enforcing these standards strictly and fairly (Dong 2007). The Southern School generally was more in favor of market regulation of labor markets, less government intervention in firm operations, and the use of private contracts to regulate the employment relations of highly skilled workers who wield impressive bargaining power by virtue of their skills and education. They assumed that more realistic standards would be easier to implement and enforce.

Opponents of this position, in the Northern School, included Professor Chang Kai of Renmin University, who argued publicly for the imposition of greater government control and intervention into labor-management relations, partly because of the "immature" nature of Chinese labor markets and worker organizations, including the trade union. Widespread violations of labor laws and abusive working conditions required that the Chinese government take a more direct role in firm-level labor policies. Northern School scholars often noted that the labor supply in China far outstripped demand; therefore, if things are left to the market, exploitation and abuse would only continue for a very long time (Liu 2006).

Neither side dealt very explicitly with the problem of enforcement and implementation. The Southern School argued, as did the EU-Cham, for better enforcement of existing laws, but it did not explain how this could be achieved. Proponents of the Northern School pointed to the increased powers of the trade union in the new law. Unfortunately, although the new law does increase the powers of the trade union, it does not shift the incentive structure of trade unions, particularly at the local and firm levels, toward the greater protection of workers. Others argued that the deficiencies in legislation were related to problems in implementation, in particular, the excessive reliance on administrative enforcement and the dearth of effective legal penalties, which reduces the power and authority of Chinese law (Liu 2006).

The debate between the Northern and Southern Schools echoed the public furor that erupted during and after the period of public comment on the draft law, regarding the nature and intention of the comments submitted by the foreign business associations. The larger issues pointed out by EU-Cham and Am-Cham were already being hotly debated among the experts themselves: Why are Chinese labor laws not enforced? How should China balance social protection with labor market flexibility? Which international models for labor regulation are most suited to China at its current stage of development? The entry of the foreign business organizations into this ongoing debate through their public comments on the draft law sharpened the rhetoric and raised the stakes of the discussion. Although some domestic experts contested the right of these organizations to make comments that could affect the outcome of Chinese legislation, these comments received scrupulous attention and raised public awareness of the potential impact of the law.

The controversy over the draft law and the attempts by foreign business associations to influence key elements of the draft were reported widely in the domestic and international media.[9] A news article in the *New York Times* in October 2006, nearly seven months after the period of public comment, ignited debate in the United States (Barboza 2006). Domestic and international labor advocacy groups picked up the debate and began to make public comments and draw up reports on the drafting process and the role of foreign investors in it. The public story on the law was now set: a classic example of footloose and fancy-free capital putting pressure on national legislative agendas to weaken domestic standards and ensure competitive and flexible labor markets for their enjoyment. Global Labor Strategies, a Washington, D.C.-based labor NGO, wrote a full report on the foreign investor response to the draft law (Global Labor Strategies 2007).[10] Workers Rights Consortium, an NGO fighting sweatshop conditions in university-licensed apparel, also issued a lengthy report on the issue (Nova 2007). In these public statements, Western NGOs came out in support of the draft law and opposed attempts by foreign business associations and foreign investors to lobby against more protective labor standards in China. These NGOs were also at least cautiously supportive of the expanded role of the trade union proposed in the later drafts of the law (in particular the March 2006 draft that was available for public comment). Despite their misgivings about the nature of the ACFTU as a distant approximation of a real trade union, these NGOs supported the draft law in the hope that the ACFTU would be transformed by new power and responsibilities. The NGO shift was strengthened by the dramatic decision of the Change to Win consortium of U.S. labor unions to send a high-level delegation to China for the first time in 2007. As one of the delegation members stated on his blog after that visit: "[s]o in our view, if we are to have leverage with multinational corporations that employ both Chinese and U.S. workers, and if we are to stop the race to the bottom, we must engage with the 177 million-member ACFTU" (Change to Win 2007). The public debate around the law also strengthened the hand of the ACFTU and improved its international reputation.

After the period of public comment ended in April 2006, the NPC undertook another full revision of the law. The new draft was finished in December 2006, but it was not subject to further formal public comment. Nevertheless, some organizations continued to monitor the drafting process and issue new comments. Am-Cham drew up comments on the final draft but did not release them publicly. The US-China Business Council continued to make its comments on the drafts publicly available on its website.

Note that this account of the formal drafting process leaves out much of the informal lobbying and politicking behind the scenes. For example, large SOEs were not active participants in the formal process, but they made their opinions heard through the relevant ministries and bureaus. Many labor-subcontracting companies that would have been adversely affected by new restrictions on labor subcontracting in the March 2006 draft made their opinions heard via the Ministry of Personnel, which regulated some of the higher-end labor-service companies. These voices, while influential, were not heard in the public discussion of the labor contract law controversy. In addition, among Chinese domestic entrepreneurs and business leaders from Taiwan and Hong Kong, there was debate both in the media and in the meetings of the Chinese Political Consultative Conference, an advisory body with many important leaders outside the CCP.[11]

In Tanner's account of lawmaking in the 1990s, he argues for the "garbage-can model" of legislation in which "organizational goals are often unclear, decision-making processes and inter-organizational relationships are ill-defined and rapidly evolving, and the stream of policy proposals flows more freely than ever" (Tanner 1999). Tanner finds the "organized anarchy" of Chinese lawmaking to be chaotic, unsystematic, and open to fairly fundamental changes as new actors (especially policy intellectuals) find openings for policy entrepreneurship. Since 2005, following the drafting of the Labor Contract Law, we have found Tanner's diagnosis not only accurate but also prescient on changes in the legislative process since the 1990s as lawmaking has become more open to participation from a wide range of actors, including policy intellectuals, foreign and domestic NGOs, business associations, and the media.[12]

To better understand the end result of this tumultuous drafting period, we focus here on five hot-point issues in the law and how these issues were addressed in different drafts of the law. Although there was some consensus about the problems that existed, the drastic differences from draft to draft and the absence of one guiding philosophy or goal indicate a substantial degree of disagreement and perhaps even confusion among the actors involved in the drafting process. Due to space constraints, we do not deal exhaustively with all the issues in the law; instead, we deal with the issues that were of most concern for employers, as exemplified by their public comments. These concerns were mainly concentrated in five areas: restrictions on fixed-term contracts, work rules and firm decision making, trade union rights and responsibilities, use of labor subcontracting, and restrictions on layoffs.

Restrictions on Fixed-Term Contracts

A main concern of the NPC, the State Council, and the ACFTU was the marked decline in labor contract time period since the promulgation of the labor law in 1994. In 1995, enterprises were encouraged to sign five-year contracts with employees, and many former permanent workers (workers hired under the "iron rice bowl") had the right to sign open-ended contracts. Chinese labor law does not permit "at-will" employment, and therefore any decision to terminate a contract relationship must show cause. If a worker is fired while in his or her third year of a five-year contract, the firm must show that it has just cause for the firing and it must also pay severance compensation. To avoid these restrictions, many firms shifted from long-term contracts to short-term contracts of two years, one year, or several months. Workforces were easily trimmed by simply not extending/renewing the contract once it expired. Prior to the Labor Contract Law, no severance compensation was required upon expiration of the contract.

This shift to short-term contracts and increased employment insecurity worried the government greatly because it had the potential to lead to massive unemployment in an economic recession or crisis. Firms were not required to hold on to workers once the contract term expired, and even a minor economic slowdown would exacerbate the serious Chinese employment pressures. Workers laid off through contract expiration would join large numbers of urban youth, older laid-off workers from the state sector, and insecure migrants in the unemployed pool. Various drafts of the Labor Contract Law attempted to end the practice of short-term contracts. This issue was one of the few to show a clear trend from less protective (more flexible) while the law was under the MOLSS drafting authority to much more protective (much less flexible) as drafting moved to include the ACFTU, the State Council, and the NPC. The final version of the law mandates open-ended contracts after two fixed-term contracts, which now makes the termination of workers much more difficult. Given that all terminations must show cause, this new restriction has led to a further increase in the number of labor disputes. These new restrictions on fixed-term contracts are the most important changes to labor relations in China since the passage of the 1994 Labor Law. If implemented strictly, they severely would restrict the employer's flexibility and would gradually reverse much of the employment flexibility first put into place by the 1994 law.

Work Rules and Enterprise Decision Making

Foreign business associations paid great attention to the March 2006 draft clauses on work rules, which vastly expanded the participation of the trade union (or other employee organizations) in setting out rules and company policies. The March public comment draft mandated that rules unilaterally set by the company would be void and that decision making on rules would then pass to the employee organizations to set on their own. The March draft also used language that granted the trade union veto power over rules (*taolun tongguo*) rather than a merely consultative role, as has been the case in the Labor Law of 1994.

Changes in subsequent drafts, however, took away these enhanced powers. The final version of the law does require trade union participation in the rule-making process, but it does not require union approval. In addition, unilaterally set rules are no longer void unless they violate the law. These changes reflect a tendency in the drafting process to grant the expanded powers and responsibilities to the trade union in the March 2006 draft but then to reduce those powers in subsequent drafts and in the final version.

Trade Union Rights and Responsibilities

The March 2006 draft granted the trade union an expanded role in firm-level decision making; the final version, however, trims these powers and generally does not significantly change the role of the trade union at the firm level from the previous law, although it is more precise about the role of the trade union in enterprise decision making. The final version also augments the role of the trade union through the addition of a new section on collective contracts. It is unclear why this change occurred, in particular why so many clauses on collective contracts were added to this law, which was supposed to be the guiding law on *individual* labor relations. Both the MOLSS and the NPC had in the past spoken of a forthcoming collective labor contract law that would further regulate the labor relationship by setting collective standards and mechanisms for collective bargaining. Given the internal bargaining and debate, the ACFTU may have given up some of the firm-level powers proposed in the March 2006 draft in exchange for new powers in setting collective contracts. These clauses are particularly noteworthy for their emphasis on local collective mechanisms and industry-wide collective contracts. Given that the powers of the trade union are severely constrained for structural reasons at the firm level, this compromise might be a good start for the gradual transformation of the ACFTU.

While the changes in the new law regarding the union are not dramatically different from the earlier powers set out in the Labor Law and the Trade Union Law, they are accompanied by much greater national level support for the ACFTU and, in particular, for ACFTU organizing efforts in foreign-invested firms (Watts 2006; Chan 2008). It is widely believed that the Wal-Mart organizing drive in 2006 and 2007 was supported by the highest levels of the CCP and state. Therefore, even though the legal responsibilities of the trade union have not widened considerably, the ACFTU and its related unions may have greater power to seek the enforcement and implementation of laws that have long been on the books in support of trade union involvement in firm decision making.

Labor Subcontracting and Informalization

The use of subcontracted (or dispatched) labor through labor-service companies is widely practiced in China and in some cases is used by employers to evade the normal social welfare/insurance burdens required by law. Workers employed indirectly through labor-service companies generally have lower standards of compensation and are hired to work for short-term periods. Some firms have transferred substantial parts of their operations to subcontracted workers or apprentice workers (*shixigong*), who are not protected by the law to the same degree as formal workers. Concerns regarding this trend are similar to the government concern about short-term contracts more generally: the creation of a very unstable and insecure labor force and the increased ability of employers to evade government regulations on social insurance responsibilities. The first drafts on the law from the MOLSS favored a less protective model of regulation. With the March 2006 draft, however, we see the restrictions on labor subcontracting increase significantly. This draft mandated that firms could employ workers on subcontract only for a one-year period, after which they must hire the worker directly. If the subcontracted worker is not hired, the firm is no longer permitted to fill that position with subcontracted labor. Am-Cham and other foreign business associations protested these restrictions with vigor, even using the specter of the bad old days of the planned economy:

> In a market economy, remaining competitive is one of the most basic prerequisites for the survival and growth of enterprises. The form of dispatched labor is a

> form of allocating human resources in a market economy....Because dispatched labor has such positive values, the government should not ban it but guide and regulate it as a normal form of employment through laws and regulations so that it can better serve the needs of the socialist market economy. Just as government leaders have recently pointed out on many occasions, the problems arising in reform can be solved only through further reforms. Banning dispatched labor would only lead enterprises back to the days of low efficiency where a company must have every function performed by its own employees. (Zimmerman 2006)

There are strong reasons to believe that the opposition by foreign business associations to these restrictions is not the whole story behind the later changes in the December 2006 and final June 2007 versions. These changes significantly weakened the very protective clauses of the March 2006 draft, including the removal of clauses that would have, in effect, banned labor dispatch and clauses that required long-term contracts between the dispatching firm and the worker. There are important interests in the Ministry of Personnel, the MOHRSS, and in large SOEs that benefit from labor dispatch and would have been adversely affected if all subcontracted workers were transformed into regular contract workers. Although the last two drafts removed some of the most onerous restrictions and weakened the obligations of employers to temporary workers, the final version of the law reinstated some of these protections, in particular increasing the employment security of dispatched workers and regulatory oversight of these subcontracting firms. The marked changes in protections from draft to draft, even at the very end of the drafting process, indicate considerable internal disagreement on the issue.

Guidelines on Layoffs

The final issue, clauses guiding large-scale layoffs, also shows a trend of less protective (MOLSS draft) to more protective (State Council, ACFTU, and NPC draft) to a mishmash of increased protection with key restrictions taken out or weakened (final version). These clauses are important because they guide the early termination of existing labor contracts rather than the expiration of labor contracts that are full-term. The December 2006 draft weakened the role of the firm trade union in the layoff process, but added more detailed regulations on permissible reasons for layoffs. The December draft also continued to mandate greater protections from layoffs for workers with longer-term relations and hardships at home. The final version continued in the same vein of the December 2006 draft by enlarging the permissible reasons for layoffs to include technological upgrading and management shifts. Layoffs are still more difficult in terms of new procedural requirements involving the trade union and the local authorities than was the current practice; however, the permissible reasons to lay off workers are expanded.

Passing the Law

The successive drafting of four of the five hot-point issues in the Labor Contract Law exhibits the tendency of moving from less protection (MOLSS 2005 draft), to more protection (State Council, ACFTU, and NPC March 2006 draft), and back to less protection (December 2006 and May 2007 drafts, and the June 2007 final version). Nevertheless, the final law is more protective than the 2005 draft initially produced by the MOLSS and thus reflects an attempt to maintain protections added by the ACFTU and the State Council while responding to the concerns and criticisms of employers, including the public statements of foreign business associations and the informal lobbying and pressure from SOEs and other state bureaucracies.

Although the Labor Contract Law was originally scheduled to be voted on during the March 2007 session of the NPC, it was delayed for a few months as the NPC worked through the impact of the public controversy. In late June, the Standing Committee of the NPC passed the Labor Contract Law after a new scandal erupted over the widespread use of child and slave labor in brick kilns in Chinese central provinces. The media coverage of the extreme exploitation of children and kidnapped adult workers ignited a public furor in China. During the debate over the draft Labor Contract Law in the Standing Committee of the NPC, proponents of quickly passing the law linked it explicitly to the brick kiln scandal ("NPC Standing Committee" 2007). Some domestic observers, while noting that the Labor Contract Law dealt only peripherally with the issues uncovered in the scandal, argued that quick passage of the was one way for the government to demonstrate its attention to and concern over issues of workplace conditions.[13] The final version of the law also increased the legal liabilities of government departments that do not fulfill their regulatory and supervisory roles.

Public discourse regarding the law focused on the opposition and criticisms of the foreign business associations, so that support for the law was equated with support for Chinese workers while opposition to the law was equated with opposition to the improvement of Chinese labor rights. Support for the law also signaled support for the ACFTU and an expanded role for the ACFTU in labor relations. Concerns voiced by the Southern School of labor law regarding the problems of enforcement and implementation (reiterated by EU-Cham in particular) were largely ignored. But the final law did include important new protections, especially restrictions on fixed-term contracts and provisions empowering the trade union.

Local Implementation and Bottom-Up Enforcement

The 2008 Labor Contract Law went into effect several months before the collapse of Lehman Brothers and the cascading financial crisis in the United States. The subsequent recession sharply reduced U.S. consumer spending and the export orders of Chinese firms. By the end of 2008, the Chinese government announced that 20 million migrant workers had lost their jobs. Layoffs and bankruptcies continued well into 2009 despite a large government stimulus program that targeted SOEs and large infrastructure projects. The double whammy of a new well-publicized protective law and an economic downturn led to a rapid and unprecedented rise in labor disputes. The number of arbitrated labor disputes reached 693,000 by the end of 2008. Some labor-intensive manufacturing centers on the coast reported increases in disputes as high as 300 percent. In 2008, China entered a new period of increased labor conflict and contention as firms and workers absorbed the significance of these changes. Although the new protections have proven to be exceedingly difficult to implement and enforce within the current political structure, they raised standards and expectations regarding workplace rights during the period of economic crisis.

Given the concern of local governments to mitigate the effects of the crisis on their local economies, many localities issued local explanations and regulations that had the effect of weakening the employee-friendly aspects of the national law. Local courts were the most active government institutions, issuing explanations and interpretations of the national law. In the media, there were criticisms of this as leading to the "regionalization" and "loopholization" of national law ("Special Report" 2008). Localities with large concentrations of foreign direct investment and labor-intensive manufacturing have been the most proactive in this regard, with High Court explanations of the laws from Shanghai, Jiangsu, Zhejiang, and Guangdong.[14] A key notion in these post-2008 local responses is that the protection of *both* workers' rights and employers' lawful rights and interests is essential to maintaining stable labor relations and continuing industrial and economic development. This language is a marked change from a year or two earlier when the central government spoke of industrial upgrading and leaving poor-quality jobs behind ("Reflection on Implementation" 2008). The Supreme People's Court issued a guiding opinion in July 2009 that reiterated this more ambivalent stance toward the protection of the newly enshrined rights in the Labor Contract Law.

In addition to the downgrading of strict implementation of the law, and in the wake of the rapidly increasing numbers of labor grievances, the central and local governments pushed dispute measures that ended in mediated or negotiated settlements. The 2008 PRC Law on Mediation and Arbitration of Labor

Disputes (which lowered the barriers to sue) had already emphasized the need to first exhaust all consultation, negotiation, and mediation avenues to resolve labor disputes.[15] As the number of disputes climbed in 2008, the reliance on mediation increased. Mediation was pursued not only as a way to reduce pressure on arbitration committees and courts but also to allow for a greater degree of compromise. In most cases, this meant that the aggrieved workers gave up or reduced some of their claims. These two shifts after the promulgation of the law—local regulations weakening the law and dispute resolution processes deemphasizing the law—were both responses to mitigate the effects of the law at a time of economic fragility and uncertainty. Nevertheless, neither response effectively controlled the number of workers who might choose to invoke the law.

The publicity and debate surrounding the Labor Contract Law in the domestic media meant that many workers had at least a vague sense that their rights have been increased and that the state was generally sympathetic toward their plight. As part of a long tradition of legal dissemination campaigns during the reform era, this law was another legal weapon that Chinese workers could use against unjust employers. In response to layoffs and terminations in the wake of rising costs and rapidly declining export orders, Chinese workers responded with a wave of filings against their employers. The number of disputes in 2008 reached nearly 700,000, double the rate in 2007. Individual cities and development zones with large manufacturing sectors reported increases up to 300 percent. Guangzhou had over 80,000 labor disputes in 2008, a 264 percent increase from 2007. Local governments and courts struggled to meet the caseload and delays of up to one year were not uncommon. In 2008, some Shanghai cases took close to two years to reach a resolution in the courts ("Labor Dispute Cases Suddenly Erupt" 2009; "Explosion in Disputes" 2009).

In addition to the large increases in arbitrated cases, Chinese courts were also deluged with labor cases. These suits included contested arbitration decisions and disputes that had never reached arbitration because the arbitrators' heavy caseload led them to pass some suits directly to the courts. (Recall that arbitration is compulsory for some labor disputes, but is not binding and can be appealed in court by either side.) The Supreme Court of China reported a 97 percent increase in the number of labor cases over the course of 2008. In 2009, this trend continued with nearly 170,000 cases in the first half of the year, an increase of 30 percent from the 2008 high ("Last Year Provincial Courts' Labor Disputes" 2009; "Cases Soar" 2009). The president of the Guangdong Provincial Higher Court reported that the Guangdong courts received over 76,000 new labor cases in 2008, up 157 percent from the previous year (Ibid.). The basic level court in the industrial zone of Tangxia in Dongguan city reported that by November 2008 each judge had received over 1,000 cases. More than half of the annual caseload was made up of labor disputes, most often migrant workers asking for worker's compensation, overtime pay, or severance compensation (Zhao 2008). Courts in Jiangsu Province, outside Shanghai, reported similarly high increases; in Jiangyang city, labor cases at the court increased 300 percent. Court officials called for new measures to handle disputes earlier and to manage the large spontaneous protests that occurred when factories suddenly closed or initiated mass layoffs ("New Characteristics" 2009).

The wave of filings initiated by workers against their employers can be seen as a type of bottom-up enforcement of the new law in direct response to the lackluster official measures to implement and enforce it. Workers with grievances against employers and armed with a new awareness about the law demanded that the state intervene. This bottom-up push for better enforcement of the new law was an important antidote to the perennial problem of weak legal implementation by local governments that are beholden to the interests of local employers.

Conclusion

Legislative decisions that reflect the apparent commitment of the Chinese state to social equality, social justice, and goals beyond increasing the growth rate have had a big impact on the social perceptions of the rule of law. Legislative commitments to increased social protection have encouraged workers to claim these rights in the dispute process despite lackluster implementation of the law by local governments in the wake of the economic crisis. Since 2008, the numbers of labor disputes and labor conflict have continued to rise quickly. Lack of attention to mechanisms for enforcement and implementation of the law, however, have added to workers' growing frustration with the efficacy and fairness of the legal system. In this sense, the raising of standards without any concomitant improvement in institutional capacity has contributed to rising expectations and diminished outcomes at the workplace and in the courts.

A key gap in capacity is the lack of a collective body to represent the collective interests of workers. Although some proponents of the law placed hope in the transformation of the ACFTU into a more committed protector of workers' rights, the law did not change the current structural or political constraints of the trade union as laid out in the Trade Union Law of 2001. The trade union is still under the administrative direction of the CCP at the central level, under the direction of the local party-state structure at the local level, and under the control of firm management at the firm level. The monopoly position of the ACFTU on representation is also unchanged. The most likely arena for ACFTU transformation is at the local industrial or regional union level because these unions can begin to sign collective contracts with employer representatives and offer protections to workers in smaller firms that often do not have a union presence (Cheng Liu 2007). This transformation, however, would require significant support from other government branches and the local party. It also requires that viable employer associations operate in a capacity to negotiate and bargain on the behalf of firms in the same industry or region. As the legislative process shows, the power and organizational capacity of the ACFTU far exceeds any other organization of employers.

The new mass line in legislation means that conflict and contention over lawmaking is no longer restricted to the inner halls of the NPC and the State Council. Although foreign business associations were roundly criticized in the press for their comments and criticisms of the draft law, their participation was a catalyst to greater public debate and participation in the drafting process. The final law was a compromise between the divergent interests of increased social protection and enhanced flexibility, but such a compromise did not lead to the government goal of legislated harmony in the workplace. Workers responded to the lack of forceful implementation by local governments with a bottom-up wave of grievance filings, overwhelming the arbitration committees and the courts. The passage of the new Labor Contract Law has heralded in a new era of disputes, strikes, and contention.

Chapter 4

Social Policy and Public Opinion in an Age of Insecurity

Mark W. Frazier

Scholars have commonly turned to Karl Polanyi's double movement paradigm to interpret the development of welfare policy in China (Wang 2008; Lee 2007; Polanyi 1957). In this view, the introduction of market forces into labor relations in the 1990s led to social dislocation and impoverishment for large portions of the labor force, to protests fueled by demands for subsistence wages and job security, and to increased employment insecurity for a growing proportion of the urban population. These problems then led to policy responses on the part of the Chinese government that provided some measure of protection against the operation of the unfettered labor market. In Polanyi's double movement paradigm, market forces are unleashed on society and, in response to the resulting turmoil, states quickly introduce labor and social legislation to provide buffers against the raw forces of capitalism—or, in the terms used by social scientists, to "embed" the market.

The dismantling of the socialist workplace institutions of lifetime employment and employer-provided benefits in the Chinese state sector and the subsequent informalization of large segments of the labor force (Albert Park and Fang Cai, chap. 2 in this volume) makes a compelling analogy with the rise of industrial capitalism and labor markets in early nineteenth-century England (see also Lu Zhang, chap. 6 in this volume). The concept of the double movement helps us understand the timing of social and labor legislation, but it does little to explain the forms and design of market-embedding social legislation. We know that states respond to the commodification of labor, but how they respond and to whom they respond are also of considerable importance.

The Chinese government in the 1990s attempted to transform labor relations with a two-pronged strategy. With the introduction of labor legislation (Mary Gallagher and Baohua Dong, chap. 3 in this volume), Chinese leaders sought to provide a legal foundation for such issues as employment relations and dispute resolution. A second and related strategy was to create a postsocialist welfare policy to provide adequate social protections both to those laid off in the process of state enterprise reform and more generally to workers in the marketized economy who faced increased employment insecurity due to the imposition of the labor contract system in 1995. A number of important studies have examined how workers in China responded to the legalization of labor relations (Gallagher 2005a; Lee 2007; Cai 2006). These studies suggest a growing awareness of provisions contained in the new labor laws, with an ambivalent view of the efficacy of labor dispute mechanisms. The response of workers to the transformed Chinese welfare system is less clear. Do workers view the new welfare regime as a legitimate attempt by the Chinese government to provide adequate protection from risks such as unemployment, workplace injury, and old age? Do they make rights claims to such social protections? Or do workers generally assess the new welfare regime as a weak appendage of the market economy, providing few if any social protections?

This chapter uses public opinion data to explore how urban workers understand social policies and how they perceive the Chinese state and its agents in offering protection from various risks in a market economy. The discussion is centered on old-age pensions in particular, which became the primary compensation that state-owned enterprises (SOEs) used after mass layoffs (through early retirements) in the 1990s. As the analysis shows, the attitudes of urban workers are in part a legacy of state socialism, but the demands on the Chinese state to provide pensions and other social welfare measures also stem from workers' experience in a highly competitive and insecure market environment. Marc Blecher (2002) has shown that urban workers seem to accept the principles of market allocation of labor. Although such market hegemony is met with a degree of resignation or acceptance, workers also demand that the Chinese government provide them with a measure of protection from the risks that they face in the labor market.

Contention and Compensation

The dramatic reduction of the state enterprise sector in the 1990s created unemployment and informalization on a vast scale. Urban SOE workers lost not only jobs but also benefits that had once been delivered by their SOEs. Widespread but localized protests followed, in which unemployed SOE workers demanded that the government provide them with adequate compensation, even subsistence living wages, for its having revoked the socialist promise of lifetime employment and permanent benefits. The targets of these labor protests tended to be local state officials and SOE managers, who frequently enriched themselves by turning over the public property of SOEs to private developers. This pattern of labor contention, in which SOE workers used labor laws to frame their grievances yet eschewed cross-factory or horizontal strategies of mobilization, has been labeled "cellular activism" (Lee 2007). These struggles between the local state and SOE workers influenced the structure and emphasis of the new Chinese welfare state.

The inability to deliver pension payments on time and in full to the growing number of jobless SOE workers who had retired (often early) during SOE restructuring led to widespread protests and to broader threats, symbolic and real, to the Chinese Communist Party (CCP) claim to maintain social stability (Hurst and O'Brien 2002). Until the early 2000s, SOEs remained largely responsible for paying pensions to their retirees, and many failed to do so. From late 1997 to May 1998, the amount of money that pensioners were owed in delayed pension payments rose from 3.75 billion to 8.7 billion yuan (Hu 1999, 14). Between the first half of 1998 and the third quarter of that year, the number of provinces whose local governments paid out more in pensions than they had collected in social insurance revenues rose from seventeen to twenty-five (Hu 1999, 15). By year-end 2000, according to an All-China Federation of Trade Unions (ACFTU) publication, accumulated pension arrears totaled 7.1 billion yuan owed to 3.8 million pensioners. This represented 13.9 percent of the 27.2 million retirees nationwide, according to the ACFTU calculations. Of the 43,617 firms that owed unpaid pensions to retirees, 21.7 percent were located in the northeast provinces of Liaoning, Jilin, and Heilongjiang (All-China Federation of Trade Unions [ACFTU] 2002, 90). Although central government regulations in 1999 and 2000 compelled local governments to take over the responsibility for paying pensions to local retirees, this transfer did not absolve SOEs of their delinquent payments. As bankruptcies of money-losing SOEs accelerated in the late 1990s, the problem of unpaid pensions grew more severe. Pension protests targeted SOEs as well as local government officials who had invoked mass layoffs and early retirements without providing adequate funding for jobless SOE workers.

The pension protests appear to have subsided by the mid-2000s, as local government officials began injecting enough social insurance revenues—and in the case of poor regions, central government subsidies—into the disbursement channels so that retirees could pick up their pensions at local post offices and banks. By the late 2000s, most of the 49.5 million retirees from enterprises in China received their benefits in full and on time. Large-scale protests in response to unpaid pensions declined, in part as a result of urban governments' continuously increasing in pension benefits and in part due to the commitment by the central government to transferring funds to rust-belt areas whose urban governments had difficulties paying pensions on time.[1]

Pensions became the dominant form of welfare provision in China. Each year, urban governments spend more on benefits for approximately 50 million retired factory workers and 12 million civil servants than they do on education, urban construction, public security, public health, or any other budgetary category. In addition to 404 billion yuan ($49.1 billion) in social insurance pension benefits that local governments paid out in 2005, they also spent about 106 billion yuan ($12.9 billion) from fiscal accounts for civil servant pensions. In 2006, urban government spending on social insurance pensions rose to 490 billion yuan ($59.5 billion)—nearly 25 percent in one year alone. These pension benefits were financed through the payroll contributions of a reported 152 million urban workers in 2007; however, the remainder of the Chinese workforce, approximately 618 million workers, were largely without pension rights because they were not legally eligible or their employers evaded the law (Ministry of Human Resources and Social Security [MOHRSS] 2007). This large majority included many workers employed informally at urban workplaces. Their informal status denied them access to workplace-provided social insurance and saved employers the fees that should have been paid to local social insurance funds. Because most pension expenditures are financed through social insurance contributions, they do not show up on the tax revenue and expenditure reports of urban governments. Still, revenues for social insurance pensions, which totaled 509 billion yuan in 2005, exceeded even the most lucrative source of budgetary revenue for urban governments—the business tax, which drew in 410 billion yuan that year.

Those left jobless by SOE restructuring in the 1990s rather successfully voiced their demands for pensions and used subsistence rights to frame their grievances, but migrant workers a decade later in the high-growth regions took a different approach. For them, pensions were a dubious form of social insurance that their employers provided in the form of wage deductions turned over to the social insurance agencies (SIAs) of urban governments in the cities where migrant workers were employed. The highly mobile migrant workers did not see the value of paying into accounts in cities that did not recognize them as legal residents. Although migrants were permitted to withdraw their own individual payments from social insurance funds when they returned to the countryside or moved to a new job in another locality, migrants were not able to recoup the much larger payments that enterprises made in their names. There were also few institutional mechanisms to permit the movement of social insurance funds from city to city or from city to countryside. In 2007, reports from southern Chinese manufacturing centers such as Shenzhen and Dongguan told of migrant workers lining up at the offices of local SIAs to withdraw their accumulated savings from personal retirement accounts. Press reports explained that migrants were "cashing out" (*tuibao*) because they suspected that local SIAs would not transfer the funds in their personal retirement accounts to their next place of work or residence (*China Labor News* 2008). As the global recession spread in late 2008, mass layoffs of migrants added pressures on local officials to distribute pension and other social insurance funds to migrants who were returning home.

Beginning in 2004, labor disputes with employers over rights to social insurance coverage exceeded disputes over wages and labor contracts. In 2000, national labor dispute statistics classified 31,350 labor disputes in 2000 as arising over "social insurance and welfare" issues. This made up just over 25 percent of the total number of cases for that year (Ministry of Labor and Social Security [MOLSS] 2000, 429). By 2004, the number of labor disputes said to involve social insurance and welfare issues had risen to 88,119; this had become the leading cause of labor disputes, exceeding the number of disputes over wages and labor contract terminations. Social insurance disputes amounted to 33.8 percent of total labor disputes (MOLSS 2005b, 525–26). Given the increasing use of agency employment and other forms of contracting by the middle of the decade, and the frequent abuse of social insurance by such contracting firms, it is likely that at least part of this increase in disputes over social pensions arose from the rapid informalization of labor during this time.

Labor legislation in 2008 attempted to remedy the shortcomings in social insurance provision. Under the Labor Contract Law, labor service agencies that provided large pools of contract labor to companies were required to extend pension and other social insurance to their employees. The law also mandated that employers make labor contracts with no termination date under certain conditions, generally when the employee had accumulated ten years of service, had already signed two fixed-term contracts with the same employer, or was ten years from retirement. The last stipulation was clearly an attempt to deter employers from creating early retirements through the nonrenewal of labor contracts for workers in their fifties and nearing retirement age (sixty for men, fifty-five for women in white-collar occupations, and fifty for women in production jobs).

In another legal development, the National People's Congress (NPC) released the text of the draft Social Insurance Law (SIL) for public comment in late 2008, after drafts of the law had stalled in the Standing Committee of the NPC for nearly fifteen years. The draft SIL attempted to deal with the problem of rural residents and migrant workers being largely excluded from coverage under health care, pensions, and other programs that urban residents received. The NPC reported receiving 70,501 responses (*yijian*) from citizens in all thirty-one provinces and from social sectors including urbanites, workers, civil servants, students, soldiers, farmers, migrant workers, and retirees (National People's Congress [NPC] 2009). The draft SIL provided social insurance coverage for migrant workers and made their coverage portable across regions. It also gave pension and health insurance rights to peasants whose land had been sold and gave subsidies for health insurance coverage to those receiving minimum income transfers, to those with disabilities, and to anyone over age sixty from a low-income family. The SIL draft became law in October 2010. Its passage could provide important legal grounds for government agencies, the ACFTU, and workers to file claims against employers who do not provide mandated coverage.

Whereas the term *pension reform* in other countries refers to efforts by governments to reduce expenditures or even privatize pensions, the Chinese reforms led to soaring pension expenditures and reinforced the expectation that the state should assume a central role as the financial and administrative provider of pensions. The reforms may have even increased such expectations among the urban Chinese workforce. These attitudes are not entirely the result of a lingering orientation of dependency instilled from having worked in SOEs; they are also the reasonable expectation that a stronger state role is needed to protect workers from the risks of the labor market and increased employment insecurity in the age of labor contracts. The discussion that follows supports this contention through three central claims: (1) urban residents continue to view the state as holding primary responsibility for financing pensions, (2) they view pension rights as being tied less to employment status than to citizenship, and (3) they place surprisingly high levels of trust and confidence in the ability of the Chinese government to provide pensions.

Public Opinion and Social Policy

In this section, I analyze the results of a social survey conducted in Beijing in early 2005 as well as focus group discussions with manufacturing workers in six Chinese cities during the same year. The data analysis compares the outlooks of pensioners, workers, and the unemployed on a range of questions dealing with pensions and the responsibility of the state, the employer, and the individual in financing future old-age income needs. The data come from the 2004 Beijing Area Study (BAS), conducted in spring 2005. The BAS has been conducted on an annual basis by the Research Center for Contemporary China since 1995. The survey includes a standard list of questions related to Beijing residents' assessment of the Chinese reform policies, as well as demographic data such as individual and family income and expenditures. Each year the BAS includes a special section of several questions related to a current issue, and the 2004 BAS included a special section on pension reforms.[2]

In March 2005, under the sponsorship of Horizon Research, a series of six focus groups was carried out with manufacturing-sector employees in six cities—SOE workers in Beijing, Changchun, and Nanjing, and workers employed in nonstate enterprises in Beijing, Nanjing, and Foshan. The focus groups consisted of eight individuals recruited from different firms throughout each city. Chinese moderators employed by Horizon led the focus group discussions, which lasted from 90 to 120 minutes.

In the data analysis that follows, the 593 respondents in the BAS were categorized as retirees (n = 216), unemployed (n = 99), and working (n = 278). Table 4.1 displays basic demographic information for these groups. The average age of the retirees in the sample was only 56.3, well below the legal retirement age for men and just above the retirement ages of 55 and 50 for white-collar and blue-collar women. Women represented 65.3 percent of the retirees. Retirees also had an average of 10.5 years of education and had a significantly lower average household income than those who were working. The ninety-nine respondents in the sample who were either unemployed or between jobs had on average 10.1 years of education and lower monthly household incomes than retirees. Men made up the majority of the working and the unemployed groups in the sample.

Of the 278 respondents in the BAS who were classified in the working category, only 28 (10.1 percent) said they did not have pension coverage. Among the unemployed, as expected, the coverage rate was much lower, with 39.4 percent lacking pension coverage. Among the 217 retirees, 143 (65.9 percent) reported that they received social insurance pensions. This difference of seventy-three is accounted for by the fact that at least sixty-seven of the retirees came from employment in government, party, and other public-sector workplaces

TABLE 4.1
Demographic data from Beijing Area Survey (BAS), March 2005

	Working (n = 278)	Retired (n = 216)	Unemployed (n = 99)	Total (n = 593)
Age (years)	43.05	56.33	45.33	48.27
	(7.93)	(5.81)	(7.12)	(9.38)
Education (years)	12.51	10.52	10.12	11.39
	(2.97)	(2.92)	(2.61)	(3.08)
Household income (yuan/month)	5,244	3,099	2,281	3,968
	(8,310)	(6,249)	(6,226)	(7,377)

Notes: Means reported for each group. Values in parentheses are standard deviations.

that would have made them eligible for civil service pensions rather than social insurance pensions. Of the 143 who reported receiving social insurance pensions, only 4 (2.8 percent) said that they had experienced a delay in receiving pensions, whereas 27 retirees (18.9 percent) reported that they frequently or sometimes worried about delays in receiving their pensions.

Bringing the State Back in as Welfare Provider

One of the crucial questions in the political debate over pensions is who bears the primary responsibility for the old-age needs of citizens. The mix of occupational, private, and state-financed pensions varies considerably across countries, and public opinion surveys also show considerable variation in the level of support for the state as the primary provider of pensions. A question posed in the Eurobarometer survey of respondents in fifteen EU member countries asks respondents from which source they think that pensions should mainly come: the state or public pensions, occupational (i.e., employer and employee contributions), and private channels such as insurance companies. The 2001 Eurobarometer found that 57 percent of respondents favored public pensions as the main source of pensions, with 7 percent choosing private channels (Janky and Gal 2007, 5).

The 2004 BAS included the same question, and the results were not dramatically at variance with the respondents in the Eurobarometer. As shown in table 4.2, nearly 62 percent of the BAS respondents said the state should be the primary provider of pensions, whereas 33.8 percent indicated that employers and employee contributions should form the main source of pension provision. Only 1.4 percent favored private pensions as the primary source of old-age income. This puts the BAS respondents in a category comparable with the Eurobarometer respondents in France and the United Kingdom, 30–35 percent of whom selected occupational or private pensions as the primary sources (Janky and Gal 2007, 15). In a survey of Shanghai respondents (n = 540) that I conducted in 2005, albeit using different sampling methods from those used

TABLE 4.2
Views on responsibility for pensions (%)
How do you think pensions should be provided: by the state, by employers and employee contributions, or by private contracts between individuals and companies?

State	Employers and contributions	Private contracts	Other	Total (n = 589)
61.8	33.8	1.4	3.1	100.0

in the BAS, only 50.0 percent of Shanghai respondents selected the state as the primary provider of pensions and 49.5 percent chose occupational pensions.

Table 4.3 uses a multinomial logistic regression model to analyze variation in the BAS responses based on the variables of age, income, education, gender, and employment category (retired, unemployed, or working). The coefficients presented in Table 4.3 (in which "mainly by the state" is the reference category) highlight a number of significant points. Of greatest interest is the distinction between those who preferred the state and those who preferred employer and employee contributions to serve as the main source of pensions. The coefficients show that older respondents were much more likely than younger ones to place responsibility on the state for providing pensions than any other categories of responses. Moreover, the unemployed were much more likely than retirees or the employed to place responsibility on the state for providing pensions rather than on employers and employees. (This finding is consistent with analyses of Eurobarometer data, in which those currently employed were more likely to support employer-employee contributions as the primary source of pensions; Janky and Gal 2007, 6.)

TABLE 4.3
Multivariate analysis: Views on responsibility for pensions
How do you think pensions should be provided?

	Mainly by employers and employee contributions			Mainly by contracts between individuals and companies		
	β	Significance	Exp(β)	β	Significance	Exp(β)
Intercept	−0.239 (.896)	0.790		1.997 (3.151)	0.526	
Age	**−0.025** (0.013)	0.061	0.976	**−0.132** (0.044)	0.003	0.876
Income	0.000 (0.000)	0.829	1	0.000 (0.000)	0.145	1
Education	0.010 (0.032)	0.761	1.01	0.042 (0.141)	0.765	1.043
Retirees	0.036 (0.280)	0.898	1.037	2.274 (1.262)	0.072	9.718
Unemployed	**−0.759** (0.286)	0.008	0.468	0.591 (0.972)	0.543	1.806
Women	−0.159 (0.198)	0.423	1.172	−1.949 (1.134)	0.086	7.024

$\chi^2 = 34.7$
Significance < 0.010
−2 log likelihood = 934.9
Nagelkerke $R^2 = 0.071$

Notes: Multinomial logistic regression results, in which the reference category is those who said pensions should be provided "mainly by the state." "Other" response category is not shown. Values in parentheses are standard errors. Significant coefficients ($p < 0.05$) shown in boldface. Response categories were coded 1 = mainly by the state; 2 = mainly by employers and employee contributions; 3 = mainly by contracts between individuals and companies.

The focus group discussions among manufacturing-sector workers and retirees revealed much about why Chinese workers might want to maintain a strong state role in the provision of pensions and other social welfare measures. (See table 4.4 for demographic information about the focus group participants.) In all six focus groups, participants expressed the view that the state and employers had abandoned welfare provision and that it was now up to the individual to pay for his or her medical expenses, to save for pensions, and so on. "The trend now is for individuals to pay [for social welfare needs]. The state and the enterprise don't care about you" (Beijing private enterprises, #3). "These days the best thing is just to rely on oneself" (Foshan private enterprises, #4). "Relying on others isn't realistic" (Foshan private enterprises, #2). Many participants conveyed the sense that they could lose their jobs at any time, which highlights the link that respondents make between increasing employment insecurity (especially the danger of informalization) and the need for the state to guarantee the provision of social insurance. "I have to raise my daughter, I'm over 40, I have a 3-year labor contract, and I don't know what will happen after the third year. How will I educate my child?" (Foshan private enterprises, #5). In addition, participants expressed anxieties over how to cover hospital expenses should they or family members be struck by an illness or suffer an accident.

Contrary to the stereotype that Chinese citizens retain traditional beliefs regarding children supporting their parents in old age, the focus group participants did not claim that they expected to rely on their children for financial support. Many participants (among them, some who had already retired) pointed out that they could not possibly ask their children, who were struggling with young families of their own, to provide financially for them (Beijing private enterprises, #3). Respondents also uniformly stated that they were concerned about the low-quality housing in which they lived.

Respondents in the BAS also voiced strong support for the role of the state in social security (referring not just to pensions but also to employment and other social protections). As shown in table 4.5, a majority of 71 percent strongly agreed or agreed with the statement that "China is a socialist country; the state should have full responsibility for providing social security." The ordered probit regression displayed in table 4.6 shows that male respondents and those with higher education were more likely to disagree with the statement, but for those respondents who fare less well in the competitive and insecure Chinese labor markets, there is strong support for government provision of social security.

Rights Consciousness

Table 4.7 shows several responses regarding legal rights to pensions. The BAS found strong support for universal pension coverage for all Chinese citizens.

TABLE 4.4
Focus groups composition

	Position	Age	Gender		Position	Age	Gender
	Beijing private enterprises March 13, 2005				Beijing state enterprises March 13, 2005		
#1	Retired	38	F	#1	Production worker	46	M
#2	Staff	47	M	#2	Production worker	47	F
#3	Staff	40	M	#3	Production worker	32	M
#4	Production worker	53	M	#4	Production worker	51	F
#5	Retired	50	F	#5	Production worker	46,	M
#6	staff	45	F	#6	production worker	37	M
#7	Production worker	47	F	#7	Skilled worker	46	F
#8	production worker	30	M	#8	Skilled worker	36	M
	Nanjing state enterprises March 12, 2005				Nanjing private enterprises March 12, 2005		
#1	Skilled worker	35	F	#1	Staff	41	F
#2	Skilled worker	36	M	#2	Production worker	38	F
#3	Skilled worker	38	F	#3	Skilled worker	40	M
#4	Skilled worker	42	M	#4	Staff	45	F
#5	Production worker	41	F	#5	Production worker	45	F
#6	Production worker	44	M	#6	Production worker	51	M
#7	Production worker	52	F	#7	Production worker	53	M
#8	Staff	54	M	#8	Production worker	54	M
	Changchun state enterprises March 19, 2005				Foshan private enterprises March 13, 2005		
#1	Skilled worker	33	F	#1	Production worker	31	
#2	Retired	52	F	#2	Skilled worker	38	
#3	Skilled worker	37	M	#3	Skilled worker	38	
#4	Production worker	35	M	#4	Staff,	42	
#5	Production worker	30	M	#5	Production worker	43	
#6	Staff	41	F	#6	Staff,	49	
#7	Retired	53	F	#7	Retired	56	
#8	Production worker	43	M	#8	Retired	53	

Notes: F, female; M, male.

TABLE 4.5
Views on social security in a socialist country (%)
We're a socialist country; the state should have full responsibility for social security.

Strongly agree	Agree	Disagree	Strongly disagree	Total (n = 601)
27.6	43.4	24.8	4.2	100.0

Respondents were also asked to consider the degree of Chinese economic development and whether universal pension rights were currently attainable. Support for pensions based on citizenship was strongly curbed under this statement. ("China is not prosperous enough for all citizens to receive pensions.")

TABLE 4.6
Multivariate analysis: Views on social security in a socialist country
We're a socialist country; the state should have full responsibility for social security.

	β	Significance
Age	−0.005 (0.006)	0.406
Education	**0.050** (0.016)	0.001
Income	0.000 (0.000)	0.058
Men	**0.216** (0.097)	0.026
Retirees	−0.110 (0.129)	0.395

$\chi^2 = 38.3$
Significance = 0.000
−2 log likelihood = 1,380.7

Notes: Ordered probit regression results. Values in parentheses are standard errors. Significant coefficients ($p < 0.05$) shown in boldface. Response categories were coded 1 = strongly agree; 2 = agree; 3 = disagree; 4 = strongly disagree.

TABLE 4.7
Views on pension rights (%)
Pensions are a basic right of all citizens.

Strongly agree	Agree	Disagree	Strongly disagree	Total ($n = 586$)
59.0	39.2	1.5	0.0	100.0

China is not prosperous enough for all citizens to receive pensions.

Strongly agree	Agree	Disagree	Strongly disagree	Total ($n = 586$)
27.3	52.2	18.4	2.0	100.0

Should (farmers, migrant workers) receive more, the same, or less in pension benefits compared to urban residents?

	More	Same	Less
Farmers ($n = 563$)	11.2	60.6	28.2
Migrant workers ($n = 561$)	8.4	66.3	25.3

Table 4.7 shows that approximately one-fifth (20.4 percent) of respondents disagreed with this statement. The notion of pension rights for all citizens, of course, relates to the fact that rural residents and rural migrants to urban areas have traditionally not been covered by urban social insurance programs,

TABLE 4.8
Multivariate analysis: Pension rights for farmers and migrants
Should (farmers, migrant workers) receive more, the same, or less in pension benefits compared to urban residents?

	Migrants		Farmers	
	β	Significance	β	Significance
Age	**0.019** (0.007)	0.008	**0.026** (0.007)	0.000
Education	**0.044** (0.017)	0.011	**0.046** (0.017)	0.007
Income	0.000 (0.000)	0.862	0.000 (0.000)	0.653
Men	0.155 0(.109)	0.157	−0.095 (0.106)	0.371
Retirees	**−0.300** (0.147)	0.041	**−0.272** (0.142)	0.056
	$\chi^2 = 12.9$ Significance = 0.025 −2 log likelihood = 904.9		$\chi^2 = 18.1$ Significance = 0.003 −2 log likelihood = 986.6	

Notes: Ordered probit regression results. Values in parentheses are standard errors. Significant coefficients ($p < 0.05$) are shown in boldface. Response categories were coded 1 = more; 2 = same; 3 = less.

although in the last decade some localities have begun to expand migrant programs. In a separate question, respondents were asked whether farmers and migrant laborers should receive pension benefits at the same levels as urban residents, at higher or lower levels than urban residents, or no pensions at all. The last row of table 4.7 shows that most respondents (60.6 percent) said that farmers should receive the same level of pension benefits. A slightly larger proportion (66.3 percent) also said that migrant workers should receive the same level of pension benefits as urban residents. Those who said migrants and farmers should receive less than urban residents were, according to the ordered probit regression in table 4.8, generally older and more educated, but when age was controlled for, retirees were more likely to support higher levels of pensions for farmers and migrants.

Focus group discussions also revealed a broad level of support for rights to the same level of pension benefits for peasants and migrant workers. Focus group participants generally felt that if pensions were based upon individuals' contributions to the nation and society, then migrant workers and peasants deserved equal treatment with urban workers (Changchun state enterprises, #2, #7, #8). The general sentiment was that, having literally built the Chinese urban landscapes, migrant workers were deserving of some form of government pension and medical benefits. Participants in the Nanjing focus groups noted with concern that peasants had no medical insurance and that if they suffered a serious illness, they could only "wait to die" (Nanjing state enterprises

#2, #7; Nanjing private enterprises, #3). This point of consensus among focus groups was consistent with the BAS results that reflected strong support for universal pension coverage.

Perhaps the strongest opinions elicited during the focus group discussions related to the issue of inequality in pension coverage and benefits. In all six focus groups, at least one participant brought up the fact that Chinese officials receive far higher benefits than do ordinary urban workers. Most often a focus group participant would raise the issue of official corruption as a sort of reference point when discussing his or her current livelihood and thoughts concerning retirement. Some participants stridently objected to the fact that officials enjoyed high salaries, low expenses (since their food and housing was virtually free), and generous retirement benefits courtesy of the state budget. "What qualifications do they have to get so much money?" asked one participant (Beijing state enterprises, #1). A forty-two-year-old Nanjing factory worker complained that "officials can still be working at age 80 and not necessarily be thinking about retiring—it's really unfair. We workers at the bottom levels don't have any sense of security" (Nanjing state enterprises, #4).[3] Focus group participants also noted that the family members of retired cadres also receive free medical care and other perks.

Confidence in the State

Table 4.9 shows that BAS respondents possessed a high degree of confidence in the future of Chinese public pensions. Only 18.6 percent of the respondents reported that they were not very or not at all confident about the future of the Chinese pension system, and 12.5 percent stated that they were very confident. The ordered probit regression model in table 4.10 shows that, after controlling for age, education, income, and gender, retirees were more likely to express confidence in the future of pensions than those still active in the labor market (i.e., unemployed or working). This finding among Beijing retirees is potentially very significant if replicated in further surveys with samples from elsewhere in China. It suggests that SOE retirees, despite having had their social contract revoked by the state, are nonetheless confident that the state can provide them with pensions.

TABLE 4.9
Confidence in the future of pensions (%)
How confident are you in the future of social pension insurance?

Very confident	Somewhat confident	Not too confident	Not at all confident	Total (*n* = 570)
12.50	68.90	16.80	1.80	100.0

TABLE 4.10
Multivariate analysis: Confidence in future of pensions
How confident are you in the future of social pension insurance?

	β	Significance
Age	−0.004	0.599
	(0.007)	
Education	0.002	0.927
	(0.017)	
Income	0.000	0.841
	(.000)	
Men	−0.112	0.297
	(.107)	
Retirees	**−0.355**	0.015
	(0.146)	

$\chi^2 = 14.2$
Significance = 0.014
−2 log likelihood = 981.5

Notes: Ordered probit regression results. Values in parentheses are standard errors. Significant coefficients ($p < 0.05$) are shown in boldface. Response categories were coded 1 = very confident; 2 = somewhat confident; 3 = not too confident; 4 = not at all confident.

Focus group discussions showed a more nuanced view of the ability of the Chinese state to provide pensions. Some participants based their confidence on the fact that the state would be compelled to provide pensions to prevent social unrest. A Beijing worker reasoned, "If you can't get a pension, the state will be in chaos. This affects a large number of people, and if they don't get pensions, how will the state not be in chaos?" (Beijing private enterprises, #1). A forty-five-year-old Nanjing private enterprise worker also argued that pensions were much too important for social stability for the government not to take measures to see that pensions were paid, whatever the cost (Nanjing private enterprises, #4). But others, especially those in the private sector, said they were not so confident. "I pay money but I don't know whether it will have any value [for future pension benefits]" (Foshan private enterprises, #4). Pension policy was always changing, some noted, and this led to uncertainty (Foshan private enterprises, #5, #2).

One of the crucial links between public opinion and the capability of local government agencies to administer pensions by collecting social insurance fees from employers and workers is the extent to which citizens trust these agencies. After explaining to respondents that central and local government agencies were in charge of managing pension funds and that commercial insurance companies were in charge of managing commercial pension funds, surveyors asked respondents to rate the levels of trust in central and local government agencies as well as in commercial insurance companies.

TABLE 4.11
Trust in government agencies and commercial insurers (%)
Central and local government agencies as well as commercial insurance firms are responsible for collecting pension insurance contributions, administering pension funds, and distributing pension benefits. In general, how much do you trust each to handle pension administration?

	Not at all	Not very much	Neutral	Somewhat	A lot
Local government (n = 593)	1.3	12.8	10.6	62.4	12.8
Central government (n = 593)	1.7	6.6	7.3	59.7	24.8
Commercial insurance firms (n = 590)	7.1	36.9	31.9	22.5	1.5

Note: Percentages do not add to 100 due to rounding.

Table 4.11 shows the results of the degree of trust that Beijing respondents placed in central and local governments as well as in commercial insurance companies to manage pension funds. A strong majority of respondents (84.5 percent) said that they somewhat trusted or very much trusted the central government to administer pensions, and about the same proportion (85.2 percent) placed some or a high level of trust in local governments to administer pensions. This finding is somewhat surprising, given that local governments are usually regarded as having more problems with corruption than the central government agencies. In Beijing, which has had its share of corruption scandals among local officialdom, perhaps residents were nonetheless willing to trust the local government to handle pensions. A more plausible explanation for the convergence in levels of trust between the central and local governments is that respondents were able to draw a strong distinction between the way that government agencies versus commercial firms handled pensions. As reported in table 4.11, respondents expressed very low levels of trust in commercial insurance agencies, with only 24 percent stating that they somewhat or very much trusted their ability to administer pensions.

Across occupational groups, workers and retirees were divided on the issue of trust. The ordered probit regression in Table 4.12 shows that retirees were more likely to express lower levels of trust in local government to administer pensions than were workers. The relatively lower levels of trust in local government among BAS respondents who were retirees, compared to workers and unemployed, could be a reflection of their relatively more positive assessment of the central government or their consideration of past cases of corruption among Beijing municipal officials (we would expect workers to have also expressed this concern, however). In my analysis of the Shanghai survey data (mentioned earlier), there was no significant difference in levels of trust toward the local government among retirees and workers (although women

TABLE 4.12
Multivariate analysis of trust in government agencies and commercial insurers
In general, how much do you trust central and local government agencies and commercial insurance firms to handle pension administration?

	Local government		Central government		Commercial insurers	
	β	Significance	β	Significance	β	Significance
Age	**0.021** (0.007)	0.001	0.009 (0.007)	0.190	−0.004 (0.006)	0.560
Education	0.023 (0.016)	0.166	−0.008 (0.016)	0.622	0.022 (0.016)	0.151
Income	0.000 (0.000)	0.849	0.000 (0.000)	0.897	0.000 (0.000)	0.520
Men	−0.103 (0.101)	0.305	0.022 (0.101)	0.829	**−0.249** (0.096)	0.010
Unemployed	−0.106 (0.137)	0.439	−0.176 (0.137)	0.199	−0.137 (.131)	0.292
Retirees	**−0.292** (0.144)	0.043	−0.129 (0.144)	0.371	−0.037 (0.137)	0.790
	χ^2 = 12.0 Significance = 0.061 −2 log likelihood = 1,297.7		χ^2 = 3.7 Significance = 0.719 −2 log likelihood = 1,276.0		χ^2 = 12.2 Significance = 0.057 −2 log likelihood = 1,531.5	

Notes: Ordered probit regression results for each category. Values in parentheses are standard errors. Significant coefficients ($p < 0.05$) shown in boldface. Response categories were coded 1 = not at all trust; 2 = not very much trust; 3 = neutral trust; 4 = somewhat trust; 5 = trust a lot.

were more likely to express lower levels of trust in local government than were men). Regarding the central government, Shanghai retirees were more likely than workers to express lower levels of trust in its administering pensions. In short, Beijing retirees placed lower levels of trust in their local government than did Beijing workers; Shanghai retirees placed lower levels of trust in the central government than did Shanghai workers.[4]

The results in table 4.12 also show that there was no significant difference in levels of trust among retirees and workers regarding commercial insurance firms or the central government. Commercial insurance companies were viewed as untrustworthy across both groups, and the central government was regarded as trustworthy across both groups. The only significant variable in the model for trust in commercial insurance companies was gender—males were more likely to express lower levels of trust in commercial insurance for retirement needs than were women.

The findings of high levels of trust and confidence in public pensions should be qualified by the content of focus group discussions, which revealed a low level of satisfaction with pension benefits. Focus group participants uniformly and strongly agreed that retirement would bring a substantial decline in livelihood. One participant in the Nanjing focus group of state enterprise workers stated that "once you retire, your living standards definitely decline" (Nanjing state enterprises, #8). Others also felt that they would at best receive a pension providing them with barely enough to live on and that they would lack any prospects of obtaining a postretirement job capable of supplementing their income (Nanjing state enterprises, #5, #7; Changchun state enterprises #2, #1). In some cases, focus group participants were recently retired workers, who in their early fifties had their own as well as family members' medical costs to support. One fifty-two-year-old plastics factory worker (Changchun state enterprises, #2) estimated her monthly expenses at 500–600 yuan, which could barely be met with her pension; if she needed medicine or medical care, the money would have to come from elsewhere.

Conclusion

Polanyi's double movement paradigm, in which governments create social legislation to embed the market as they simultaneously promote the diffusion of market forces on society, says nothing about the types of legislation that emerge from this process. As the preceding discussion suggests, that question can be answered for China by taking into account the historical and institutional context of the Chinese transition to markets, as well as the attitudes and beliefs of the population. The way that the Chinese government sought to embed labor markets was in part a reaction to the instability posed by mass layoffs in the state sector in the 1990s and the increasing employment insecurity that was enshrined in the labor contract system that was legalized in 1995. The dismantling of the large parts of the state sector and with it the all-encompassing exclusive welfare coverage for full-time SOE workers has been replaced by new norms of equal access to coverage for health care and pensions. The principle of equal access to social insurance for all employees of urban enterprises receives only lip service from many employers in the vast landscape of the Chinese labor market, but the normative shift is significant. As many studies have shown, for decades the Chinese state has maintained policies that created a highly stratified or segmented labor force (Walder 1986; Perry 1994). Although the core of the state-sector workforce remains protected under preferential welfare programs run by the large SOEs that dominate sectors such as energy and telecommunications, even these employees are under the same rules for pensions and other social insurance as workers in private sector and foreign-invested firms, regardless of their size or profitability. In addition, the continuing informalization of Chinese labor threatens to undermine the modest advances in social insurance in recent years. Labor service companies and other contracting firms allow the enterprises and employers that use them to evade regulations requiring all employees of urban enterprises to provide social insurance coverage.

Against this tide of informalization, public opinion appears firmly behind the idea of welfare rights and coverage based on citizenship rather than employment. Indeed, this support for social insurance as a citizenship right may be the public's hedge against the rising tide of informalization and the loss of welfare benefits that accompanies informal employment. The public opinion data analyzed here, although limited in its scope to views about pensions, suggests that urban workers in China place a strong emphasis on the state provision of pensions and that they view pension eligibility as a basic right. The focus group discussions also revealed a keen awareness of the failings of the state to meet pension and other broader welfare obligations to migrants and peasants, as well as a sense of injustice in the generous medical and pension benefits accorded to state officials. This is the broader context of urban public opinion in which a range of social policies under Hu Jintao were launched after 2003. These new programs included rural medical cooperatives, rural and urban minimum living payments (*dibao*), the abolition of school fees in rural areas, and the expansion of social insurance programs for health care and pensions, among others.

In large part, the central government has escaped blame for the failings of its social policies to protect citizens against the risks of market forces. The local governments, which are charged with implementing most of the Chinese social policies, are also required to finance these programs. Thus, any shortcomings and injustices are seen by the public as largely the result of local government malfeasance and corruption. Yet tolerance by Beijing of a highly fragmented pension program also places fundamental constraints on its ability to redistribute welfare funds from rich to poor areas (Frazier 2010). It is too early to determine the effect social policy measures of the Hu administration on the public perception of the ability of the CCP to cope with demands for greater social protection. But if the early indications regarding pensions provide tentative clues, the public assessment of other social policies is likely to be ambivalent. On the one hand, these policies appear to be creating cash transfers of a sort (although pensions are based on social insurance rather than outright transfers from taxes) to eligible recipients. On the other hand, the awareness of inequalities in pension and other welfare provision creates in the mind of the public a demand for broader coverage and for capable government agencies to handle the new programs. If measures to expand health care and other social insurance coverage to the nearly one-half of the urban workforce who lack such protections are met with successful countermeasures by enterprises to hire informal labor and to evade the costs associated with expanded coverage, there is some likelihood that the central government, and the CCP itself, will no longer be able to escape blame for Chinese social policy shortcomings.

Part II

Transformation of Employment Relations in Industries

Chapter 5

Enterprise Reform and Wage Movements in Chinese Oil Fields and Refineries

Kun-Chin Lin

As Mary Gallagher, Ching Kwan Lee, and Sarosh Kuruvilla (chap. 1 in this volume) point out, there has been a qualitative transformation in labor relations in China since the mid-1990s. The state has led a process of deconstructing socialist labor relations to facilitate the commodification of state-owned productive assets and human resources. The structure and ownership of firms were redrawn with corporatization, privatization, and market liberalization while workers were forced to reckon with the end of their iron rice bowl tenure.

This chapter examines the impact of state-led organizational restructuring in the state-owned oil and petrochemical industries that are so central to the rapid economic development of China. My focus is on understanding the movements in wages in this industry. Comparing wage scales before and after the 1998–1999 restructuring of the Chinese oil and petrochemical industries, I show how a pattern of relatively stable increases and narrow wage gaps among employees in the first decade and a half of reform rapidly gave way to a dramatic escalation of wage differentials after restructuring took place.

Restructuring has not yet led to a free-market determination of wages. Instead, political imperatives continue to place constraints on price-setting in state-owned enterprises (SOEs). The central government, to reduce exposure to loss-making operations and unsustainable labor forces, sold off most non-strategic SOEs or devolved them to local authorities. The retained enterprises were placed under asset management companies, and their corporate governance and organizational structures were transformed through restructuring plans that aimed to carve out a profitable core of assets and workforce from the black-box operation of the past. The end result was the creation of a core-periphery divide in the industry, with stable employment at the core and temporary and informal employment in the larger periphery.

How can we best understand and explain these changes? I propose a network organizational approach to map out the constituent parts of an oil field or refinery and their forms of resource exchange, which shape the state-appointed managers' degree of freedom to direct state-owned capital to meet labor demands. The sociological analysis of interorganizational networks puts forth the notion of centrality as a measure of socioeconomic power of certain nodes of dense connectivity in the network.[1] As applied to the case study presented here, centrality describes the network characteristic of decision-making units that coordinate high transaction volumes, gather resources from formal and informal ties, and exercise a high degree of flexibility in directing the exchange relations in the administrative and corporate networks in large state-owned conglomerates. I focus on financial and labor centralities. *Financial centrality* refers to the concentration of financial resources for wage payments, where they are deposited, pooled, and augmented; *labor centrality* refers to the organizational locus of chronic overstaffing or low productivity of workers.

The organizational locations of these two centralities strongly shape the interactions of internal and external labor markets, which impose constraints on the overall wage-payment bill and wage-scale adjustments. Prior to 1998, the petroleum administrative bureaus (PABs) that oversaw the oil fields or refineries and a wide range of related work units represented the loci for the overlap of both financial and labor centralities—a condition that enabled managers to harness resources to support wage inflations and sustain workforce expansion. The asset restructuring of 1998–1999 established an institutional divide between capital-intensive core subsidiaries and labor-intensive noncore firms within each production site of the national oil corporations (NOCs) and, thus, radically reshaped interfirm network relations. Financial centrality has since been moved up to the corporate headquarters in Beijing, whereas labor centrality has been devolved and concentrated in the noncore parts. As a result, the burden of cost reduction has fallen squarely on the noncore while the core leveraged profitability to justify wage hikes for employees. I point out the inherent risks in this arrangement from the instability of network relations, posing enduring problems for location-specific labor market formation and sector-specific industrial governance.

Discontinuous Change in Wages in the Chinese Oil Industry

According to Christopher Erickson and Sarosh Kuruvilla, a transformation in labor relations involves changes in the "deep structure," defined as "basic principles" of labor relations that may include "attitudes toward and definitions of property rights in the workplace, employer/employee relative status, individualism versus collectivism, and the nature of exchange in the labor market" (1998, 18).[2] A transformation can be characterized by the speed of change relative to past changes and the scope of dissemination and degree of diversity in experimentations of forms. At times, rapid change and a sudden proliferation of varying forms of experimentation produce a discontinuous change; at other times, incremental changes may still lead to a transformation as cumulatively they eventually alter the deep structure (Erickson and Kuruvilla 1998, 11–12).

China is a case of discontinuous transformation and not the incremental transformation implied in conventional narratives of gradualism in market reform. Wage movements and wage-grade differentials in state-owned oil fields and refineries in China followed a path-dependent trajectory of incremental change up to the mid-1990s, but were then overtaken by a discontinuous transformation since 1999.[3] The experience of oil and petrochemical producers illustrates the national context of increasing difficulties and the final abandonment of a universal wage framework for the SOEs.

Wage Movements in Chinese Oil Fields from the 1980s to the Mid-1990s

In the immediate post-Mao period, Chinese reformers were centrally concerned with reestablishing order in urban industries and workplaces following the Cultural Revolution, which in practical terms meant delegitimizing ad hoc and radical political processes and reinstitutionalizing Soviet-style national wage scales (e.g., the "eight-grade system" from the 1950s; Lin 2008c). In 1985, Beijing laid down a national framework for the industrial-wage structure that introduced employee incentives pegged to the performance of the enterprise as a whole as well as to individual markers. This framework took effect in the context of increasing enterprise autonomy, managerial-responsibility contracts, decentralized administration of wages, and the de-linking of the wage structures of administrative and production work units in the state-owned sectors. The local political effect of these enterprise reform measures was to foster a workplace-based "growth coalition" among managers and workers in pursuit of fixed-capital accumulation and wage inflation, which explicitly defied the national wage guidelines and confounded the macroeconomic management and fiscal integrity of the central government. Repeated attempts in the early 1990s to cap the floating component of wages and to adjust the classification of the types of work and methods for assessing personal merits to the complexity of tasks failed to stem the tide of upward wage pressure. Studies of wage levels from the mid-1980s to the mid-1990s spoke uniformly of the lack of responsiveness of wage movements to market forces and the apparent distorting effects of institutionalized bargaining activities between government officials and the enterprises under their jurisdiction, and between managers and workers in SOEs.[4]

The natural resource extraction and processing sectors have traditionally enjoyed relatively high wages compared with the industrial average. Even as early as 1955, petroleum workers earned the highest average monthly wage of 109.89 yuan, with a highest-to-lowest grade wage ratio (3.18) above the industrial average (3.1) (Hoffman 1968, 18). Starting with the three major oil fields of Daqing (in the province of Heilongjiang), Shengli (Shandong), and Liaohe (Liaoning), oil fields implemented the 1985 wage framework about a year after its passage. Although the data are far from complete, it appears that prior to 1999 the wages of oil and petrochemical workers increased steadily and with controlled disparities.[5] The ratio of the administratively set salary at the highest wage tier to that of the lowest wage tier in oil fields had varied, but not linearly toward greater disparity. In 1985, the ratio was 7.3 for cadre wages, 3.15 for technicians, and equally small for workers. Under the 1993 unified wage-grade system, the ratio had become 7.5 (the highest grade of 639 yuan per month to the lowest grade of 84 yuan) for all workers; a year later, parallel wage tracks for administrators, technicians and "operators" (relatively unskilled workers and service providers) were reintroduced with policy constraints on disparities limiting the ratios to 6 for administrators (660 yuan per month for the highest grade to 110 yuan for the lowest), 5.5. for technicians (655 yuan to 120 yuan), and 5.4 for operators (460 yuan to 85 yuan).[6] These numbers reflect a downward trend from the greater disparity under the 1993 system.

Reflecting the general trends across all industries and ownership types, oil fields rewarded seniority handsomely (Peng 1992; Hu, Li, and Shi 1988; Gustafsson et al. 2001). A worker with twenty-one to twenty-five years of experience earned an additional 6 yuan per month; one with twenty-six to thirty years earned and extra 8 yuan; and one with thirty-one years or more earned an extra 10 yuan. Given that wages for technical workers ranged from 37 to 123 yuan per month, these bonuses could become sizable. Ex-workers who retired before the 1984 wage reform got an extra 17 yuan in monthly subsidies. In 1989 and 1992, the retirees got additional 10-yuan increases in subsidies per month. Although the pensioners gained in the short run, they lacked long-term and institutionalized means of obtaining cost-of-living adjustments in the context of rapid economic changes (Hurst and O'Brien 2002).

Despite the introduction of performance linkages, market forces did not penetrate decision making regarding wages (Xie and Hannum 1996). The PAB, which administered the main oil field or refinery complex and its associated production and service units in a given locality, was where the buck stopped under the traditional planned economy. At the level of the PAB, central and local states assessed and adjusted the aggregate wage bill. The actual disbursement of wages within the firm followed the wage grades set nationally and adopted with some modification by the PAB. In actuality, however, a significant part of wage distribution became a black-box operation. The PAB contained three lower tiers of administration: the core oil field or refinery unit, large production teams, and small teams. Each of these levels exercised discretion in interpreting and modifying formal wage structures. Under pressure, the work units within the PAB colluded to hide information and extract concessions from state planners.[7] During this period, workers easily persuaded managers to constantly revise upwardly their wages and bonuses.[8]

Given a fiscal environment of soft-budget constraints and their greater autonomy over personnel and wage decisions, state-appointed managers had no overt reason to object to workers' demands. In fact, while most oil fields were operating in the red in the early 1990s, there were minimal attempts to cut labor costs by either reducing wages or eliminating workers (see tables 5.1 and 5.2). Since China became a net oil importer in 1993, leading to the prioritization of the development and conservation of domestic resources by Beijing, upstream companies had benefited from more favorable central government policies, such as price adjustments and financial support from state-owned commercial banks. As a result, oil fields began to grow again and pretax profits rose. Refineries enjoyed a golden age in the first half of the 1990s. With administrative prices converging with global prices and crude imports becoming available, domestic banks loaned freely as Chinese petrochemical producers geared up to meet rising domestic demand and exports.[9]

The absence of wage reductions or layoffs as instruments of cost reduction also reflected the continuing ambivalence by Beijing toward undercutting the livelihood of its industrial constituency; for example, the State Council regularly prefaced decrees for enterprise restructuring with stern comments on the preservation of the workforce and securing the income level of discharged workers. Workers were asked to leave voluntarily with fat severance packages and promises of unending additional support when needed (Lin 2009). As a cumulative result of these practices, aggregate wage bills by 1995 represented 20–30 percent of the total cost of Chinese oil companies (Liu 1998, 7). This percentage was much higher than that for efficient producers in the West or in Japan and suggested to central reformers the existence of substantial slack in resource utilization, which became a point of reform focus and contention in the next period.

Wage Movements in Chinese Oil Fields since the Late 1990s

The macro- and microeconomic contexts for wage determination took an unpredictable turn in the second half of the 1990s. Competition between SOEs

TABLE 5.1
Number of employees in extraction and processing sectors, 1990–2006

Year	Extraction of petroleum and natural gas (thousands)	Processing of petroleum; coking; processing of nuclear fuel (thousands)
1990	740	442
1991	727	491
1992	778	761
1993	1,232	679
1994	1,166	712
1995	1,280	719
1996	1,252	761
1997	1,165	742
1998	1,123	677
1999	1,024	629
2000	809	617
2001	736	570
2002	779	566
2003	862	526
2004	885	508
2005	875	552
2006	931	555

Source: MOLSS (1991–2007).
Note: Year-end totals shown.

TABLE 5.2
Average annual earnings of workers in extraction and processing sectors, 1990–2006

Year	Extraction of petroleum and natural gas (yuan)	Processing of petroleum, coking, processing of nuclear fuel (yuan)
1990	3,160	2,921
1991	3,516	3,106
1992	3,845	3,528
1993	5,007	4,563
1994	7,507	6,538
1995	9,238	8,426
1996	10,727	9,153
1997	12,127	9,657
1998	12,707	11,094
1999	14,318	12,917
2000	16,614	15,335
2001	18,695	15,854
2002	20,663	17,357
2003	23,082	20,733
2004	26,316	22,951
2005	30,018	25,494
2006	33,180	28,335

Source: MOLSS (1991–2007).

and collective and private firms and between Chinese and foreign producers went up several notches as the national economy and most sectors switched from a state of chronic shortage to surplus. Liberalization pressures increased with the preparation by China to join the World Trade Organization. Industries faced overcapacity problems, falling prices for their outputs, snowballing indebtedness, and in 1997 a massive influx of cheap imports from neighboring states suffering in the Asian financial crisis. To combat these mounting competitive pressures, Beijing backed a two-pronged bailout package to recapitalize the SOEs (San Nian Tuokun, or "Three Years out of Trouble") and privatize most state-owned medium-size enterprises (Zhua Da Fang Xiao, or "Grasping the Large and Letting Go of the Small") (Zweig 2001). From 1998 to 1999, the State Council implemented a major restructuring of the oil and petrochemical industries to establish two vertically and horizontally integrated (onshore) NOCs, the China National Petroleum Corporation (CNPC) and Sinopec, which then underwent further asset reallocation to create core and noncore subsidiaries under the parent companies. The core firms—PetroChina (under CNPC) and Sinopec Listed (under Sinopec)—were then put up for initial public listings on the global and domestic stock markets (Lin 2006).

For every oil field and refinery, the former PAB was divided into a core subsidiary (called here the core) that concentrated the most valuable and profit-generating assets and a relatively lean workforce drawn from the former SOEs, and a noncore company (the noncore) that held most of the loss-making assets and the surplus workforce, including those work units involved in production and technical services for the oil fields and refineries, as well as in the provision of social services and local public goods including canteens, hospitals, schools, and residential compounds.[10] Financially, the core units are designated profit centers; that is, their primary responsibility to the headquarters is to generate a set level of profits. In contrast, the noncore units are designated cost centers with duties to control the overall and labor costs, keeping them below levels specified by the top financial executives of the parent holding company. Equal in legal stature as independent persons, the core and noncore companies in each production site engage in contract-based exchanges mediated in Beijing by the corporate headquarters. In practice, the core net payment for the noncore contractual services constitutes the desired cost level of the noncore as it seeks to break even (see table 5.3).

The watershed asset restructuring of the oil and petrochemical sectors was followed by a discontinuous transformation of the wage regime in response to new ownership demands. First, the State Council (technically, state asset companies created by the State Council) took up a new role as the dominant shareholder of the new corporations, focusing on improved corporate extraction of and control over surpluses from the subsidiaries (Lin 2007). Second, as

TABLE 5.3
Organizational characteristics of NOC core and noncore subsidiaries, 2000

Organizational characteristics	Core subsidiaries (oil companies)	Noncore subsidiaries (oil bureaus)
Asset profile	0.75 of total profitable assets	0.25 of total profitable assets
Labor-cost profile	0.25 of total labor force	0.75 of total labor force
Market orientation	National and international	Local
Organizational goals	Profitability and cost reduction	Stability and restructuring
Sources of revenue	Production and sales; dividends	Contractual earnings for services to the listed part; government transfers
Financial principles	Production units as cost centers; simplified, transparent; centralized accounting	Former administrative units as profit centers with legal-person status; independent accounting
Principal-agent relations	Central state asset management company as the dominant shareholder of the listed company; publicly listed in domestic and international stock markets	Central state asset management company as the sole shareholder of the noncore company

Source: Author's summary of data from China National Petroleum Corporation ([CNPC] 1998).
Notes: NOC, national oil corporation.

the corporate headquarters of listed companies came under pressure to register profitability and take on the appearance of Western-style corporate governance, they regularly offered promises of massive layoffs and efficiency-oriented wage reforms to appease nonstate investors (see table 5.4). Exploiting the new institutional cleavage between core and noncore parts, central state and elite corporate interests designed transfer pricing through the squeezing the cost levels of the noncore subsidiaries to generate profitability for the core-listed companies. The manipulation of wage rates and spreads reflected this agenda.

At the moment of restructuring and accompanied wage reform in 1999, managerial income in oil fields and refineries fell into a broad range of 50,000–180,000 yuan per year (a wage differential of 3.6, lower than in earlier periods).[11] The initially narrow disparity was soon overtaken by opportunities for rewarding managers and core employees enabled by the new partitions of assets and workforce.[12]

Trends in compensation closely followed the new institutional divisions in the NOCs after the 1998–1999 restructuring. Employees of the core subsidiaries of the NOCs enjoyed an overall rising wage distribution, exceeding that of the industrial averages (both extraction and processing industries are considered). If we use the industrial averages (see table 5.5) as proxies for the noncore unlisted firms, the increasing disparity between core and noncore becomes clear. More direct evidence of general wage stagnation in the noncore can be

TABLE 5.4
Number of employees in NOC-listed companies, 1999–2007

	1999	2000	2001	2002	2003	2004	2005	2006	2007
PetroChina-listed company	480,012	441,612	422,554	419,598	417,229	424,175	439,220	446,290	466,502
Sinopec-listed company	N/A	508,168	443,808	418,871	400,513	389,451	364,528	340,886	334,377

Sources: Company 20-F and 6-K reports to SEC, 1999–2007, www.secinfo.com.
Notes: N/A, not available; NOC, national oil corporation; SEC, U.S. Securities and Exchange Commission.

TABLE 5.5
Average annual wages, 1999–2006

Year	Sinopec (yuan)	PetroChina (yuan)	Oil and natural gas exploration[a] (yuan)	Processing[a] (yuan)
1999	N/A	16,264	14,318	12,917
2000	18,756	20,566	16,614	15,335
2001	21,185	21,876	18,695	15,854
2002	24,733	25,336	20,663	17,357
2003	31,130	30,901	23,082	20,733
2004	34,893	35,188	26,316	22,951
2005	37,311	44,058	30,018	25,494
2006	45,995	59,667	33,180	28,335

[a]Industrial average.

TABLE 5.6
Comparison of average wages of Sinopec Holding Group and Sinopec Listed Company, 1999–2004

	1999	2000	2001	2002	2003	2004
Sinopec Group						
Total number of employees	1,017,600	1,156,500	906,200	896,700	845,100	767,600
Wage and salaries (millions of yuan)	16,768	19,973	19,968	19,002	20,886	22,013
Average wage and salaries per employee (yuan)	16,478	17,270	22,035	21,191	24,714	28,678
Sinopec Listed Company						
Average wage and salaries per employee (yuan)	18,756	21,185	24,733	31,130	34,893	37,311

Sources: Sinopec Yearbook (various years); Company 20-F and 6-K reports to SEC, 1999–2007, www.secinfo.com.

Note: SEC, U.S. Securities and Exchange Commission.

calculated from data on the entire Sinopec Group (the parent holding company, including both the noncore and core subsidiaries), which shows that from 2000 to 2004 the aggregate wage bill was kept relatively constant, with workforce reductions permitting incremental increases in the average wage of Sinopec employees (see table 5.6). It is unfortunate that the NOCs do not release separate data on noncore employees, which would allow an explicit comparison of trends in worker compensation.[13]

The observed steady increase in company contributions to employees' social security and pension plans (see tables 5.7 and 5.8) may appear to be a continuation of the wage-padding behavior of the old SOEs. As previously explained, this financial stability is the outcome of the strategy by the headquarters to create a privileged bundle of assets and employees via the core-noncore division. Lacking data on the noncore firms, we cannot tell if the remaining noncore

TABLE 5.7
Average annual corporate contributions to employee retirement plans, 1999–2002

Year	Sinopec (yuan)	PetroChina (yuan)
1999	N/A	3,677
2000	2,674	4,318
2001	3,060	4,480
2002	3,953	5,026
2003	4,699	5,256
2004	5,757	5,837
2005	6,224	7,067
2006	7,023	10,408
2007	8,392	12,313

Note: N/A, not available.

TABLE 5.8
Average annual corporate payments for social security costs, 1999–2007

Year	Sinopec (yuan)	PetroChina (yuan)
1999	N/A	6,785
2000	1,620	12,110
2001	1,843	11,236
2002	2,309	13,387
2003	2,492	15,936
2004	2,647	17,406
2005	2,263	23,505
2006	2,555	28,080
2007	3,861	38,701

Note: N/A, not available.

workers have attained a similar, although at a lower level, stability in compensation. If so, this would mark a departure from the uncertainties of the late 1990s, when social welfare and in-kind benefits became highly contentious and unpredictable with work unit attempts at variously titled severance (*xiagang*) packages.[14]

Within the core firms, upper managers have reaped increasing rewards (see table 5.9). Starting in 1999 with the low 3.6 ratio between the highest and lowest salaries, the wage differential skyrocketed to 22.86:1 in 2005, 68.44:1 in 2006, and 91.67:1 in 2007 for directors of Sinopec, and 8.42:1, 39.33:1, and 39.33:1 for supervisors in the same years. The aggregate salaries (including wages, certain allowances, and in-kind benefits) of the top five highest-paid Sinopec corporate officials rose from 1.4 million to 4.5 million yuan between 2001 and 2007; for the PetroChina top earners, it rose from 1 million to 3.6 million yuan in the same period. The pro-management bias is reflected in

TABLE 5.9
Wage differentials for directors and supervisors in Sinopec, 2005–2007 (RMB'000)

	2005	2006	2007
Wage differential for Sinopec directors			
Highest	480	616	825
Lowest	21	9	9
Differential	459	607	816
Wage differential for Sinopec supervisors			
Highest	202	354	354
Lowest	24	9	9
Differential	178	345	345

Sources: Company 20-F and 6-K reports to SEC, 1999–2007, www.secinfo.com.
Notes: RMB, renminbi; SEC, U.S. Securities and Exchange Commission.

the NOC contributions to employee retirement schemes. The PetroChina annual contribution to its top-five earners' pension plans rose from 22,740 yuan in 2001 to 148,154 yuan in 2007, which was 1.02 times and 2.41 times that of the average company contribution to employee pension plans. Regrettably, no data are publicly available for comparisons to wages and benefits of the top managers in the noncore firms.

Explaining Discontinuities in Wage Regimes

The discontinuous transformation in wage movements since the late 1990s poses an analytical challenge to the literature. There are four major approaches in China studies for explaining changes in labor relations and specifically wages in the reform era: policy-driven, market-logic, bureaucratic politics, and state-society.[15] Most economists writing on Chinese labor relations take central policies and their variable implementation as the main exogenous forces shaping labor market distortions (e.g., labor market segmentation).[16] Politically oriented accounts often rely on time-honored bureaucratic analysis to explore tensions between competing ministries and elite political patrons and in the principal-agent relations between central agencies and subnational governments, which undermine coherent and progressive reform policies.[17] And the state-society paradigm has generated detailed studies of complex dynamics at the two interstices (Migdal, Kohli, and Shue 1994): (1) officials and enterprises under their jurisdiction and (2) managers and workers in a work unit.[18] Typically, long-term particularistic relations are posited as the key mechanism for resolving differences in interests and resource needs between the dyadic pair of governmental and firm-level actors.[19] At times, SOEs are depicted as a community in which moral economic norms govern wage decisions.[20] Specifically, rewards for political loyalty from "activist" employees (Walder 1986) and seniority and egalitarianism form a lasting basis of fair compensation for the majority of workers. These norms supposedly vitiate policy changes that are intended to induce performance-based incentive schemes.[21]

These approaches succeed to varying degrees in explaining why state-sector wages are resistant to policy stimuli, but they do not provide as adequate an account of change as our case studies of discontinuous transformation clearly need. First, empirical analyses show that the policy-controlled component of industrial wages decreased in importance in the 1990s as bonus and in-kind payments rose in relative share of total compensation (Child 1994).[22] Most analysts simply attribute the decline to greater managerial autonomy and adherence to firm-level egalitarian norms. Yet it remains a mystery as to how SOEs were able to amass and allocate financial resources for particular patterns of extra-policy and nonmarket compensations, and how these resources might be redirected to create greater wage disparities among firms within an industry or within a firm.

Second, the existing accounts lack specific causal mechanisms for the shift from incremental changes to discontinuous transformation in wage determination. If workplace norms bonded state-appointed managers and workers and facilitated the tasks of management, why did the central reformers or state managers go against these norms in the late 1990s (Meng 2000, 100)? In other words, how did firm-level egalitarian norms endure the vicissitudes of policy changes in the first two decades of reform, only to fall apart with state-engineered enterprise reform and sectoral consolidation in the late 1990s? What changes in the organizational environment of the firm produced the accelerated pace of wage movements and sectoral or geographical diversification in wage rates?

The importance of sectoral and location-specific variations is often noted but has been inadequately explored in existing explanatory approaches. In statistical tests of wage variations, industrial dummies have consistently tested most significant over time.[23] Donald Hay and colleagues (1994) found that, as marketization proceeded in the second half of the 1980s, industry dummies in price-adjusted wages scored high in significant magnitudes. In contrast, and somewhat surprisingly, firm-level institutional variables such as the degree of managerial autonomy, type of managerial contract responsibility system, and the existence of financial difficulties for firms failed to register any significance for wage differentials.[24] The insignificance of these variables suggests that further contextual information on the firm and the market structure is needed to uncover the intervening factors

In addition, locality-specific factors have also registered consistent impacts on wage variations (Child 1994, 194).[25] John Giles, Albert Park and Fang Cai

(2006), for example, found variations in wage arrears and in health and pension benefits across cities. Also, Yu Xie and Emily Hannum (1996) discovered regional variations in earnings inequality, and William Hurst (2004) suggested broad patterns of regional differences in enterprise reform outcomes, levels of compensations, and welfare provision. For large-SOE managers, local political economy imposes operational costs and resource constraints that surely differ between, say, Fushan and Shanghai (Smyth, Zhai, and Wang 2001; Tobin 2003). But how exactly do these locality-specific, external considerations affect intrafirm pricing decisions? And how might we incorporate the importance of bargaining dynamics and particularistic relations between individual enterprises and their political patrons or supervisory agencies in the analysis of sectoral or locality variations?

To start addressing these questions, I propose a network organizational approach that focuses on transactions at and across the boundaries of the firm and that explicitly accounts for particularities in industrial organization and in local market and political relations. Variations in wages, in turn, stem from the internal capital and labor markets of the firm, conditions of the dynamic networks relations of authority and exchange relations surrounding individual state-owned production units. By targeting both these internal markets and the interfirm and local government-business relations, corporatization and the core-noncore restructuring of the oil and petrochemical industries in the late-1990s disrupted preexisting constraints on wage adjustments, leading to wider disparities over time.

Mapping the Network Organizational Characteristics of Oil Bureaus

In the next sections, I offer a broad framework for network organizational analysis of the key authority and exchange relations governing Chinese oil fields and refineries, with an emphasis on identifying the financial and labor centralities that constrain intrafirm pricing decisions. Network analysis developed in the empirical context of understanding the specific environment factors of firms in advanced industrial societies that affect strategic behaviors, such as interlocking directorates with bank representation, mergers and joint ventures, subcontracting relations, agglomeration effects in industrial districts, political activities of corporations, and post-Fordist structural changes in production methods.[26] Network is understood as both structure and practice, and its effectiveness depends on socially embedded processes of legitimation and signification in addition to domination via the control of resource distribution (Sydow and Windeler 1998; Dobbin 2004; Wellman and Berkowitz 1988). Conceptually broad-ranging, the network analysis literature nonetheless presents a specifically targeted approach for empirical research: (1) describe networks of relations, (2) identify key patterns in such networks, (3) trace the flow of resources through them, and (4) discover the effects on individuals connected to the networks in specific ways (Wellman and Berkowitz 1988, 16). Technically, this research agenda faces data challenges in mapping a complex industrial system—as a starter, we would need a huge database on ownership and control and on inter-firm interactions! This chapter does not offer a networkwide analysis for the oil and petrochemical sectors because such data are extremely hard to obtain and verify in China. But this analysis does specify the local and particular properties of the firm-centric social structure without losing sight of its embeddedness in the greater industrial system.

To map the key relations and resource flows in and across the networks surrounding an oil field or refinery, I highlight three types of exchange relations and distinguish between financial and labor centralities. First, exchanges among the various subsidiaries, production and service units, and firms in the industry and the local economy can be broadly characterized as resource-based, authority-driven, or contract-bound (Granovetter 1994, 464–65). Resource-based exchange can be formal or informal and based on market signals, barter under shadow prices, or social capital (e.g., trust). The general assumption is that resource-based exchanges transpire in accordance with the mutual economic interests of the partners in the network. Authority-driven exchange, in contrast, derives from superior-subordinate role relations and again freely crosses the formal-informal divide and need not be state-centric or redistributive in nature. Authority is expressed through decrees, and its effect is not issue- or transaction-specific. Contract-bound exchange is a hybrid form, supposing a compromise of self-interests. Its enforcement draws on the external authority of the legal and broader social normative institutions. Contract-bound exchange negates some of the arbitrariness of authority-driven exchange in order to stabilize the terms of exchange, and with a longer duration it provides flexibility for actors to counteract the vicissitudes of market signals. Although contracts are transaction-specific, a set of contracts may reinforce firm-level price distortions and constrain the contracting parties' broader calculus in resource allocation.

Shifts in the nature and frequency of exchanges among the units of the networks due to corporatization and restructuring have led to shifts in the location and density of financial and labor resources in oil fields and refineries.[27] Recall that *financial centrality* refers to the organizational locus of financial resources for wage payments—where they are accumulated, kept, pooled, and augmented. Network characteristics create channels for as well as barriers to the movement of financial resources to targeted firms and employees. *Labor centrality* refers to the concentration of labor surplus and bottlenecks in exchange with the local labor markets. Persistent rigidities in human resource redeployment in SOEs arise as work units find limited opportunities to reallocate underused manpower within the corporate hierarchy or to displace workers directly on to the local and national labor markets.

As the organizational maps show, in the earlier period of enterprise reform, the oil field and refinery constituted the focal point of both financial and labor centralities, and the overlap allowed the party secretary and oil-field executives to apply financial slack directly to support wage demands. But the core-noncore partition since 1998 has lifted financial centrality above the level of the core and noncore subsidiaries while confining labor centrality to the noncore, thus undermining the ability of managers to sustain equitable wage growth and surplus manpower.

Shifting Network Relations from Administrative to Corporate Hierarchy

As basic administrative units under the national oil and petrochemical companies, the pre-1998 Chinese PABs were embedded in two interfirm networks: (1) the national "socialist production hierarchy" of SOEs (Walder 1992) and (2) a location-specific set of firms brought into contact with an oil field or refinery through the vertical (*tiao*) and horizontal (*kuai*) administrative-authority relations that governed the work units (Schurmann 1968). The first hierarchy largely determined the amount of resources commanded by the firm, as well as planned investment and subsidies from the state, residual claims over output and revenue, and degrees of soft-budget constraints. The rank of a firm in this hierarchy also correlated with its bargaining power vis-à-vis other SOEs in informal bartering situations. Within the constraints of this hierarchy, constant bargaining took place between state managers and ministerial and local governmental authorities over resource distributions in the second, more diffused network that included other firms in the locality and workers benefiting from the businesses related to the SOEs. As a result, managers entered into exchange relations with local SOEs or affiliated firms and relinquished important controls over property rights and employees to outside demands. On the plus side, interfirm networks did not merely constrain managers in fulfilling the planned targets but also provided entrepreneurial opportunities. By building network bridges across "structural holes" (Burt 2004) and combining information from disparate groups that would not otherwise have communicated, managers could overcome chronic problems of material input shortages, unreliable suppliers, and distribution channels and could reallocate (in limited ways) surplus labor.[28] This adaptive strategy has been well documented in comparative socialist economic studies.[29]

The 1998–1999 restructuring disembedded Chinese NOCs from these networks through three key strategies: (1) replacing administrative (planned) resource allocation with corporate hierarchical coordination; (2) instituting contract-based exchanges among subsidiaries, with prices determined by the Beijing corporate headquarters; and (3) reducing the autonomous exchange relations of individual work units with other firms and local governments. The simplification in network relations meant vastly different resource constraints for the core and noncore subsidiaries. The noncore is saddled with the overwhelming pressure of making adjustments. Charged by the headquarters to keep down costs, the noncore units have been driven to haggle with local officials in matters of labor discharge, social welfare, and privatization of assets, such as schools, hospitals, hotels, and restaurants formerly owned or controlled by the PAB. These issues are more often than not addressed in a confrontational manner, with local officials seeking to preserve rent-seeking niches while resisting fiscal or social liabilities (Lin 2008a). At the same time, the corporate headquarters have placed restrictions on noncore units regarding access to local banks and barter or trade relations with downstream producers in the region. These shifts in network relations have resulted in intense network isolation for the noncore, leaving managers in these firms with few options for the reallocation of the workforce.

In contrast, corporate headquarters have enhanced the role of the core units as profit centers by linking their output directly to internal allocation mechanisms. Refineries obtain oil from the oil producers within the parent holding firm and via imports through direct allocation by the headquarters. Therefore, core companies no longer need to concern themselves with developing independent interfirm network relations because its resource exchange relations are now managed at the regional, national, and international levels by the redistribution and trading channels of the parent company.

Network Organizational Maps of National Oil Corporations

Network organizational maps offer a compact view of relationships among primary establishments, their affiliated businesses, governmental units, and banks. The diagram maps the hierarchies, labor markets, and the types of exchanges involved. Summarizing the discussion here and the secondary literature, figures 5.1 and 5.2 offer stylized network maps of the pre-1998 CNPC and the post-1999 CNPC (the parent holding enterprise) and a typical oil exploration and production location that is home to the core-listed subsidiary (PetroChina) and the noncore counterpart (CNPC-owned firms).

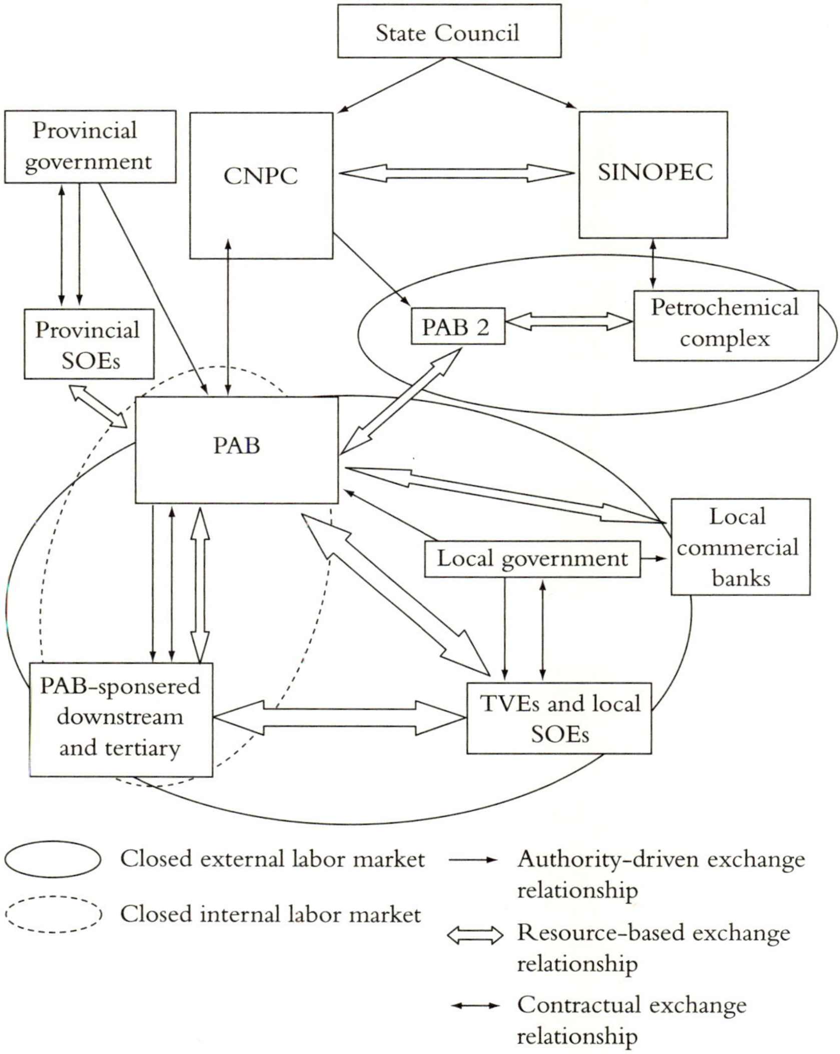

Figure 5.1 The pre-1998 national oil corporations. CNPC, China National Petroleum Corporation; PAB, petroleum administrative bureau; SOEs, state-owned enterprises; TVEs, town and village enterprises.

Relocating Financial and Labor Centralities

With corporate restructuring, core and noncore firms experienced a significant divergence in network relations from their common starting point as work units under the PAB. These changes in the nature of networks and boundaries of

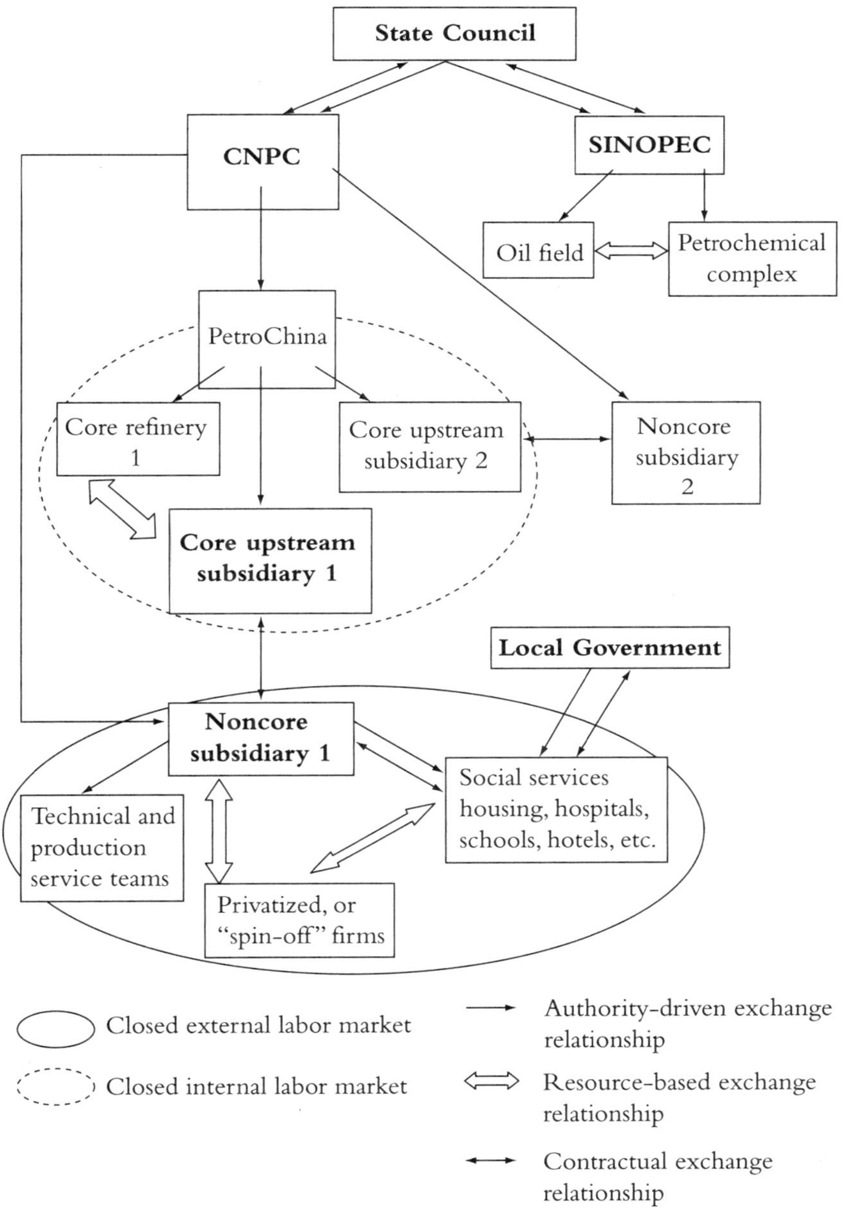

Figure 5.2 The post-1999 national oil corporations. CNPC, China National Petroleum Corporation.

firms have had direct impacts on the location of financial and labor centralities, which in turn affects the managers' ability to set wages.

Before corporate restructuring in 1998, financial centrality fell squarely on the PAB, where party-state leadership coincided and served as a point of negotiation with local governmental and ministerial authorities, as well as a check point of regulated access to local labor markets. The PAB also formed the locus of capital accumulation because its leaders crafted complex exchange and financial schemes in order to submit to the central ministry a simple quota output equal to or greater than the expected PAB contributions to the Five-Year Plan. The locating of financial centrality at the level of the PAB reflected the intentions of the planners in implementing the managerial contract responsibility system (essentially a series of contracts between the SOE managers and the central and local planners), which ensured guaranteed outputs for the command economy while providing state-appointed managers with sufficient incentives to exploit private information to capture local market opportunities. Provided a degree of political and operational insulation from the contractualization of the authority relations with the central planners, the PAB formed the hub from which spokes of contractual and resource-based exchange relations emanated (see fig. 5.1). Thus, it came as no surprise that, at the national level, CNPC and Sinopec as administrative firms were largely unable to deal with the financial problems of wage inflation, inadequate investment in some operations and overinvestment in others, mounting indebtedness, and interenterprise arrears over time (Lin 2008b).

After the 1998–1999 restructuring, the locus of financial centrality was centralized—removed from the PABs—and shared between the CNPC and PetroChina headquarters to achieve the primary corporate objective of maximizing the profitability of the publicly listed company (see fig. 5.2). PetroChina and the CNPC governed their respective core and noncore establishments by issuing financial decrees: profit targets for the core and cost reduction targets for the noncore (Lin 2008b). To sever the subsidiaries from their past financial network ties, the headquarters shut down the numerous PAB local bank accounts, created a consolidated account to which the headquarters had direct access and overriding authorization, centralized debt management and lending decisions, and prohibited further interenterprise arrears (Lin 2006).[30] The headquarters also maintains a tight rein over the value of contracts between the core and noncore parts, which enables it to achieve the desired financial indicators for domestic and foreign stockholders. Beijing has further supported this financial centralization by limiting state-owned commercial banks to negotiating debt-reduction measures (i.e., debt-equity swaps) and additional loans in a centralized manner with the headquarters rather than individual PABs and by offering policy benefits to the parent holding companies, such as industry-specific subsidies and exemptions from having to pay dividends to the state asset management agencies.[31]

Top-down manipulation of resource-based, authority-driven, and contractual-exchange relations interacted with the internal and external labor markets to create a similarly disruptive shift in labor centrality.[32] Before 1999, the entire PAB was essentially a closed labor market because it drew on state-assigned college graduates, engineers, and managers to fill its technical and administrative ranks. When oil fields and refineries expanded during cycles of investment boom, the PAB recruited locally for relatively unskilled workers. The children of permanent employees found jobs within the PAB and its affiliated tertiary enterprises, contributing to the swelling labor costs. Social norms favored closed employment relationships, that is, terms of employment that covered a set of tasks or a job for an indefinite period of time. Workers were dismissed only in exceptional circumstances, and thus the initiative for ending the contract was with the worker.[33]

There was significant self-interested rationality in perpetuating closed employment relations. Given the highly imperfect local and regional labor markets, it was useful for managers to develop firm-specific skills and mobilize workers for collective rent-seeking. SOEs did not necessarily offer outputs that were valuable from the point of view of the market, but as social organizations they sustained the livelihood of workers and the career advancement of cadres. In an important sense, they offered group rewards, in particular relatively egalitarian wage increases and a wide-range of social benefits for "collective consumption" (Bian 1994, chap. 8).[34] These two sets of motivations were reinforcing in that a stable and content workplace helped cadres pass their performance evaluations. In essence, workers and managers colluded to extract benefits from state agencies that had highly incomplete knowledge of PAB operations.[35] Given the nature of the collective goods supplied, we could readily predict that the PAB would suffer free-riding problems, such as wage increases that were insensitive to individual contributions.

The restructuring of NOCs in 1998–1999 into core and noncore companies split asunder the overlapping closed external and internal labor markets of the PABs, creating a closed internal labor market in the core company and pushing toward an open external market for workers in the noncore company. Corporate headquarters mandated massive and multiphased (with an annual quota) layoffs in the noncore units and attempted to create a competitive intersubsidiary market for technical and production services as a breakthrough process for freeing up slack labor. With reduced reciprocal exchanges with local officials and reduced interactions with firms in similar structural positions or downstream firms, noncore firms also lost access to neighboring internal labor markets to mediate excessive labor pressures. Ironically, the more restrictive the local external labor market, the greater the likelihood of contention between the pressured noncore firms and anxious local governments, which understandably expect pillar SOEs to absorb excessive laborers or pay for unemployment benefits and pensions in tough times.[36]

The internal labor market of the noncore also became increasingly rigid as Beijing pushed for clearer property rights and welfare entitlement claims between the PABs and affiliated businesses. Before 1998, PABs negotiated reductions of the workforce by investing in the upfront costs for their employees to start private businesses, many of which seemed risk-free given the continuing partial ownership and management support from the PAB and the social welfare and in-kind household benefits for ex-workers (Lin 2009). These proliferating affiliated businesses—tertiary-sector and downstream enterprises—blurred the boundaries between intrafirm and interfirm exchanges. The Daqing and Karamay PABs were able to place several thousands of workers by investing in such firms in their respective high-technology and commercial zones (Lin 2008a). Starting in the mid-1990s, these firms have been subject to categorical privatization. Additional spin-offs were implemented as part of asset restructuring since 1999.[37] Andrew Walder has pointed out that in the 1980s large enterprises reaped "processing fees" from affiliated small enterprises by selling surplus supplies and outsourcing state projects (Bian 1994, 160). These fees translated into slack financial resources for managers and workers (Solinger 1989). With the demise of these transitional organizational forms, an important source of slack and an outlet for surplus labor were closed down.

The shifting of labor centrality from the PAB as a whole to the noncore subsidiaries, accompanied by the recentralization of financial controls by the headquarters, dismantled the prior organizational constraints on wage hikes for the core employees. We could interpret the rising wages of core companies during the past decade as the continuation of the wage-padding norms of the past. The rent-seeking and collective goods are now collected at the higher levels of the corporate headquarters for the benefit of a transterritorial group of core subsidiaries rather than at the location-specific PABs.[38] The higher wages may also signal trust in a time of divisive reform politics and of career and role uncertainties, with the intent to deepen core employees' commitment within new organizational boundaries.[39] We can reasonably expect core employees to be rewarded for going along with the exploitation of their noncore ex-colleagues.

In sum, by mapping out the forms of exchanges and their cumulative effects on financial and labor centralities, we go beyond the usual analytical dichotomy of capital versus labor to show how capital serves labor and vice versa.[40] Studies of soft-budget constraints of SOEs (Kornai 1992; Steinfeld 1998) may suggest a relatively low price of capital as compared to labor, but we should keep in mind that socialist work units reinvest profit, incur debts, and vie for state allocation of fixed-capital investment partly to provide security against temporary or chronic wage-fund shortages. Thus, the demand for capital is strongly linked to the maintenance of the social and political demands of the industrial workforce, and the value of capital could be captured more fully by estimating the opportunity costs of having to discharge or reduce the wages of SOE employees. In short, the relative prices of capital and labor do not suggest economic efficiency or a priori developmental importance but, rather, reflect the strategic deployment of these resources in tandem to sustain the organizational processes of industrial networks.[41]

Conclusion

In the discontinuous transformation of wage movements in Chinese oil fields and refineries in the late-1990s, abruptly rising wage differentials among the various work units and between management and workers closely followed shifts in the organizational boundaries of the firms. The impact of these shifts on the relative prices of capital and labor exhibit sectoral and geographical variations brought about by specific institutional configurations of corporate relations and local market structures. Generally speaking, the firm-level process of wage determination has been liberalized by the lifting of central government regulations on wage standardization across sectors and regions, greater exchange with the open labor market, and convergence of the state-owned sector with the private and foreign-invested sectors in terms of employment.[42] The earlier egalitarian norms appear to have been swept away by these changes (Tomba 2002; Solinger 2002, 2003). The broader social effects of increasing wage and bonus disparities—in particular in policy-protected oligopolistic industries—have been noted by both Chinese and foreign scholars.[43]

The network organizational approach offers insights into social consequences of the state-led commodification of labor in China. In particular, my findings address three well-developed research agendas: (1) industrial governance and impact on macroeconomic management, (2) labor market formation, and (3) collective representation and mobilization of labor.

The NOC extraction through top-down financial controls and local containment of labor surpluses injects elements of instability into the oligopolistic structure of the Chinese oil and petrochemical industries. As wage disparities increase, there may be aggregate pressure on the headquarters to further obtain government subsidies and regulatory support to stabilize the resources needed to ease the burdens shouldered by the noncore in order to safeguard rewards for the core. This redistributive agenda has become contentious in recent debates over profit-sharing arrangements between NOCs and the State Council, with negative implications for fiscal and macroeconomic stability as NOCs resist price adjustments and tax reforms (Lin 2008c). It remains to be seen whether a new regulatory structure will be established to sort out the problematic oligopolistic relations of NOCs. Whether the solution favors pro-competitive liberalization or bureaucratic encroachment of corporate decisions, it will no doubt underscore the interventionist role of Beijing beyond its nominal shareholder responsibilities.

Regarding labor market formation, I have suggested that it is not as useful to imagine a dichotomy between nonmarket labor relations within SOEs and market relations outside them. Instead, I have paid attention to how changes in the organization of firm and interfirm exchange relations have redrawn the boundary between internal and external labor markets. Back in the 1990s, the informalization (Solinger 1998, 2001) of employment terms took center stage as firms found this to be the most flexible way to mobilize and relocate human resources at the margins of the firm and local labor market. In the oil and petrochemical sectors, the cost-saving benefit of this option has been severely negated by the asymmetric contractual terms between core and noncore enterprises. Thus, the heavy use of temporary workers by noncore firms does not necessarily translate into more stable wages and benefits for permanent employees; instead, it has served only to increase the informalization at the periphery.

Network analysis also makes clear that experiments in collective representation at the firm level, which made little headway in the 1980s and 1990s, make even less sense within the new corporate context (Li 2004; Howell 1998). New organizational divisions intended to disrupt past ties have isolated the noncore from the core and from other firms in the formerly socialist production networks. This isolation has fueled a countermovement, expressed as disagreements over notions of entitlement, fairness, and efficiency. In response, factions of managers and workers have forged new cross-cutting allegiances, which have formed the social and psychological bases for sustained collective action and inactions (Lin 2009). These allegiances, however, do not divide neatly along class lines or role differentiations, and thus they may not respond to the traditional approach to collective representation.[44] I predict that workers will find it easier to mobilize outside the formal representation framework, with the aim of capturing or disrupting resource flows in the new network.[45]

Chapter 6

The Paradox of Labor Force Dualism and State-Labor-Capital Relations in the Chinese Automobile Industry

Lu Zhang

The rapid rise of China to become the largest automobile-producing nation and market in the world made newspaper headlines at the end of 2009. Despite the extensive interests in the booming Chinese automobile industry, little attention has been paid to the 2.9 million Chinese autoworkers who are making those headlines. These workers are the focus of this chapter. Most existing research on the changing labor relations in reform China focuses either on labor-intensive manufacturing in the sunbelt in southern China or on declining state-owned enterprises (SOEs) in the rustbelt northeastern China. This in-depth case study of the automobile industry contributes an important case for comparison; here we have a capital-intensive pillar industry experiencing rapid expansion and restructuring with both heavy state and global capital involvement through joint ventures.

The main argument is that growing competition in the Chinese automobile industry since the mid-1990s has driven the major Chinese automakers to move toward a leaner and meaner workplace to cut costs and increase staff flexibility. They have generally replaced permanent and long-term state workers with young, urban-bred, formal contract workers under renewable short-term labor contracts. At the same time, more and more automakers have introduced *labor force dualism* by deploying a large number of temporary workers (hired through labor dispatch agencies) alongside the formal workers on assembly lines but subjecting them to different treatment. In the second and the third sections of this chapter, I describe in depth this process of industrial restructuring, changing workplace, and transformation of production workforce in the

Chinese automobile industry since the mid-1990s. I highlight the emergence and expansion of labor force dualism and agency employment (labor dispatch), and the recomposition of formal and temporary workers under the dualist system.

Labor force dualism was implemented in an effort to solve the problem of providing employers with flexibility in hiring/firing while at the same time obtaining cooperation and loyalty from the core (formal) workers. But it has had notable unintended consequences. On the one hand, labor force dualism has detached formal workers from temporary workers and has kept the former relatively quiet so far. On the other hand, the dualistic system has also radicalized a new generation of temporary agency workers to actively protest against discriminatory treatment. Moreover, shop floor dynamics are very much conditioned by global processes. Intense competition at a late stage of the product cycle of world automobile production has driven management to reduce the privileges of formal workers in wages and job security. As a result, the current consent of the formal workers with management, based on material gains, is declining. Workers' bottom-up resistances, in turn, have forced management to pull back from labor force dualism and improving working conditions for temporary workers. In the fourth section, I examine the workers' resistance to the labor force dualism and the management responses, pointing to the paradox of labor force dualism in labor control and the radicalization of a new generation of temporary workers.

Shop floor and global processes are themselves conditioned by national political processes. By locating the case of autoworkers' resistance within the broad dynamics of national politics, I show in the fifth section how the bottom-up pressure of rising labor unrest incited by the informalization of employment has induced the central government to step in to regulate and stabilize labor relations through labor legislation reforms, including the enactment of the Labor Contract Law. Yet the unintended impacts of this new labor law on labor dispatch reveals the boundary-drawing strategy of the state among its working population and a relational and dynamic relationship among the party-state, labor, and capital in reform China.

In the concluding section, based on the empirical evidence from the automobile industry, I discuss the dynamics of evolving state-labor-capital interrelations in reform China. I emphasize the legitimacy leverage of Chinese workers and the role of bottom-up labor resistance in counterbalancing the adverse effects of unregulated markets by holding the authoritarian regime responsive to popular demand.

The data used in this chapter derived from sixteen months of fieldwork at seven major automobile assembly enterprises in six Chinese cities between 2004 and 2009.[1] I chose the seven case-study enterprises based on the following combined criteria of case significance and research feasibility.[2] First, the

TABLE 6.1
General information of the case-study automobile factories, 2006

Company name	Number of employees	Sales (thousands of units)	Ranking (sales)	Ownership type	Location (province)
Venus	6,569	413	1	JV	Shanghai
Saturn	12,531	352	2	JV	Shanghai
Jupiter	9,284	350	3	JV	Jilin
Mars	18,000	300	4	SOE	Anhui
Earth	3,049	43	N/A	SOE	Shandong
Mercury	5,600	260	6	JV	Guangdong
Uranus	3,096	N/A	N/A	SOE	Shandong

Notes: JV, joint venture; N/A, not available; SOE, state-owned enterprise.

seven selected enterprises were all large-scale assembly plants with high volume output and large numbers of employees. They held competitive market positions, and five of them were among the top six passenger carmakers in China in 2006. All of them received strong government support and had substantial financial and organizational resources. The logic of choosing stronger auto assembly enterprises lies in the fact that automobile enterprises of this type are usually more able to promise their employees job security and better treatment given their competitive market position and substantial resources. If we find that practices at the major auto enterprises do not live up to the promises of employment security, then it is even less likely that firms with fewer resources and less government support will do so. Second, the seven case-study enterprises represent the two major ownership types in the Chinese auto assembly sector: two SOEs and five joint ventures (JVs) with foreign partners from the United States, Germany, and Japan.[3] Third, the seven cases are also located in distinct geographical regions, including three major automobile production bases in China (Changchun, Shanghai, and Guangzhou) as well as both brownfield and greenfield factories. Finally, the choices of the case enterprises were also largely determined by my ability to gain access to the factories and to conduct fieldwork with minimal management interference (see table 6.1 for a summary of the general information of the case-study enterprises).

I spent at least 1.5 months at each of the seven selected enterprises, visiting production lines, collecting company files and employee newsletters/periodicals (*yuangong qikan*), and conducting in-depth interviews with a total of seventy-seven formal contract workers, seventy-three temporary workers, thirty managers, and twenty factory party and union leaders at and outside factories.[4] To examine the role of the state (especially the lawmaking process and the impacts of the new labor laws), I interviewed thirty-eight local labor bureau officials, trade union staff, and labor dispute arbitrators at both the municipal and district levels in five cities (Beijing, Shanghai, Guangzhou, Qingdao, and Yantai). I also collected related archival and documentary data.

Foreign Investment, Industrial Restructuring and Changing Workplace in the Chinese Automobile Industry

Over the past two decades, the Chinese automobile industry has grown dramatically. Production output increased almost twenty times, from 0.71 million units in 1991 to 13.79 million in 2009. The development of the automobile industry in the reform era can be characterized as a state-led triple alliance[5] through the establishment of centrally sanctioned JVs between foreign multinationals and large SOEs. By the early 2000s, all the major world automakers had built JVs with one or two Chinese partners to make and sell vehicles in China.[6] The proportion of auto SOEs declined from 100 percent at the beginning of the Chinese market reform to less than one-third of total output in 2001, whereas JVs by large SOEs and foreign carmakers occupied 97 percent of Chinese passenger-car production and market share in 2000. This domination declined after 2004 as the indigenous Chinese automakers, such as Chery, Geely, and Chang'an, grew quickly. But Sino-foreign JVs still occupied 74 percent of market share in 2008 (CATRC 2000–2007; Liu 2009).

Those JVs have had a major impact on the organization of production. They have imported advanced machinery and technology, global standards, and Taylorist and lean production practices[7] to maximize profits. By the late 1990s, the basic organization of production at the major Chinese automobile assemblers was characterized by mass assembly lines and standardized operation, with lean production techniques, such as the just-in-time (JIT) inventory and delivery system, visual control system, quality circles, and teamwork.

At the same time, as a "pillar industry" of strategic importance,[8] the development of the Chinese automobile industry in the reform era has been closely guided and monitored by the central government. The use of foreign direct investment (FDI) in the auto sector has been cautious. For instance, the creation of new assembly JVs in China has to be approved by the center, and foreign automakers are not allowed to build wholly owned assembly plants or to own a majority stake in assembly JVs.[9] Moreover, by controlling the personnel decisions of senior (Chinese) management at the JVs through the cadre-manager personnel system, the central government has been able to ensure that those JVs carry out the economic, political, and social agenda concordant with the goals of the party-state. Given the more interventionist role of the state in the auto assembly sector, it is no coincidence that we find the resilience of some SOE characteristics at leading Chinese auto JVs. Indeed, until the mid-1990s, the auto assembly sector was still a centrally controlled and largely protected monopolist sector dominated by a few preselected JVs with high-level profitability (Gao 2002). Workers at large auto JVs and their state-owned Chinese partners were known to enjoy high wages, generous benefits, and stable employment in this period (Chin 2003). Even workers at less profitable SOEs were able to receive guaranteed employment and a full coverage of social welfare provisions typical in large work units (*danwei*) (cf. Walder 1986; Lu and Perry 1997) under government protection and soft budget constraints (Harwit 1995; Treece 1997).

Starting in the mid-1990s, however, the broader structural change in the Chinese system—including the deepening of SOE and labor reforms in the urban areas and the government industrial policy change to prepare the automobile industry to meet the challenge of the accession of China to the World Trade Organization (WTO) led to a large-scale restructuring of inefficient SOEs and layoffs in the auto assembly sector. The 1994 automotive industrial policy called for the consolidation and rationalization of the auto assembly sectors through mergers and reorganization (*jianbing chongzu*) with "large ones taking over smaller ones." To bring labor productivity in line with the standards set by "international market rule" (Treece 1997), between 1994 and 2000 the major domestic auto groups carried out a series of enterprise restructurings by streamlining organizations, laying workers off, shifting main products and markets, and reaching out to foreign partners to built new JVs.[10]

More dramatic enterprise restructuring came from growing competition. The loosening of entry barriers in the auto sector under the Chinese WTO agreement and the fast-growing domestic private auto markets invited another round of massive foreign investment, as well as new domestic entrants in the late 1990s and early 2000s. It was estimated that between 2000 and 2005 the prices of an average sedan model dropped 30 percent and that the average life cycle was shortened by half compared to the 1980s and 1990s. The average profit margin of a Chinese passenger carmaker was approximately 11–12 percent in 2000, yet it had dropped to merely 3–4 percent by 2005.[11] Clearly, the days of "windfall profits" in the Chinese auto assembly sector had gone, and China "had suddenly become the toughest market in the world" (Dyer 2005).

To cope with the tougher new environment, the major Chinese automakers quickly moved toward a leaner and meaner workplace with new strategies to maximize profits and minimize production costs. In the organization of production, there was a convergence among major Chinese automakers in combining lean production and Fordist/Taylorist mass production techniques with a labor-intensive strategy by employing a large number of semi-skilled young workers working in two or three shifts nonstop on mass assembly lines. In labor and employment policy, automakers have generally reduced employment security and sought more labor flexibility in hiring and firing.

The results of the industrial and enterprise restructuring were impressive. The total output increased by almost 1 million vehicles, from 1.4 million vehicles in 1994 to over 2.3 million vehicles in 2001, and it more than tripled in the next

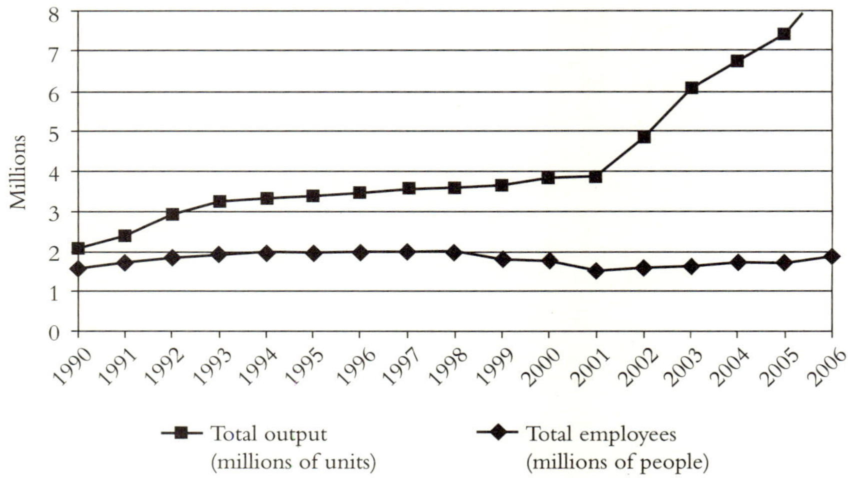

Figure 6.1 Annual output and number of employees in the Chinese automobile industry, 1990–2006

five years and reached 7.3 million vehicles in 2006. At the same time, the total number of employees in the automobile industry (including parts and accessories) declined from almost 2 million in 1994 to 1.5 million in 2001, and it only slightly increased to 1.65 million in 2006 (CATRC 2002–2007) (see fig. 6.1).

This unique Chinese pattern of fast expansion and modernization of automobile industry without a significant increase in employment,[12] reflected the fact that the full take-off of the Chinese automobile industry was a simultaneous process of "leaning out" of inefficient SOEs and unmaking the old generation of state workers, and quickly expanding the JVs and making a new generation of industrial workers. As such, even though the numerical change of employment in the automobile industry did not seem that dramatic, the social composition of production workforce had been largely transformed after the restructuring.

The Transformation of Production Workforce and the Emergence and Expansion of Labor Force Dualism

The transformation of the production workforce in the Chinese automobile industry involved two processes: (1) the replacement of permanent or long-term state workers with new urban-bred, young, formal contract workers under short-term renewable labor contracts, and (2) the introduction of labor force dualism by tapping a large number of rural and urban youths as temporary (agency) workers through labor dispatch agency firms.

The replacement of permanent state workers was carried out relatively smoothly through early retirement, reassignment, and buyouts and did not cause overt labor unrest. My fieldwork suggests that three main factors could explain the relatively smooth downsizing in this first round of restructuring. First, most state-owned automobile assemblers had substantial financial and organizational resources accumulated in the pre-reform era, which allowed them to pay the redundant workers more generous early retirement benefits and severance compensation or to transfer some of the redundant workers to other (less well-paid) jobs in service firms spun off from the main enterprise, thus softening the direct blow of downsizing.[13] Second, at many old SOEs, management relied on the trade union and party factory committee, which in turn relied on the accumulated goodwill and political commitment of older workers, to convince those who were to become redundant that the reform was in the collective interest and that they should therefore step aside without making a major fuss. Third, the central and local governments were more interventionist in monitoring the restructuring process at large automobile SOEs and JVs of strategic importance. My interviews with managers and local government officials suggested that, in the auto assembly sector, enterprise restructuring proposals often had to be approved by the central or local governments. And one of the important considerations was whether redundant workers would be properly settled. When restructuring was proposed through setting up new JVs, there were often requirements that the new JVs to absorb redundant workers from their Chinese partners.

At the same time, the leading Chinese automobile enterprises, especially those newly built JVs, kept hiring new formal workers directly from colleges and vocational schools with short-term (one- to two-year) renewable labor contracts. The replacement of veteran workers with young short-term formal contract workers led to a dramatic drop in the average age and seniority of production workers. For instance, after restructuring, Earth managed to reduce the total number of its employees from 4,600 to 3,000 and lowered the average age of production workers to twenty-nine, meanwhile increasing output by more than 50 percent.[14]

The Emergence and Expansion of Labor Force Dualism

The second important aspect of workforce restructuring was the adoption of labor force dualism by using a large number of temporary workers alongside formal workers on production lines. Formal workers enjoyed high wages, generous benefits, and more secure employment under renewable labor contracts.

TABLE 6.2
Comparisons of labor force dualism at the selected automobile plants, 2006

				Formal workers		Agency workers	
Company name	Year founded	Labor force dualism	Ownership type	Number	Contract terms[a] (years)	Number	Working terms (renewable)
Jupiter	1991	Yes	JV	10,000	2-2-2-2-2-nonfixed	3,000	1 year
Saturn	1985	Yes	JV	9,050	2-2-3-3-nonfixed	3,219	3 months
Earth	1993	Yes	SOE	3,170	1-1-2-3-3-nonfixed	400	1 year
Mars	1997	Yes	SOE	18,000	1-1-1-1-3-3-nonfixed	6,000	3 months to 1 year
Venus	1997	No	JV	6,767	1	N/A	N/A
Mercury	2002	No	JV	4,000	1	N/A	N/A
Uranus	1998	No	JV	5,000	1	N/A	N/A

Source: Interviews with production workers and managers at the selected automobile assembly plants in 2006 and 2007.

Note: JV, joint venture; N/A, not applicable; SOC, state-owned enterprise.

[a]A *non-fixed-term labor contract* is a labor contract for which the employer and the employee have agreed not to stipulate a termination date. The Labor Law of 1994 states that an employee can propose to sign a nonfixed-term labor contract with his or her employer if he or she has been working for the employer for a consecutive period of no less than 10 years. The Labor Contract Law of 2008 adds that an employee can negotiate a nonfixed-term labor contract if the renewal occurs after the consecutive conclusion of two fixed-term labor contracts (Labor Contract Law, Article 14).

By contrast, temporary workers were only paid one-half to two-thirds the wages of formal workers for the same or similar work, with very few benefits and little job security. Among the seven studied automobile factories, four adopted labor force dualism with a large number of temporary workers (see table 6.2). Indeed, labor force dualism had become a widespread practice in the Chinese auto assembly sector by the early 2000s.

According to the managers I interviewed, the main reasons for using temporary workers were to contain labor costs and increase labor flexibility. The human resources managers at Neptune and Jupiter estimated that for the cost of hiring a formal contract worker, adding in all the social insurances and benefits, they could hire at least three or four temporary workers. Management desire to increase staff flexibility was emphasized more by the automakers built relatively earlier and that therefore had a large number of non-fixed or long-term contract employees. For instance, Jupiter had nearly 10,000 formal employees in 2006, and approximately half these workers had non-fixed or long-term (of three years or longer) labor contracts. The factory started using temporary workers in direct production in 1996. By 2003, the number of temporary workers had reached 3,000. When Jupiter encountered a market downturn in 2004, it dismissed approximately 1,000 temps without laying off any formal workers.

When the markets started recovering in 2005, the factory quickly rehired 500 agency workers to meet the production demand.[15]

Yet, unlike the conventional core-periphery model (Atkinson 1987) or the "flexible firm" formula (Kalleberg 2001, 2003), under which the segmentation between core and periphery workers corresponds directly to functional and numerical flexibilities, the Chinese version of labor force dualism deploys both formal and temporary workers on assembly lines performing identical tasks but subjecting them to different treatment. Why, then, did some automakers keep a segment of more expensive and relative protected formal workers whose jobs could be performed by temporary workers? Why not simply use all temporary workers or give short-term labor contracts to all production workers?

My interviews with managers indicated that an implicit motivation for adopting labor force dualism was to use temporary workers as a buffer to contain potential conflicts and labor disputes that would have been caused by laying off formal contract workers. As a manager at Neptune indicated, the company would rather use frequently rotated agency workers to gain flexibility than deal with the trouble likely to be caused by laying off their own formal workers. In his opinion, "frequent layoffs of our own formal employees could harm the harmonious labor relations and the good publicity of the company."[16]

That may also explain why those newly built greenfield plants did not bother to use labor force dualism. Without the burden of a large number of veteran state workers, they simply recruited young workers directly from plenty of technical vocational schools and gave one- or two-year labor contracts to all line workers.

But unlike the Japanese labor dualism, which offers real employment security to the core labor force in exchange for cooperation and loyalty meanwhile creates a large buffer of a low-cost and flexible workforce in the lower rungs of the supply network (Sako and Sato 1997; Chalmers 1989), we see in table 6.2 that there was a general decline in job security of the young generation of formal contract workers. As such, the Chinese labor force dualism has inherent contradictions and limits in soliciting commitment and consent from the core segment of formal contract workers as we shall discuss in more details below.

The Social Composition of the New Generation of Chinese Autoworkers

After restructuring, production workers accounted for 60–80 percent of the total formal contract employees. The remaining were white-collar managerial and technical staff.[17] Among the formal production workers, except for a small portion of skilled veteran workers (most in their thirties and forties) with non-fixed (permanent) or long-term labor contracts, the majority were semi-skilled or unskilled urban-bred youths in their early twenties with one- to two-year renewable labor contracts. The young generation of formal workers had relatively high educational qualifications, given that all the automobile factories studied required a minimum of twelve years of education for newly hired formal production workers. More than half of the formal production workers I interviewed had vocational high school training or junior college education (fourteen years of education). Approximately 90 percent of the formal workers interviewed had at least middle-level skill qualifications (equivalent to semi-skilled) as measured by national vocational technique qualification exams. As a human resources manager at Venus emphasized, "We have a very strict screening process when hiring new workers to ensure the quality of our workforce. We believe that only high-quality workers can make high-quality cars."[18] Yet despite their relatively high qualifications, approximately 70–80 percent of formal production workers were working at repetitive line-operating positions that required some basic training of a week or two. Only approximately 20–30 percent of production workers were maintenance workers, technicians, and team leaders, who were defined by management as the "real" skilled core production workforce.

The mismatch between formal workers' educational qualifications and work reflected the contradictory impacts of changing production organization on labor. On the one hand, continuous automation and standardization reduced the required skill levels for many line positions. On the other hand, the integrated JIT production system and flows of assembly production required "disciplined and committed workers capable of working cooperatively."[19] The specific labor requirements had mixed impacts on the prospects for job security and for the bargaining power of autoworkers.

The social composition of temporary workers in the automobile industry has changed as well. In the early 1990s, most temporary workers were previously peasants hired directly by the automobile factories in relatively small numbers to cope with seasonal production changes.[20] Most peasant workers at SOEs were recruited from the nearby countryside or townships in cooperation with local labor bureaus from the suburbs and nearby countryside as a type of "rural redundant laborer export" (*nongcun fuyu laodongli shuchu*). These peasant workers usually had three-month to one-year labor contracts, and they were paid approximately 50–70 percent of the wages of formal contract workers for doing the same work. But peasant workers were ineligible for the pensions and social security benefits that urban workers were entitled to because of their rural household registration status (*hukou*). At this stage, the boundary between formal contract workers and temporary workers was easy to maintain based on the state-enforced rural-urban household registration system that has long relegated rural residents to second-class citizenship and limited their access to good jobs in cities (Solinger 1999).

Since the mid-1990s, labor dispatch (*laowu paiqian*),[21] a more flexible and (employer) worry-free type of employment, expanded rapidly in almost every sector in China. The automobile factories started using agency workers on a large scale. Labor dispatch is a typical triangular type of employment that separates the legal contract employment relationship (between labor dispatch agencies and agency employees) from the workplace management relationship (between client firms and agency employees). Unlike peasant workers, agency workers sign labor contracts with the labor dispatch agencies and are sent to work at the client automobile factories under (renewable) service agreements ranging from three months to one year. Because agency workers are not directly employed by the automobile factories they worked for, they can be "returned" (dismissed) to the labor dispatch agencies anytime without severance compensation. There is no job security at all for agency workers. By using agency workers, automakers can reduce their responsibilities for temporary workers to the minimum. As of 2006, it was estimated that over 80 percent of the temporary workers at Chinese automobile assembly factories were agency workers. The remaining temporary workers included some previously hired peasant workers and a growing number of student apprentices working as full-time temporary workers.[22]

Most agency workers were under the age of twenty-three and had an average of nine to twelve years of education. Unlike peasant workers, the agency workers consisted of both rural and urban youths. Approximately 70 percent of agency workers were local rural youths from the suburbs and countryside close to the automobile factories; approximately 20 percent were student agency workers recruited through vocational-school-type labor dispatch agencies all over the country,[23] and the remainder were local urban youths who were unable to find formal employment. As such, the boundary that demarcated temporary workers from formal workers based on rural-urban *hukou* status became blurred. Management tended to emphasize education and skills as the new yardstick to draw the boundary between formal and temporary workers. But in many cases, the new temporary agency workers had similar education and skill levels to the formal workers. Thus the recomposition of temporary workers delegitimized labor force dualism based on the rural-urban *hukou* system, and contributed to rising activism among the new temporary agency workers against unequal treatment at the workplace.

The evidence presented so far shows a clear move toward labor flexibility and informalization of employment in the Chinese automobile industry since the mid-1990s. Fieldwork in the steel- and white-goods-manufacturing sectors found a similar trend.[24] The startling fact that one-third to one-half of production workforce at the leading Chinese automobile factories (key enterprises in a capital-intensive "pillar industry") were now temporary agency workers indicates the scale and depth of the informalization and reduced employment security in China by the late 1990s and the early 2000s.

The Paradox of Labor Force Dualism: Workers' Resistance and Management Dilemmas

Labor force dualism was implemented in an effort to solve the problem of providing employers with flexibility in hiring/firing while at the same time obtaining cooperation and loyalty from the core (formal) workers. But it had notable unintended consequences. On one hand, I found labor force dualism had detached formal workers from temporary workers and had kept the former relatively quiet, despite their serious and growing grievances. On the other hand, the "new" temporary agency workers were radicalized and actively pushed back against unequal treatment. Workers' resistance, in turn, forced management to pull back from labor force dualism and to improve conditions for temporary workers. To understand this shop floor contention and the contradictions of labor force dualism, we first need to examine the nature and extent of the bargaining power and the grievances of formal contract workers and temporary workers, respectively.

Growing Discontent among Formal Contract Workers

Bargaining Power and Grievances

The scale and concentration of automobile production in the twentieth century has recurrently allowed autoworkers to achieve effective workplace bargaining power. This power derives from workers enmeshed in tightly integrated production processes, in which a localized stoppage in one node can cause disruptions on a much wider scale than the stoppage itself (Silver 2003, chaps. 1–2). The increased scale and concentration of automobile production in China over the past decade has also increased the potential workplace bargaining power of Chinese autoworkers. For one thing, Chinese autoworkers are concentrated in factories of enormous size. The Volkswagen plant in Shanghai has approximately 15,000 employees. More impressive still is the concentration of around 100,000 autoworkers employed by the FAW Auto Group in its various factories within the FAW auto city, a 12-square-kilometer district in the city of Changchun, where over 300,000 FAW employees and their families work and live.

Moreover, the widely adopted JIT techniques in the Chinese automobile production have indeed increased the vulnerability of production to any interruptions in the flow of parts to the assembly line by eliminating the buffers built into the traditional Fordist system and have thus boosted the potential workplace bargaining power of Chinese autoworkers. For instance, at one of the automobile assembly factories I studied, management introduced JIT production methods despite a very poor labor-management relationship, reflected among other things in the widespread acts of petty sabotage by workers. In the end, to keep production flowing smoothly, management felt obliged to eliminate its experiment with JIT production methods and return to a system with greater built-in supply buffers.[25]

The increasing workplace bargaining power of Chinese autoworkers goes hand in hand with growing workplace grievances rooted in the grueling nature of the lean and labor-intensive mass production paradigm. Working conditions at the major Chinese automobile factories are characterized by repetitive and tedious work, heavy workloads, an intense work pace, and long working hours. At the auto assembly plants I studied, production lines usually operate in two shifts of ten hours each, except for those machine maintenance workers and repairmen who work three shifts of eight hours each. During the peak seasons, many plants run two shifts of twelve hours each. That makes most workers feel exhausted. Approximately 89 percent of workers interviewed considered the current production pace[26] to be "very intense." More than 85 percent of the workers in their twenties did not think they could sustain the current production pace for such long working hours when they reached their forties.

Moreover, lean production created a more demanding and stressful workplace that required workers to work longer, harder, and faster, with more pressure and responsibility but little real empowerment and autonomy over their own work (Parker and Slaughter 1995). For instance, after the implementation of *kaizen* (continuous improvement) activities, the body shop of Jupiter increased its line speed from 85 seconds per sedan to 75 seconds between August and October 2006. Together with overtime, production output more than doubled while the number of workers was reduced from 121 to 105.[27]

Physical working environments are considered relatively good at the leading Chinese automakers, especially at the large JVs. Workshops are clean, bright, and air-conditioned; flexible devices were installed to help workers choose comfortable postures at work. But there are still particular parts of automobile production that are dirty, strenuous, and damaging to workers' physical health. For example, workers at body shops, the most unfavorable place, where car bodies are welded together, complained about the bad air quality, unbearable welding heat, and noises damaging their hearing.[28]

Wages and Job Security

Chinese autoworkers, especially those working at large automobile assemblers are also known for their high wages and generous benefits compared to other manufacturing workers in China. It is argued that high wages are one of the main reasons for the hegemonic consent of Chinese autoworkers with management (Chin 2003). A close examination of the wage and labor market conditions in the Chinese auto assembly sector, however, suggests a more complicated picture. First, formal autoworkers did earn significantly higher wages than did other manufacturing workers in the same localities; however, formal autoworkers' wages declined or remained stagnant from 2004 to 2006, whereas the local average wages in these cities grew steadily in the same time period (see table 6.3).

Indeed, more than three-fourths of the formal workers (sixty out of seventy-seven) I interviewed felt they were underpaid given the rapid growth in output and profits of their companies and the heavy work load, intense work pace, long working hours, and grueling nature of their daily work. Workers felt they were squeezed and that they did not receive a fair reward and the recognition they deserved for their work. As a formal worker at Mars resentfully commented,

> It is not just about money; it is how you feel about how you are treated by the company! You feel they [the company] really do not care about you as a worker. They [managers] promised to increase our wages when the company becomes more profitable. But after all these years of fast growth, the pay checks and bonuses of managers and salesmen have got bigger and bigger. We workers still earn that little! It is us, we front-line workers who make the cars, do the heaviest work, and generate the profits for the company! But we are the least paid and cared for here! That is not the right way to treat employees![29]

This strong frustration of relative deprivation has been found in the major waves of autoworkers' struggles worldwide.[30] Workers were even more indignant about the increasingly enlarged wage differences between workers and managerial staff. For instance, position wages at Earth were divided into ten grades and thirty-six scales, with the highest being ten times that of the lowest. Moreover, because the bonus wages were linked to position wages, the difference in monthly income between management and workers could be even larger. Thus there is no reason to assume that high wages in and of themselves guarantee workers' consent and commitment.

The new formal contract workers with short-term labor contracts were also concerned about their job security. As previously discussed, despite the variations in labor contract terms by individual factories, most newly hired formal contract workers can sign only one- to two-year renewable labor contracts. As a formal worker who had one-year labor contract at Earth commented, "There's no job security nowadays as long as you work for others. They [managers] can let you go simply by not renewing your contracts. You have to plan for yourself."[31]

TABLE 6.3

Monthly monetary wages of formal and temporary workers at the selected automobile enterprises compared to local average wages (RMB *yuan*)

	Saturn			Jupiter			Earth			Mars						
Year	Formal worker	Temp worker	Local average*	Formal worker	Temp worker	Local average	Formal worker	Temp worker	Local average	Formal worker	Temp worker	Local average	Uranus	Local average	Venus	Local average
2004	5,000	2,500	2,250	3,000	1,500	800	2,917	2,200	1,000	n/a	n/a	n/a	1,500	600	5,500	2,250
2005	3,500	2,000	2,300	2,500	1,500	900	2,583	1,600	1,100	1,000	600	700	1,500	700	4,000	2,300
2006	4,000	1,700	2,500	3,000	1,800	1,000	2,667	2,000	1,200	1,000	800	800	2,000	800	4,000	2,464
2007										1,200	900	800	n/a	n/a	n/a	n/a

* The local average wages of manufacturing workers were calculated based on the median value of the estimations by the interviewees at the selected automobile plants.

Note: Table 6.3 was based on the author's interviews with production workers in the summers of 2004 and 2005 and between September 2006 and July 2007. The monthly wage data did not include wages of group leaders and managers.

Certainly in market economies anywhere, employment security depends first and foremost on whether the given economic sector is in strategic ascent or decline.[32] The Chinese automobile industry has been expanding over the past fifteen years, and there have been no large-scale layoffs since the first round of industrial restructuring. Most formal contract workers had renewed their labor contracts with their employers during the past several years. Especially at those firms adopting labor force dualism, the buffer of a large (and demarcated) temporary workforce provided formal workers with some sense of job security. This is perhaps one of the main reasons for the relatively quiescence among formal contract workers in the automobile industry.

Nevertheless, with the increasing competition and the shrinking of profit margins in the automobile sector in China since early 2000s, there was a general expectation among the managers I interviewed that additional cost-cutting measures and another round of restructuring were likely to occur in the near future. Moreover, recall that the required skill levels for many line operators had been reduced due to automation and mechanization, it seemed more feasible for management to fill those line positions with temporary workers. Indeed, according to the annual survey conducted by the Chinese Automotive Manufacturer Association in 2005, management at the major Chinese automobile assemblers expected to increase the number of unskilled line operators by 50 percent while reducing the skilled line workers by 60 percent from their current production labor force (see table 6.4). Meanwhile, there was a growing demand for maintenance workers and technicians to keep the machines running properly. These changes in demand for levels and types of skilled workers in the Chinese auto assembly sector accorded with the general trend in the world automobile production, in which the progressively mechanized assembly line has reduced workers' tasks to "baby-sitting" machines and responding to machine problems (Ishida 1997).

As such, although there was a certain portion of formal production workers who had growing marketplace bargaining power based on employer demand for their specific skills, the skill-based marketplace bargaining power of most

TABLE 6.4
Current and desired percentages of workers in the Chinese automobile industry

Skill ranking	Current percentage	Desired percentage	Expected recruitment change
Unskilled and semiskilled (operator)	25.27	38.42	Increase 50%
Maintenance/technician	2.17	23.10	Increase 10 times
Skilled (operator)	55.6	21.81	Decrease 60%

Sources: China Association of Automobile Manufacturers ([CAAM] 2005).

line operators was weak. There were growing feelings of insecurity and lack of commitment among the young generation of formal workers who had short-term labor contracts. For example, during the market downturn in 2004 and 2005, Neptune shut down several lines, cut work shifts and operation hours, and laid off over 2,000 agency workers. Although most formal workers were able to stay in their jobs thanks to the buffer of temporary workers, 90 percent of production workers experienced significant wage cuts, and many formal workers experienced anxiety about the possibility of not being able to renew their labor contracts. As a formal worker at Neptune recalled,

> No one really knew what would have happened if the company had not been able to come back on track after laying off all the agency workers. Many of us were worried it would eventually come to our turns of "letting go" if things did not get better. Especially for those whose labor contracts were to expire, people got worried if their labor contracts can be renewed. Fortunately, we came through it. But after that difficult time, many of us realized that we could not count on the company, no matter how well it is doing now and how long we have worked here. It is a market economy. Profitability and efficiency come first. No *renqing* (human feeling), no security nowadays.[33]

Lacking a sense of job security, many formal contract workers took night classes and other training programs after work to stay competitive in the job market and to prepare for the uncertain future. The interviewed managers complained about lack of loyalty and commitment and deteriorating workplace morale among the young generation of formal workers. Especially when economic incentives were cut back, there were immediate withdrawals of formal workers' cooperation. For example, a shop manager at Venus mentioned that when the factory reduced its annual bonus in 2005, workers complained fervently and there was a 30 percent higher redo rate during the first quarter of production.[34]

As their wages and job security declining, formal workers became increasingly discontent. Given that more cost-cutting measures and possibly another round of restructuring were widely expected among the managers by the time of interview, it is very likely that the protection and privileges of formal contract workers in the Chinese auto assembly sector will continue to decline. As such, it is hard to say how far management will be able to maintain a relatively quiescent formal workforce.

Temporary Workers Push Back

Temporary workers, who are often perceived as weak, vulnerable and docile to management control due to lack of job security, took management by surprise with their feisty resistance to the unequal treatment under labor force dualism. Temporary workers pushed back through small-scale, less-open, but highly disruptive forms of everyday resistance, such as sabotage, slowdowns, absenteeism, collective quitting, and, in the extreme case, strikes. For example, in June 2004, over three hundred agency workers at the Earth assembly shop stayed in their dorms and refused to go to work to protest the delay of their monthly wages. The whole assembly line stopped for fifteen hours before the problem was solved and the workers went back to work. In March 2005, some two hundred agency workers at Mars walked out during a morning shift to protest the excessive compulsory overtime and to request a wage increase. In February 2006, on the first work day after the Chinese New Year holiday, more than three hundred temporary workers at Mars did not return to work all together, and management had to send staff to work on the shop floor temporarily before the factory could find enough replacements. In fact, at Mars approximately 20 percent of assembly line workers quit every year, most of them temporaries, especially apprentices and student agency workers. In October 2006, more than three hundred agency workers at Earth went on strike again to protest a wage raise exclusively for the formal workers and demanded an equal raise.[35]

The rising resistance by temporary workers first had to do with their growing workplace bargaining power, derived from their growing numbers and concentration on assembly lines that enabled temporary workers to shut down the entire shop by acting suddenly and collectively. As one agency worker noted: "In our work team, there are 21 workers, and 12 of us are *laowu gong* [agency workers]. The whole assembly shop has 500 workers, and almost half are now *laowu gong.* If we [agency workers] stop working together, the whole lines will have to stop."[36]

Moreover, a growing number of temporary workers who had worked at the automobile factories for long tenures became the backbone of the production workforce. Some even became team leaders after working at automobile factories for over five years.[37] Thus, in both numerical and functional terms, temporary workers had gained growing workplace bargaining power.

Second, temporary workers had a keener sense of injustice and resentment about being treated as second-class workers. During my interviews, agency workers often used the words "injustice" (*bu gongzheng*), "unfair" (*bu gongping*), and the legitimate claim "equal pay for equal work" to denounce labor force dualism and agency employment. A dismissed agency worker described his bitter experience as a *laowugong* (agency worker),

> I used to wok on the P assembly line. In 2004, P model did not sell well. So starting in 2005, the managers asked those formal workers on our [P] line to either stay at home or transfer to other lines. But even those formal workers staying

> at home could still earn 2000–3000 *yuan* per month. We agency workers were not that lucky. Most of us were simply kicked out with a compensation of one-month wage for every one year of work here. I contributed three years of my youth and energy to the company, but got almost nothing at the end! I think this dual system is so wrong! It is unfair![38]

The changing social composition of temporary workers also contributed to their rising resistance. As previously discussed, the new generation of temporary workers (mainly agency workers) in the automobile sector consisted of both local rural youth and city-bred young graduates with better education and qualifications than the average of temporary agency workers.[39]

Furthermore, most agency workers I interviewed have a strong desire to reside in the city, and they long for economic and social advancement as well as workplace dignity. But the harsh reality of being treated as second-class workers, the lack of training opportunities, and the slim chance of becoming formal contract workers made agency workers feel frustrated and resentful.[40]

The dormitory residential pattern of temporary workers also facilitated their collective mobilization. Most temporary workers live in the factory-subsidized dormitory residences adjacent to the production complex.[41] The concentrated dormitory residence of temporary workers of similar backgrounds and workplace experiences enabled workers to stay connected and mobilize effectively. For example, the two wildcat strikes by student agency workers at Earth were both initiated and organized around the workers' dormitory residence, with several hundred student workers staying at their dorms and collectively refusing to go to work.

Moreover, the ambiguous triangular employment relations and the lack of regulations in agency employment before the 2007 Labor Contract Law often led to the fraud in agency workers' pensions and social insurance as both the labor dispatch agencies and client firms tried to evade their responsibilities for the agency workers. Agency workers' grievances were thus derived from being "doubly exploited," and their protests were often explosive and morally based. My piecemeal data from Shanghai and Guangzhou suggests that labor dispute cases brought by agency workers were often filed collectively when agency workers were laid off from the client firms and both the labor dispatch agencies and the client auto firms had failed to pay for their social insurance.[42] For example, in November 2004, more than three hundred dismissed agency workers at Jupiter filed a collective labor dispute case against the automobile factory and the labor dispatch agency for their unpaid pensions and social insurance after being laid off. Although the interviewed agency workers were cynical about the effectiveness of the labor dispute resolutions handled by local officials, they had developed a good sense about the strategies to leverage the aspects of the law that could be used to their advantage. An agency worker who participated in filing the collective labor dispute case against Jupiter commented:

> We know that the law often does not work the way it says. But even if that does not work, it is good to have the labor laws on our side—we can at least file dispute cases against them [employers] when they violate the law! We have nothing more to lose since we have already lost our jobs. But the companies, especially those famous large ones, like Jupiter, are more afraid of getting involved in labor disputes. So they will often pay to get out of the trouble as soon as possible. Why? Because the government wants stability, and the large companies do not want to harm their public images for violating the law. Having the labor laws on our side is better than nothing.[43]

As these comments indicate, the labor laws and the labor dispute resolution system have empowered workers and fostered a philosophy of rights among the rank and file no matter the outcome.

The evidence also points to the limits of the temporary workers' resistance and bargaining power. For one thing, the relatively high wages[44] at the major automobile factories and the oversupplied labor markets, especially the perceived difficulty in finding formal employment, inhibited many temporary workers from openly confronting management. The absence of independent union representation and the lack of the right to strike exacerbated the weak associational power of all Chinese workers as a whole. Moreover, it remains to be seen whether the current labor force dualism and detached relationship between formal and temporary workers can be transformed into a more engaged and supportive intergroup relationship despite their different workplace experiences and backgrounds.[45]

Nevertheless, temporary workers' everyday resistance and open protests, although spontaneous, small-scale, and short-lived, did cause interruptions of regular production and losses in output. More important, they allowed temporary workers to realize their collective power to struggle for better conditions. If we look back at the experiences of labor unrest by the U.S. autoworkers in the early twentieth century and the autoworkers in Western Europe in 1950s and 1960s, we find that the first generation of migrant workers generally did not protest against the harsh conditions of work and life. The arbitrary power of management over issues such as hiring, firing, promotion, and job assignments was initially unchallenged in the automobile factories. The second generation, however, became the backbone of the militant struggles that succeeded in radically transforming relationships within the factory and society (Silver 2003, 51–52). The new generation of temporary workers in the Chinese automobile factories has begun to demonstrate their growing activism and potential for collective mobilization against workplace discrimination and management arbitrary labor control.

Management Dilemmas and the Contradictions of Labor Force Dualism

The declining consent among formal contract workers and the rising everyday resistance among temporary workers raised management concerns about the limits of labor force dualism in production labor control. In response, management pulled back and became more cautious in deploying temporary agency workers in direct production. For instance, Neptune and Jupiter restricted the use of temporary workers to unskilled line positions so that they could be easily replaced. Earth set a "15 percent rule" for hiring agency workers, which limited the number of agency workers to no more than 15 percent of the total production workforce.

Management also took various measures to accommodate and control temporary workers. The first strategy was to raise temporary workers' wages and grant them more equal access to company facilities and resources, such as free shuttle buses, meal subsidies, and company car purchase discounts. Temporary workers were also allowed to join the automobile factory unions where they worked. The second strategy was to direct temporary workers' grievances through formal channels such as factory unions and factory party committees. At Neptune, for example, union staff and party committee leaders set up monthly "heart-to-heart" meetings with randomly selected temporary workers to hear their concerns and requests. But temporary workers were not enthusiastic about those meetings. As an agency worker who once attended the monthly meeting commented, "The problem is with this unequal system, and they won't change the system anyway."[46]

Management was aware of the limits of labor force dualism in labor control and inducing workers' efforts in production. Among the thirty managers interviewed, approximately two-thirds expressed their concerns about product quality and labor control problems resulting from using temporary workers in direct production on a large scale. Although realizing labor force dualism has its inherent contradictions and limits in labor control, those who had adopted labor force dualism had difficulties in completely pulling back. The human resources manager at Jupiter responded frankly,

> We want all of our workers to stay happy with the company. But let's be realistic—the company has to first make profits. For that, we need to increase productivity and flexibility, and reduce labor cost, while still keep our workers happy. That is not easy. That's why we brought in agency workers. But there are

> some other new problems, and we will have to continue improving our management of temporary workers. We should limit the number and scale of temporary workers to certain production areas....Well, they are just not the type of workers you can count on for a long term.[47]

The dilemma faced by management regarding labor force dualism reflected the ongoing tension between the drive of capital toward profitability and management concerns for legitimacy (i.e., maintaining peaceful labor relations). On the one hand, workers' resistance to the large-scale restructuring and downsizing of many SOEs in the 1990s put the concern for legitimacy in the front of management, pushing automobile enterprises toward protecting a core segment of its labor force in an effort to seek consensual and cooperative labor-management relations. On the other hand, China entered the global competition in the mass production of automobiles at a late stage of the product cycle, when production activities were already subject to intense international competition and profit margins were already extremely thin (Vernon 1966). The profitability pressure in the Chinese auto assembly sector drove the automakers to move toward more cost-cutting measures, such as the use of more temporary workers and continuous threats to the protection for formal workers. Such measures, however, provoked workers' resistance and induced management to think twice about labor force dualism. Perhaps what makes this dualism (and labor relations in general) at the major Chinese automobile SOEs and JVs unique is that it more directly reflects the conflicts and compromises among the multiple forces of the state, (global and domestic) capital, and workers, given that those enterprises have been subjected to capitalist production and competition pressures while still being held strongly in state hands. In the other words, it exemplifies a relational and dynamic relationship between the state, labor, and capital in reform China. Such relationships are underpinned by the contradiction between maintaining legitimacy and increasing profitability and the efforts of both the state and firms to strive for a balance through ongoing boundary-drawing processes. From this perspective, the labor force dualism currently unfolding at the major Chinese automakers is indeed a transitional modus vivendi for large SOEs that are moving away from the old *danwei* system of permanent employment toward a more flexible labor system. So where is this dualism going? To answer this question, we need to go beyond the shop floor and look into the broader national political dynamics—that is, how the Chinese state has responded to the contradictory pressures of maintaining legitimacy with labor in the face of mounting labor unrest and pursuing profitability along with capitalist enterprises as marketization and commodification of labor intensified.

Counter-Countermovement from Above: The State-Led Labor Law Reforms and Boundary-Drawing Strategy

Mary Gallagher and Baohua Dong (chap. 3 in this volume) outline the processes involved in the introduction of the Labor Contract Law in 2007. In this section, I focus on the motivation of the state to do this. Particularly germane to this case, the Labor Contract Law devotes one section and eleven articles to regulating labor dispatch (agency employment). The Labor Contract Law stipulates that a labor dispatch agency is an employer and shall sign fixed-term labor contracts of no less than two years with agency workers. The labor dispatch agency must ensure that agency workers receive at least the minimum wage on a monthly basis, even when they are not placed at client firms. The arrangements between the labor agency and client firms must be governed by a formal contract detailing placements and payments, including arrangements with respect to social insurance premiums for agency workers. Moreover, the Labor Contract Law stipulates that agency workers shall have equal pay for equal work done by other workers at the client firms and that they can also join the client firm union. Apparently, the law attempts to regulate and curb this new type of informal employment and provides more protection for agency employees who are excluded from regular contract employment.[48]

What led to this countermovement from above—the state-led labor legislation—to regulate labor dispatch? How has the new Labor Contract Law affected the management decisions and practice regarding labor force dualism at the enterprise level?

As mentioned previously, the wide use of agency workers in the automobile assembly sector reflected the rampant expansion of labor dispatch and the general trend toward the informalization of labor in China since the mid-1990s. At the beginning of 2006, the piecemeal data showed that an estimated 25 million agency employees worked in SOEs and in public and government sectors, and that more than 10 million agency employees worked in the construction sector. It was estimated that the number of agency employees could be more than doubled by adding those working at the private and foreign-invested companies (Wang 2006). More worrisome to some Chinese Communist Party (CCP) officials and scholars was the trend toward the normalization and generalization of labor dispatch as the regular practice by employers across all sectors (Chang and Li 2006). In fact, because employers did not have to pay statutory employment benefits for agency employees, many SOEs and government institutions used long-term "temporary" agency workers to fill positions that had been previously occupied by standard contract employees.[49] More and more employers used formalized agency employment to sever the standard contract employment relationships with their regular employees. For instance, approximately 10 million agency employees were hired by large SOEs in the traditional key industrial sectors, such as electric power, oil, steel, machinery, automobile, and telecommunications. This number has continued to grow rapidly (Weng 2009).

Yet until the enactment of the Labor Contract Law in 2007, there was no specific labor legislation on labor dispatch. The triangular employment relationship and lack of regulations caused rampant social insurance fraud and mismanagement in agency employment. Many agency workers were left without the social insurance or employee benefits required by the government. Around the time that the new law was drafted, there was extensive media coverage about the plight of agency workers and its negative impacts on labor relations in a long term (see, among others, Zhang 2005; Wu 2005; "Protections for agency workers' rights" 2005; Chang and Li 2006; Wang 2006; Zhang 2006; Yu 2007). Several high-profile labor dispute cases involving agency employment received wide attention in China and aroused extensive debates among scholars, officials, and the general public about this relatively new type of employment.[50] The All China Federation Trade Union (ACFTU) and its local union branches conducted several surveys on labor dispatch. The resulting reports suggested that labor dispatch complicated labor relations, caused the increase of labor dispute cases, and made it very difficult to protect agency workers' rights and interests ("Protections for agency workers' rights" 2005; Tu 2007; Zhang 2007). The ACFTU was concerned about the findings and called for the relevant legislative and executive departments to regulate labor dispatch ("Protections for agency workers' rights" 2005).[51] The debates soon became politicized when top CCP officials made it clear that it was essential to stabilize labor relations in order to maintain stability and construct a harmonious society.[52] Under the general political guidelines of the Hu Jintao and Wen Jiabao administration to construct a "harmonious society," criticisms of labor dispatch and other "unstable" employment practice that could harm stability and social harmony became dominant in both public media and official discourse (Guo 2006; Lian and Chen 2007; Dong 2008; Zheng 2008).

It was within this broad political context that the Labor Contract Law took tough measures to regulate labor dispatch. Through this tough legislation, the state made a clear statement that it was making efforts to promote long-term stable employment relations and to protect workers' interests, including agency workers formerly excluded from labor law protection. To a large extent, the enactment of the Labor Contract Law was a state-led politicized legislative campaign to pacify workers and boost government legitimacy in response to the bottom-up pressures from mounting labor unrest and the popular demand for more security and protection as marketization deepened.[53] It reflected a state policy shift under the Hu-Wen administration from prioritizing economic growth at all costs during the second phase of the economic reforms in the 1990s to giving more emphasis to social equality and justice and to protection for the disadvantaged groups.[54]

This state-led labor law reforms had a direct impact on shop floor management decisions and practice regarding labor force dualism and agency employment (labor dispatch). Notably, instead of curbing labor dispatch as the legislation intended, one year after the implementation of the Labor Contract Law the number of agency employees jumped from roughly 17 million to 27 million, which accounted for more than 15 percent of the total workforce in the secondary and tertiary sectors in China (Weng 2009).

A close look at management responses at the case-study automobile enterprises provides some explanations for the unintended impact. My interviews with managers suggested that there had been a gradual change of employers' attitudes and responses toward labor dispatch since the new law was implemented. At the beginning, management was hesitant to use more agency workers given the apparently inhibiting stance of the new Labor Contract Law on labor dispatch. For instance, in January 2008 when another large automobile assembler sought to use agency workers to staff an entire plant, the plan was rejected by its Chinese parent company, a large state-owned auto group, for fear of coming into conflict with the provisions of the Labor Contract Law and harming the company image.[55] In November 2008, Chinese domestic auto sales slumped under the influence of the global financial crisis. Despite the dire market prospects, the large automakers received dictates from either local governments or their Chinese parent companies to avoid layoffs and help maintain social stability. So they cut shifts and working hours, let temporary workers go, but, nevertheless, avoided layoffs of formal contract workers. Even though the automobile industry quickly rebounded and boomed in early 2009 under the central government stimulus plans for ten key industries (including the automotive), the major Chinese automakers remained cautious in hiring more formal contract workers. Instead, they preferred to use more temporary agency workers. For instance, in October 2009, after production output almost doubled, Jupiter hired two hundred new formal contract workers, along with eight hundred temporary agency workers.[56] The reasons were not difficult to understand. According to the managers I interviewed, the new law made it more difficult to dismiss formal contract workers, yet the "2008 experience" showed "how important to have staffing flexibility in the volatile auto sector in China."[57] Meanwhile, although the new law put stricter regulations on labor agency firms, it does allow client firms to continue using agency workers in the similar way as before. As a managerial staff at Neptune commented,

> The new labor contract law does not make much difference to our company because we have always followed the labor law and the government regulations

> in treating our employees. The new law does raise the bar for labor dispatch agencies, making sure that they pay the required social security and benefits for agency workers. Relevantly, our cost of using agency workers has increased. But compared to the cost of hiring formal contract workers, it is still much cheaper. More importantly, we can still have staff flexibility.[58]

At the same time, there is evidence that agency workers' conditions had improved at those major automobile enterprises since the implementation of the Labor Contract Law. For example, the four auto assemblers using labor force dualism increased temporary workers' wages and began providing temporary workers with equal access to some of the benefits that had been exclusively for formal contract workers, such as employee car-purchase discounts (Neptune) and winter-heating subsidies (Jupiter).[59] But there were still big differences in bonuses, allowances, and benefits between temporary and formal contract workers.[60] Temporary agency workers still did not have any job security and advancement opportunities at the automobile factories where they work every day.

Nevertheless, it seems the Labor Contract Law has driven the major Chinese automakers to move toward entrenching dualism with more job security and protection for a small portion of the core formal contract workers while using more temporary workers for numerical flexibility. Notably, some greenfield auto assembly firms have also started moving in this direction as they become more mature. For instance, Mercury recruits its skilled workers and team leaders from the Mercury Training Program at a local technical vocational college, while hiring (rural) unskilled and semi-skilled line operators from the suburbs and surrounding areas of Guangzhou. The former sign two- to three-year renewable contracts and are sent abroad to train at the home plants of its foreign partner. The latter can only sign one-year renewable labor contract with very limited on-site training. In this case, the core formal workers and periphery temporary workers could become further divided, and the temporary workers at the up-tier assembly firms could be weakened.

The seemingly unintended impacts of the Labor Contract Law on labor dispatch, I would argue, were indeed an outcome of the state boundary-drawing strategy to balance and accommodate the conflicting interests of the pro-capital and pro-labor forces within the state lawmakers. This point can be seen clearly from the negotiations and compromises over the specific provisions on labor dispatch during the revision of the second draft of Labor Contract Law. As Gallagher and Dong (chap. 3 in this volume) note, the second draft was much stricter on labor dispatch than the third and the final drafts. For instance, the second draft required that a client firm sign formal labor contracts with temporary agency workers if the firm used the same agency workers for more than one year; this provision was dropped in the final draft. The main argument from employers and the pro-capital side was that if this provision were put into effect, it would harm company flexibility and competiveness and would negatively affect employment. Moreover, it would hurt temporary agency workers because employers can always stop using them before reaching the one-year term. As a Shanghai labor bureau official commented, "We need to protect our workers, but we also need to give our companies flexibility to make necessary adjustments to the market and production changes. Currently, temporary agency employment can function as a safety-valve for formal contract employment. Too harsh and too many restrictions on it will harm companies' competitiveness and eventually hurt employment for both formal and temporary workers."[61]

Although the ACFTU insisted that agency employment be regulated and controlled to better protect workers, the concerns about employment and the move to "regulate and develop" labor dispatch as a "supplementary type of employment" gained the upper hand during the debates.[62] As a result, the final draft dropped this specific provision that could have inhibited temporary agency employment. Thus, the Labor Contract Law provides formal contract workers with more job security and better working conditions, but it still excludes temporary agency workers from the regular contract employment and its associated rights, albeit with some legal protection.

This evidence reveals the state boundary-drawing strategy through legalizing (formalizing) labor dispatch and a dualist labor system of workers within the formal contract system and other workers who are not. More specifically, by requiring employers to provide their formal contract employees with more job security and protection, the state attempted to shore up its legitimacy with formal contract workers. Meanwhile, by allowing the existence of a flexible segment of temporary agency workers outside the regular labor contract system, the state granted employers a safety valve to lower labor costs and gain flexibility and profitability. In reflection, to the extent that labor force dualism can be viewed as a management boundary-drawing strategy at the firm level, the state boundary-drawing strategies have been carried out in a more systematic and institutionalized way through national welfare policies, labor policy, and legislation, and thus they have had deeper and long-term impacts on individual workers' livelihood and life chances.[63]

Notably, the central government recently began to draft Regulations on Labor Dispatching, due to the government concerns about the rapid expansion of labor dispatch since the implementation of the Labor Contract Law, which might threat formal contract employment (Weng 2009). The two debated focal issues of the draft regulation are (1) whether the regulation should specify the workplaces that can use temporary agency workers and (2) whether temporary agency workers are eligible to sign non-fixed-term labor contracts with their labor dispatch agency employers. Again, there are disagreements among the lawmakers. ACFTU has stayed assertive in "regulating and controlling" labor dispatch and has stressed that "labor dispatch should only be used at substitutive, short-term and temporary posts";[64] the Ministry of Human Resources and Social Security (MORHSS) has been inclined to "regulate" labor dispatch and has noted that labor dispatch has had positive impacts on promoting employment ("Ministry of Human Resources" 2008). The outcome is hard to predict at this moment, but it is likely to depend on the relatively emphasis of the CCP on maintaining stability and legitimacy (with labor) and promoting growth and profitability (with capital) given the specific political and economic situation.

The interaction between the top-down state-led labor law reforms and the bottom-up pressures from labor unrest and popular demand, as well as the negotiations and compromises during the lawmaking process, point to a dynamic relationship among the party-state, labor, and capital in reform China.

Conclusion: Toward a Relational and Dynamic Understanding of State-Labor-Capital Relations in Reform China

This chapter has explored how shop floor, national, and global processes interacted in complex ways to produce specific labor relations in the Chinese automobile industry under market reform and globalization. The central argument lies in the dynamic relationship among the state, labor, and capital in reform China, exemplified in labor force dualism at the firm level. I have shown how the contradictory pressures of pursuing profitability and maintaining legitimacy have driven large auto SOEs and JVs to strive for a relatively stable solution through labor force dualism, drawing boundaries between formal and temporary workers. Yet a divided labor force does not necessarily preclude robust and continuing labor movements that can lead to significant changes. As we have seen, labor force dualism has, so far, detached formal contract workers from temporary workers and inhibited them from overt protests against management. But the same labor force dualism has also sparked the new generation of temporary workers to push back against unequal treatment. Moreover, there have been withdrawals of consent and cooperation among the formal contract workers as their wages and job security declined. Workers' bottom-up resistance, in turn, induced management to make specific concessions, such as improving conditions for temporary workers.

Furthermore, although labor unrest in the automobile industry has been confined to a small number of incidents (notably, the recent wave of strikes in Honda parts factories are a new development. See Zhang 2010), the labor unrest incited by the informalization of labor is part of a much larger phenomenon in China since the mid-1990s as marketization deepened. By locating our cases of autoworkers' resistance within the broad national political dynamics, I have shown that the bottom-up pressure of rising labor unrest and disputes induced the Chinese central government to reintervene and stabilize labor relations through labor law reforms, including the enactment of the Labor Contract Law. Yet the unintended consequences of the Labor Contract Law on labor dispatch have revealed that the state have implemented a boundary-drawing strategy among its working population to strike a balance between maintaining legitimacy (with labor) and pursuing profitability (with capital). As a result, we see the major Chinese automakers moving toward entrenched labor force dualism, albeit with improved conditions for both formal and temporary workers.

The assumption underlying the party-state striking a balance between labor and capital is that, notwithstanding the prevailing views that Chinese workers are structurally weak under the one-party authoritarian system, the workers do have the leverage and willingness to struggle for change, and the CCP ruling group must respond to their grievances and demands. It has been widely acknowledged that the legitimacy of the CCP in the reform era is built on two pillars: sustaining fast economic growth and maintaining social stability. But it is often less emphasized that the centrality of maintaining stability and regime legitimacy is itself the fundamental political logic of the CCP. That is to say, the pursuit of economic growth by the CCP is not the goal but a means through which to achieve the ultimate goal of strengthening its regime legitimacy and maintaining its monopoly on political power.[65] As such, the impetus of the Chinese liberal economic reforms and marketization in the 1990s largely came from the belief of the top CCP officials that market economic reforms are tactically necessary to create the conditions for more effective state guidance of the economy and, thus, to create a stronger and more effective developmental state, rather than their intention to pursue a capitalist economy per se (Kroeber 2011).[66]

Moreover, the unique historical legacy of China—both the revolutionary and socialist legacy of the Mao years—has led to a unique party-masses relationship. The revolutionary tradition of "mass line" and "two way socialization process" of the CCP have "endowed China's subaltern strata with a self-confidence and combativeness with few parallels elsewhere," and "the continuing official adherence of the party-state to that tradition has given some legitimacy to this self-confidence and combativeness" (Arrighi 2007, 373–76). It is this unique relationship between the party-state and the masses that endows the Chinese workers an important source of legitimacy leverage that can keep the authoritarian party-state responsive to people's demands.[67]

Ironically, because of the lack of electoral legitimacy, the authoritarian regime has to be more responsive and adaptive to grievances and demands from below in fear of ungovernability. The CCP top priority of maintaining stability, and its continuing public commitment (at least in rhetoric) to its revolutionary tradition and "the legitimate rights and interests of workers" ("Hu" 2008) undergird Chinese workers' legitimacy leverage based on their potential disruptive power. This legitimacy leverage, in turn, encourages Chinese workers to stand up and protest against employers' violations of their rights in spite of their lack of independent trade unions and other electoral representative institutions.

Indeed, the feeble role of the ACFTU in representing the interests of rank and files and bargaining with employers have forced the central and local governments to directly intervene in workplace labor-employer conflicts, and most often to intervene in favor of labor to maintain social stability. As such, the localized and apolitical labor protests can be easily turned into political issues concerning social stability and regime legitimacy in the eyes of workers. That explains why the widespread, localized, and apolitical labor-capital conflicts at workplaces can command direct top-down state intervention through legislation and other formal institutional changes to pacify workers. In the other words, the Chinese workers are indeed "bargaining without union" (Zhang 2005), but they are backed up by, and making use of their legitimacy leverage over, the state to wring concessions from their employers.

To be sure, although my case study reveals the significance of Chinese workers' bottom-up struggles and legitimacy leverage to win employers' concessions even without independent unions, I am not disputing the importance of organized labor and the recent efforts noted by Mingwei Liu (chap. 8 in this volume) to build a genuine worker-representative organization to speak and struggle for Chinese workers' rights and interests. Nor am I denying that an authoritarian political system remains a formidable barrier for Chinese workers' collective pursuit of a better workplace. The important theoretical point here is, in concordance with the arguments made by James Scott (1985) in *Weapons of the Weak,* that bottom-up collective struggle in and of itself holds counterhegemonic potential, regardless of the kinds of goals that are being pursued (Meyer 2008). Chinese workers themselves have proven the simple idea that through collective struggle that the working class can continue to improve their lives and to make changes for better. It is in this regard that I argue that we should not underestimate the impacts of Chinese workers' widespread, localized, and apolitical protests, which have proved to be a counterbalancing force against the adverse effects of unregulated markets by holding the party-state responsive to popular demand. Indeed, the key theoretical insight of Frances Piven and

Richard Cloward (1977) was precisely that many of the gains made by "poor peoples' movements" do not come from the establishment of formal organizations oriented toward the capture of state power but, instead, are the result of concessions wrung from the powerful in response to widespread, intense, spontaneous disruptions from below, in response to the threat of "ungovernability" (Silver and Zhang 2009).

But to exercise such (potential) "disruptive power" from below effectively "people must also recognize that they do have some power, that elites also depend on the masses. People have to organize, to contrive ways of acting in concert, at least insofar as concerted action is necessary to make their power effective" (Piven 2008, 8). It is very important to remember that the "idea of power" itself has been an important source of workers' power (Piven and Cloward 2000, 413–14). Thus, there is an urgent need to confront neoliberal ideology and to raise workers' recognition of their own bargaining power. A good illustration of this point is the empowerment effects of the new Chinese labor laws in motivating ordinary Chinese workers to stand up and defend their labor rights through formal legal systems.[68] China's new labor laws, as recent events have indicated, are very likely to serve as the catalyst for a new wave of labor activism and militancy in China—especially if employers attempt to evade the law and if the arbitration system becomes so burdened with cases that it is unable to resolve workers' grievances quickly, encouraging them to turn instead to direct action.

A fuller answer of the roles Chinese autoworkers are likely to play awaits further analysis along these and related lines.[69] And it also awaits the future words and deeds of the Chinese autoworkers themselves.

Chapter 7

Permanent Temporariness in the Chinese Construction Industry

Sarah Swider

One well-documented consequence of Chinese economic growth has been the dramatic increase in the number of migrant workers who have moved from rural areas to the urban ones in search of jobs. The 2000 census estimated the total migrant population at roughly 144 million people, representing 12 percent of the total national population and 25 percent of the total working population (Liang and Ma 2004). The National Bureau of Statistics estimated the number of migrant workers would be 225 million by the end of 2008. Most migrant workers, if not all, work informally and make up the largest proportion of informal workers in China (see Mary Gallagher, Ching Kwan Lee, and Sarosh Kuruvilla, chap. 1, and Albert Park and Fang Cai, chap. 2 in this volume).

A burgeoning body of scholarly literature has focused on understanding the lives and working conditions of these new migrant workers. Studies have focused on migrants working in manufacturing (e.g., Lee 1998a; Ngai 1999, 2005); migrants working in enclave economies (e.g., Ma and Xiang 1998; Zhang 2001); and migrants working in various segments of the service industry, including sales (Hanser 2006), the hotel industry (Otis 2007), domestic work (Hairong 2006), and entertainment (Jacka 2006). Few studies have focused on migrants in the construction industry,[1] a surprising omission given that the construction industry is the largest employer of migrant workers. Dorothy Solinger (1999) estimates that between 30 and 50 percent of all migrants were working in construction in 1995, representing roughly 80 percent of total employment in the industry at that time.[2] Moreover, for men, who represent 60 percent of all migrants, the construction industry is a primary source of employment.

This chapter details how market forces and changes in industry configurations have resulted in a significant growth of informal employment in the construction industry, quite consistent with similar patterns of informal employment in the oil and automobile industries (Kun-Chin Lin, chap. 5, and Lu Zhang, chap. 6 in this volume). Moreover, there is considerable variation in how the employment of these informal migrants is structured. I show that the dominant employment form of mediated employment results in a state of "permanent temporariness" in which migrants are neither strongly tied to their home communities nor integrated into their host communities.

These findings are based on qualitative research conducted in Beijing in 2004–2005. In addition to participant observation at several construction job sites, enclaves, nongovernmental agencies (NGOs), and street labor markets, a total of ninety-one interviews were conducted with migrant workers, managers, labor contractors, NGO workers, lawyers, and government officials. These data are supplemented with secondary data from newspapers, scholarly journals, and organizational documents.

Industry Overview

By 2007, the construction industry in China was the third largest in the world in terms of spending, just behind Japan and the United States. During the past two decades, the industry has grown substantially. Its contribution to GDP increased from 4.3 percent in 1981 to 6.7 percent in 2002 (see fig. 7.1), and the value of gross output expanded from 34.7 billion yuan in 1980 to 1678 billion yuan in 2000, with the housing sector representing the largest percentage (see fig. 7.2).

Industry growth has been accompanied by a growth in the number of construction companies (from 57,404 in 1980 to 97,263 in 2000) and increased diversity in terms of ownership. Prior to economic liberalization, there were three main types of companies: state-owned enterprises (SOEs), urban collectives (UCs), and rural brigades (RBs). In the 1980s, RBs represented roughly 90 percent of all companies operating in the construction industry, a figure that had decreased to 50 percent by 2000. This decrease was offset by an increase in SOEs, and also, private firms, foreign companies, joint ventures, and shareholding companies. Despite this increased diversity however, public companies (SOEs, UCs, and RBs) still accounted for the major percentage of construction companies in 1999 (see fig. 7.3).

Employment in the construction industry has increased with industry growth. By 2002, the industry employed more than 38 million people, or 5.2 percent of total national employment. The structure of employment has undergone change

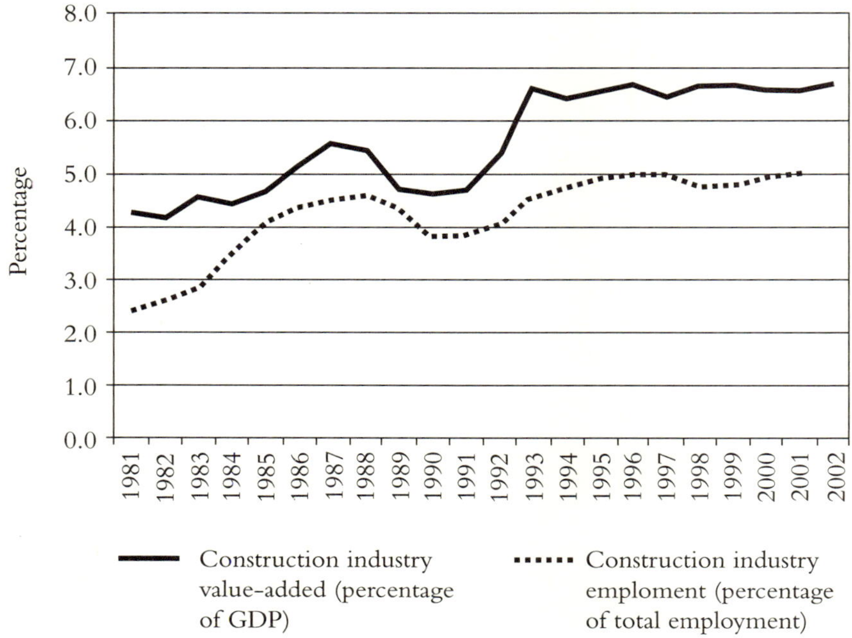

Figure 7.1 Growth of the Chinese construction industry, 1981–2002
Source: Jin (2003).

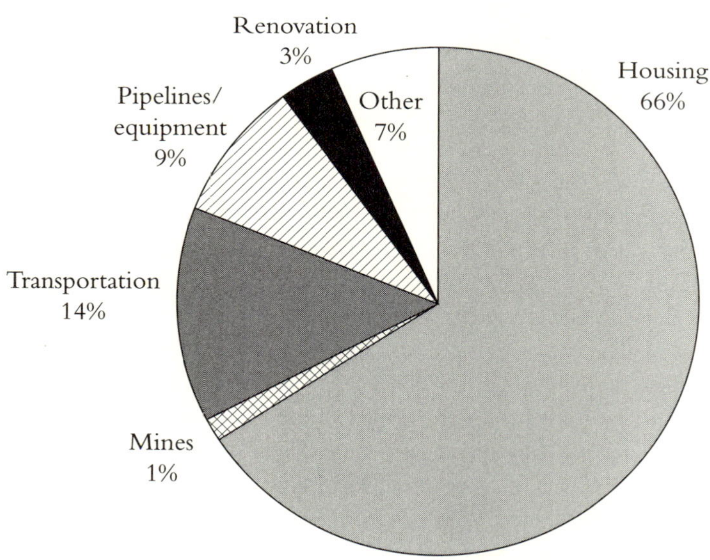

Figure 7.2 Industry segments in China, by output value, 2000 (%)
Source: National Bureau of Statistics ([NBS] 2002).

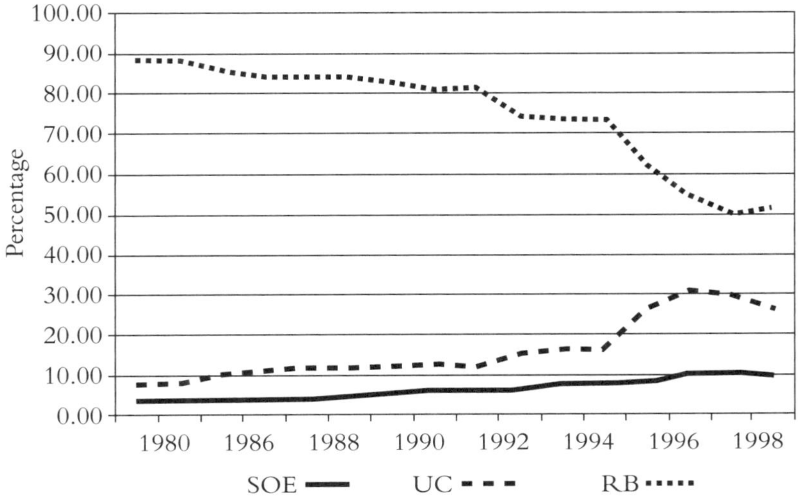

Figure 7.3 Public construction companies in China, 1980–1998 (% of all enterprises in the industry). RB, rural brigade; SOE, state-owned enterprise; UC, urban collective.
Source: Lu and Fox (2001).

however. With the growth of the industry and the entry of private firms, there was a gradual decrease in the number of SOEs and, with that, a decrease in the number of permanent urban employees. Whereas in 1980 half of all workers in the construction industry worked in SOEs, by 1999 SOEs employed only one-fourth of construction workers. The explosive growth of the industry in the 1990s and 2000s fueled a major increase in temporary employment, especially in the nonstate sector. Much of this temporary employment is completely informal, making use of the growing pool of migrant workers, although precise estimates, as noted earlier, are hard to come by. The informalization of employment (and the absence of social insurance for these workers) is particularly worrisome given the growing number of fatalities in the industry, increasing from 1,292 in 2001 to 2,607 in 2005 (Zou, Fang, and Wang 2007).

The construction industry is regulated at four governmental levels: central, provincial, county, and municipal. At the central/national level, the Ministry of Construction, in collaboration with other central ministries, oversees the industry. The provinces each has a construction commission, and at the county and city levels, construction bureaus are present. At the national level, many of the procedures and regulations governing the industry have been standardized and codified in three main pieces of legislation: the Construction Law of the People's Republic of China (1997), the Contract Law of the People's Republic of China (1999), and the Tendering Law of the People's Republic of China

(1999). In addition, a large number of administrative rules and regulations have been issued by the other levels of government. Sarah Swider (2010) notes that there is often conflict between decisions made at the national level and those at the other levels. This administrative thicket also makes enforcement difficult because it enables contracting companies to find loopholes. Efforts to regulate construction companies have proved ineffective, and many smaller construction companies operate freely in the informal market.

Historical Background

In 1951, shortly after the Chinese Communist Party (CCP) came to power, the construction industry underwent nationalization as part of the "Three-Anti" and "Five-Anti" campaigns.[3] Nationalization included a reorganization of the labor force based on the communist goal of full employment. This took the form of creating permanent, full-time, cradle-to-grave jobs that were filled through government labor bureaus (Cai, Park, and Zhao 2008).[4] This structure of full-time permanent employment was not consistent with the seasonal nature of the industry and the reality of geographically dispersed worksites. To deal with these contradictions, workers were organized into mobile units, which turned out to be a highly inefficient use of workers and resources (Chao 1968).[5]

The industry in the 1950s continued to exhibit its prenationalization configuration of a labor force duality, despite the nationalization strategy. During the 1950s, there were three main types of workers: permanent employees, temporary employees, and draft labor. Permanent employees received compensation even when there were work stoppages beyond their control, such as material shortages, bad weather, and delays in implementing projects. They were assigned to a *danwei*[6] and received benefits such as housing, education, and health care. In contrast, temporary workers were recruited from the local workforce to supplement permanent workers when needed.[7] In 1953, temporary workers represented approximately 44 percent of the total industry employment (Chao 1968).[8] These temporary workers were generally of rural origin, with low levels of education and training, and their compensation was calculated by time (per day) or under a "pay as you work," or piece-rate, system. Finally, a significant segment of the industry workforce consisted of draft laborers. Draft laborers included peasants who were mobilized during the winter when agricultural work was at a lull, military labor, and workers from labor reform camps or prisons. Draft laborers were used most extensively in public work programs and were poorly compensated.[9] Yet all these groups were formally employed.

In 1957, the construction industry was reorganized on geographical lines. There was a construction base assigned to each defined geographical area, which was assigned labor, equipment, and resources. This structure, albeit in a weakened form, still operates today and impacts the growing private sector of the construction industry (Lu and Fox 2001). These geographical bases recruited additional temporary labor, beyond their assigned labor forces, when demand increased; this temporary labor was mostly informally employed. Coupled with the political campaigns of the 1960s, which sent many workers to the countryside, the end of the 1970s witnessed a decline in the percentage of full-time permanent employees in construction and an increase in informal employment.

Construction Industry and Migrant Workers

The construction industry thus has had a history of using rural temporary workers sanctioned by the state. Not until the 1980s did we see a dramatic increase in market-driven migration, in which rural peasants left their farms to find work in the cities. This dramatic increase in migration brought about state-led reforms in the migration system as well as in the construction industry, in which a large portion of these migrants worked.

The migration system has historically been, and continues to be, shaped by the *hukou* system. The *hukou,* simply put, operates as an internal passport system that links citizenship rights and welfare benefits to an individual's local place of birth (Chan and Zhang 1999; Solinger 1999). Under the Maoist regime, the *hukou* system played a dominant role; everything, from work and housing to food and health care, was distributed based on where people were registered. People who wanted to move were required to gain government permission by requesting a change in their place of registration and their *hukou* status. Despite the unequal distribution of resources across rural and urban areas, the system was fairly effective in discouraging people from migrating without state approval.[10]

A number of reforms in the 1980s and early 1990s made it easier for rural peasants to migrate and survive in the cities. As a result, the number of migrants grew from a few thousand in the late 1970s to more than 100 million by the mid-1990s (Chan and Zhang 1999; Liang and Ma 2004). In the mid-1980s, the swelling migrant worker population in urban areas led to changes in the official *hukou* classification system, which was expanded to include a new status called "temporary migrants."[11] This new status, which required registration, sanctioned the migration from rural areas to urban areas for work.

At the same time, believing that the construction industry was well suited to absorb a significant proportion of these registered temporary migrants, the state restructured the industry. This restructuring was mainly done through an

1984 executive order, The Separation of Management from Field Operations, and an associated provision, Tentative Provisions for Construction Industry and Capital Investment Administration System Reform [1984] No. 123 (Qian and Hui 2004). These provisions reorganized the construction industry into three basic types of enterprises: general contracting companies, specialist companies, and labor-only companies.[12] General contracting companies tended to be located in urban areas and employed mainly administrative and technical workers. They typically hired qualified employees on a permanent basis.[13] These firms obtained construction contracts and subcontracted work to the labor-only contracting companies. The labor-only companies hired these temporary registered migrant workers as "field workers" to actually build the buildings, roads, bridges, and houses. With the dramatic Chinese economic growth and the concomitant growth in urban construction, employment in these labor-only companies exploded, and it did not take long for these reforms to significantly change the composition of the construction industry workforce. In 1980, there were approximately 10 million workers in the construction industry, including 7.1 million urban workers and 3 million migrant workers. By 2001, fifteen years after these reforms were initiated, urban workers had remained roughly the same at 7.3 million, but rural migrant workers had expanded significantly to almost 30 million (Qian and Hui 2004).[14] This reorganization represented a decisive step away from the pre-1978 system of labor appointments and toward a free labor market, albeit a segmented one divided between permanent urban employees in managerial, technical, and administrative positions and temporary rural workers in the field (see fig. 7.4).

What is significant however, is that the growth in the labor-only companies consisted of not only registered temporary migrant workers but also a large number of unregistered migrant workers working informally. Under informal employment, labor contractors do not properly register their workers or pay the required taxes and assessments; on the other side, workers in informal employment do not have proper documents or access to benefits and social welfare programs. In 1999, informal employment was estimated to make up 17 percent of the entire construction industry workforce (Lu and Fox 2001), and although there are no clear figures, anecdotal evidence suggests that more than 30 percent of the construction industry employment is now informal.

Although part of the reason for this growth in the informal section of the construction labor force can be traced to the large increase in the demand for construction, the large increase in available and unregistered migrant workers, and the desire of constructions firms for flexible labor, it is also true that growth in informal work can be partly traced to a response of firms to increased regulation. The state promulgated regulations to weed out bad contractors who exploited labor, as well as to control the quality and flow of the construction

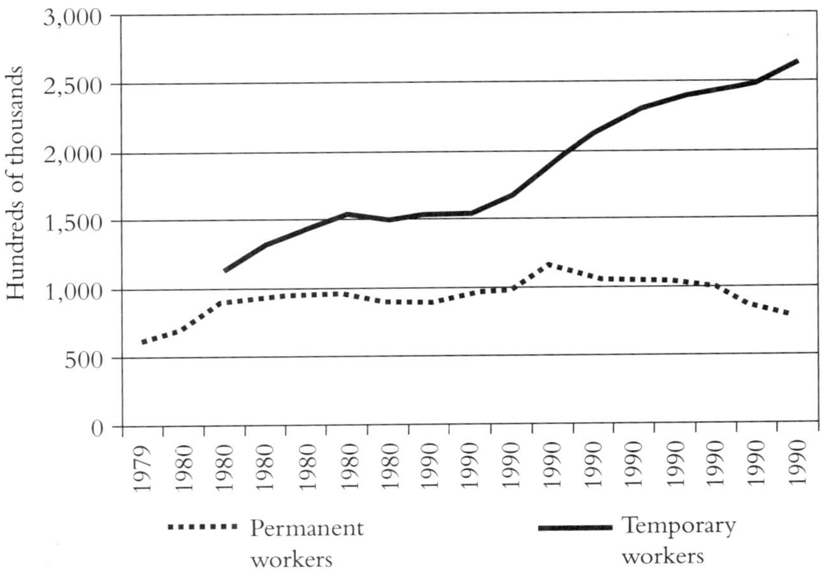

Figure 7.4 Employment in the Chinese construction industry 1978–1999 (hundreds of thousands)
Source: Qian and Hui (2004).

workforce at the local level. For example, in Beijing the government set up the Incoming Construction Force Administration Office under the Beijing Construction Commission. This office opened in 1987, and by 2001 it had fifty workers and branches in districts and counties under Beijing Municipality (Lu and Fox 2001). These offices are charged with registering workers, dealing with labor contractors, handling disputes, and providing technical training and legal assistance. Many observers, however, suggest that these regulations have not been successful in eliminating bad contractors and, instead, have had the unintended effect of pushing a large part of the construction industry underground. In other words, taken together, these reforms have resulted in a shift from the state sector to the informal sector rather than from the state sector to the private (but regulated) sector.[15]

Today, all migrant field workers are temporary migrants, but we have no idea what proportion of them is registered and what proportion works informally.[16] Registered temporary migrants often enter the city through government channels, such as government labor offices, labor bases, and registered labor companies. These registered migrants do not necessarily have an urban *hukou* (but might possess a temporary (one-year) urban *hukou*) and are more likely to work in the formal sector than their unregistered counterparts. They can be found working on special projects, such as Olympic building sites; on projects that must meet stringent safety standards, such as dams, subways, power plants, chemical factories, airports; or in joint venture companies.

In contrast, unregistered temporary workers have very different pathways into the labor market and are much more likely to work in other sectors of the industry. They tend to work on new apartment projects and mixed-use buildings; on smaller commercial ventures; and in finishing work, renovations, and repairs. As informal workers, these workers do not have working or temporary housing permits, nor do they have written contracts with their employers. This means that, in contrast to those who are legally registered as temporary workers, unregistered migrant workers have no formal right to be in the cities.

Modes of Employment in the Construction Industry

It is important to note that all informal migrant workers do not necessarily experience the same working conditions. Rather, there is significant variation among informal migrant workers on a number of dimensions, such the conditions of work, relationship to the local labor market, degree of incorporation into the cities, and wages. The best way to understand this is to examine the different modes of employment in the construction industry for migrant workers. By *mode of employment,*[17] I mean the specific pathways to employment in the industry. Each specific pathway has associated with it certain types of working conditions, certain types of labor processes, and certain implications for the level of incorporation of migrants into the cities. In addition, the mode of employment also affects migration patterns and the connection of migrants to their lands.

I have identified three modes of employment among migrant workers in informal employment in the construction industry: mediated, embedded, and individualized.[18] In mediated employment, the labor market is organized by a contract labor system.[19] In this system, labor contractors hire workers under year-long verbal contracts. The contractor covers the costs of migration and provides a yearly salary but withholds most of the wages until the end of the contract.[20] The key element here is that the labor contractor helps workers overcome barriers to migration (such as costs) and provide workers with information about and access to employment. This arrangement is only effective when hiring workers who are not already in the city, and as a result, contractors draw solely from the rural workforce. Typically, a labor contractor will hire groups of individuals from a particular village or rural township, often by working through one member of family in the village.

In contrast, in embedded employment, recruitment is largely through social networks. In this mode of employment, workers are hired from both the rural and urban labor markets, and migrants draw on networks that reach back to their hometowns and on those that extend to migrants living in the cities. These social networks are diverse—horizontal and vertical, weak and strong, and they cut across industries, occupations, and place. The diversity of these social networks increases the mobility of migrant workers in and across occupations and industries. Workers are typically hired on an informal per-job basis (rather than on a year-long contract basis). Working conditions and other aspects of employment relations are embedded in, and regulated by, mechanisms that emanate from these social networks, such as social capital, bounded solidarity, enforceable trust, and reciprocity.

Third, in individualized employment, workers find employment through spot markets. Because workers must already be in the city to participate, workers are hired solely from the urban labor market. There are at least three types of spot markets: unorganized markets, organized markets, and direct hiring. Unorganized markets usually operate in unofficially designated public spaces where workers gather and wait for potential employers, similar to street labor markets for day laborers in other countries. In organized markets, market bosses determine who can participate, and fees are collected for connecting workers to employers. Finally, in direct hiring, workers go directly to job sites looking for work. All three methods of finding work fall under the rubric of spot markets because they are made up of discrete individuals and the terms of employment are negotiated on the spot. Wages are often calculated per piece (per brick laid or per block carried) and paid at the end of the job. Employment relations under individualized employment tend to be despotic and exploitative, and, of course, informal. The harsh nature of this mode of employment is due to several factors: workers are inserted into employment relations as separate individuals, their employment is very short term in nature, and workers have no possibility of seeking recourse via the state. (See the summary in table 7.1.)

In this chapter, I focus particularly on mediated employment, which was prevalent in Beijing (where I did my fieldwork).[21]

Mediated Employment and Permanent Temporariness

Under mediated employment, the labor market and employment relations are shaped by the hiring practices of formal and informal labor contractors. Specifically, large formal labor contractors are most often registered with the government, usually take the form of labor companies, and bring from hundreds to thousands of workers into the cities to work on urban construction projects. Informal labor contractors, although they also bring hundreds of workers into the cities, are not registered with the government. The reforms in the 1990s,

TABLE 7.1
Summary of modes of employment

Mode of employment	Labor market	Employment relations
Mediated	Organized by the contract-labor system Rural labor market	Mediated by hiring practices/contract-labor system Paid by time
Embedded	Organized by social networks Rural and urban labor markets	Embedded in social networks and regulated by mechanisms such as enforceable trust, reciprocity, and bounded solidarity Paid by job
Individualized	Spot markets: unorganized, organized, and direct hiring Urban labor market	Individually subordinated Paid per piece/end of job

an attempt to regulate the market and weed out bad contractors, only had the effect of pushing smaller contractors into the informal sector.

Under this mode of employment, migrants enter into a verbal agreement with a labor contractor, often via a team leader. The basic agreement is that the migrant worker will come to the city and work for the labor contractor for roughly eleven months, returning home for a month (at most) during the New Year holiday. If the contract is renewed, the worker returns to the city to work after the New Year break. In return, the contractor pays an agreed-on amount of money for the year of work.[22] In addition, the contractor agrees to pay upfront the costs of migration, which will later be subtracted from the worker's salary. The contractor also provides shelter and food. In some cases, these are "free";[23] in other cases, there is a daily charge subtracted from the salary. Finally, the migrant worker agrees to forgo payment of his salary until the end of the contract (before returning home), with the exception of a small monthly stipend for living costs, such as hygiene products and entertainment (soap, cigarettes, cell phone, etc.).[24] (See summary in table 7.2.)

Why do migrant workers use this system? First, the existing rural-urban divide creates barriers to migration, and the contract labor system helps migrants to overcome these barriers by covering upfront costs and reducing daily living costs, as well as diminishing risks and uncertainty by providing access to jobs. These benefits help to explain why migrants participate in a hiring system that contains a high level of risk (because payment is withheld until the end of the contract). This system has two major drawbacks from the point of view of migrant workers. First, the configuration of the contractual arrangements makes the incorporation of migrant workers into the cities difficult, if not impossible. Second, the structure of the system shapes migration patterns in a way that weakens migrants' connections to their families and hometowns. These

TABLE 7.2
Summary of the contract labor system

Worker	Contractor
Agrees to work 11.5 months for contractor	Agrees to pay upfront costs of migration and starting job in city on job site (some of which is later subtracted from pay)
Agrees to forgo payment of salary until end of contract (one year)	Gives workers monthly allowance (later subtracted from pay)
	Provides housing and food (usually on job site, with some variation)

two factors, create a system of permanent temporariness that unfortunately has become a key characteristic of the lives of informal migrant workers.

Connections to the City: The Job Site as Home

By restricting the mobility of migrant workers, mediated employment shapes the development of migrants' social networks, limits migrants' knowledge about the city, and minimizes their interactions with locals. In this way, it plays an important role (beyond the broad legal barriers that apply to all migrants) in preventing migrants from becoming physically and socially integrated into their host communities. This limited mobility develops from the contract labor system, in which employers (contractors) not only provide work but also supply food and housing. As a result, the job site becomes home because workers live, work, eat, and sleep on site. In most cases, workers are forbidden from leaving the site without permission. Even when they are allowed to leave, long working hours and the arduous nature of the work leave little time or energy for wandering around the city.[25] This socially constructed constraint on movement is often reinforced by physical restraints in the form of guarded entrances and tall walls surrounding job sites.

An important impact of this limited mobility is that it shapes migrants' social networks in the cities, which tend to develop horizontally but not vertically. This means that most workers' relationships are limited to other construction workers, usually those doing the same type of work and/or from the same hometown.[26] In part, the limited nature of migrants' social networks is due to workers being hired as groups and not as individuals. These groups of workers tend to be from the same hometown or province, and when they come into the cities under a contractor, they tend to work together on the same job site doing the same kind of work. As a result, a pattern emerges in which workers interact with other migrants from the same region who are in the same occupation. Although these workers have limited mobility in terms of their lives in the cities, they are quite mobile in terms of their work. As workers move from job site to job site, their networks extend across the city and across regions but rarely outside this web of construction workers. Because their social networks do not cross into other groups of migrants with different occupations and/or hometowns (or provinces), they are usually strong, rather than weak, ties that are less effective at providing new job opportunities (Granovetter 1974).

Restricted mobility also severely limits interactions with city natives, reinforcing the divisions between these two groups. Most migrants under mediated employment have little or no direct contact with natives. Of the workers that I interviewed, not a single migrant hired under the mediated mode of employment had friends, family, or acquaintances who were native Beijingers. By contrast, migrants under other modes of employment have more opportunities to interact with natives through a range of activities, such as using public transportation, being hired by locals to do renovations or repairs, acting as consumers, and spending more time in public places.

Another notable impact of limited mobility is that it prevents migrants from gaining knowledge about life in the city. In fact, compared to other migrants (and natives), it is striking how little these workers know about the city in which they work and supposedly live. Although the average length of job tenure is difficult to ascertain, more than one-fourth of workers I studied had been working for their current contractor for more than five years, and some of them had been with their contractors for more than ten years. Still, many of them did not know how to use public transportation, were unfamiliar with the customs associated with flagging taxis, could not find their way around supermarkets, and were unfamiliar with expected behaviors in such public places as parks and malls. Furthermore, they did not know how to find housing, how to use the banking system, or how to shop.

This reality captures the way in which the perpetuation of the segmented labor force based on the rural-urban divide depends on keeping migrants temporary and preventing them and their families from integrating into their urban host communities.

Connections to Hometowns: From Tangible to Intangible

Mediated employment turns job sites into temporary homes for migrants in the cities, but it also weakens migrants' connections to their hometowns, which in turn makes these temporary homes on the job site more permanent. The impact of mediated employment on migrants' connections to their hometowns occurs predominantly through families.

The structure of mediated employment makes it virtually impossible for migrants to bring their families to the cities. Only men are hired as construction workers, and under mediated employment, these men live together on job sites.[27]

Families are not allowed to live on the job sites (which have limited space and rather primitive living conditions), and alternative housing is not an option because rental costs are prohibitive. Furthermore, because these workers move from job site to job site, often across cities, it would be difficult for families to follow them.[28] As a result, when men come to the cities under mediated employment, they migrate as individuals. Their children usually remain in their hometowns, and their wives either stay with the children or also migrate for work.[29]

Because migrants under mediated employment work under year-long contracts and cannot bring their families to the cities, they see their families only during the few weeks they have between contracts. Over time, these arrangements can significantly weaken, or destroy, family relationships. In my study, there were a number of construction workers in mediated employment who had literally lost their families as a result of these arrangements. In some cases, men had missed the opportunity to marry. In other cases, wives had left or divorced the migrant men. A typical example is Zengzeng, who, like many others, had originally come to the city to make money to build a house for his wife and son. Now, he still returns home to Henan every year, but his wife has left him and his son is being raised by his parents.[30] In more severe situations, migrant workers stop returning home and/or stop sending money home or significantly reduce the amount they send.

Family needs, such as education, health care, and housing, were among the top reasons men migrated to the cities to seek work. In interviews, migrants were painfully aware of the fact that this migration process had ultimately destroyed their families—the impetus for their migrating in the first place. Those who still had families also doubted that their hard work and sacrifice would result in a better future for their children. For example, one night in the dorms at the Xizhimen job site, I asked Gaoshan, a steel worker, about his family. One of the other migrants jumped into the conversation, noting that Gaoshan worked in the city so that he could afford the costs of his son's education, and Gaoshan proudly began talking about his son's accomplishments in college. The others started joking that his son was going to college only to end up like his father, a construction worker in the city. The joke was followed by laughter and then a somber silence. Gaoshan's sacrifice provided money for his son's education, but the reality created by the *hukou* system was still the same: if (male) peasants want to earn money, one of their few career options is to migrate to the cities and work construction. This structural constraint meant that his son, even with an education, would probably become a temporary migrant worker and end up performing manual work.

Another significant way that mediated employment weakens migrant workers' ties to their hometowns is through land contracts. When migrants leave the city for a year or longer, they might choose to rent their land to someone else who wants to farm it (Chinese peasants are not allowed to sell their land). Many construction workers who return to the cities year after year find that it makes sense to sign contracts that extend to five years. But once they contract out their land, especially for longer periods of time, they lose the security that the land would otherwise provide in giving them a fallback option to return home if things do not work out in the city. Moreover, the migrants I interviewed noted that, even though construction work is difficult, farming is backbreaking. Accordingly, the very option of doing construction work in the city rather than farming creates a psychological distance between these migrants and their land. When workers talked about returning home, their plans did not focus on farming but, rather, on starting a business (even if the business was related to agriculture). Also, many of the younger men on the job site had no connection to farming and the land because they had chosen migration and construction as their first job.

As the distance between migrants and their hometowns grow, the relationship shifts from being tangible to intangible. Even as migrants became permanently temporary in the city, their most common topic of conversation is family and hometowns. They continue to miss their families, yearn for home-cooked meals, and remember past holiday celebrations.

In sum, there are two different processes occurring under mediated employment that cause permanent temporariness. First, arrangements under mediated employment prevent workers from becoming integrated into the cities, reinforcing temporariness. Second, mediated employment separates migrants from their families and agricultural work and makes it difficult for them to maintain strong connections with their hometowns. Over time, their relationships and connections to their families, communities, and their land weaken, and, in some situations, erode completely. Together, these processes produce a state of permanent temporariness among migrants.

The New Permanent Temporary Migrants

Permanent temporariness emerges out of migratory patterns that are shaped by the mode of employment—in this case, mediated employment. Permanently temporary migrants represent an emerging migratory pattern that does not fit neatly into the traditional sojourner-settler model and related theories about migrant workers and the labor market (Piore 1979). In his seminal work, *Birds of Passage,* Michael Piore suggests that migratory patterns are linked to the structure of job opportunities. He argues that migrants are drawn into the secondary labor market, in which jobs are unstable, temporary or seasonal, unskilled, and low-wage. This market is a good fit for migrants because they are "target earners." Target earners plan to stay only long enough to make a certain amount of money, and they arrange their lives to save as much as possible, as quickly as possible, and then return home once they have met their target. As a result, migrants become sojourners who exhibit circular migration patterns in which they repeatedly travel back and forth between their home and the host communities where they work to earn money. In contrast, settlers are those who intend to stay permanently. According to Piore, this group includes refugees and many migrants who are in enclave economies. He demonstrates that enclave economies produce settlers rather than sojourners because they offer steady jobs and advancement for first-generation migrants.

Clearly then, Piore links specific segments of the labor market (the secondary labor market and enclaves) with specific job structures (temporary work vs. more permanent work). My study, in contrast, indicates that there may be more diversity than Piore assumes within the secondary labor market. In particular, in contrast to the dichotomy between sojourners and settlers, I found that mediated employment creates a new migratory pattern resulting in permanent temporariness. The temporariness of these migrants is quite different from the traditional understanding of temporary migrants and certainly not of the kind described by Piore. To be sure, Piore stresses the temporal aspect of migration that is created as migrants move back and forth between two areas with different levels of economic development, keeping their stay in the host community short-term. According to Piore, "It is chiefly the temporary character of the migration stream that makes these migrations between industrial and underdeveloped areas of value to industrial society and equips the migrants for the particular roles that they play in industrial society. Unfortunately, from this point of view, the migrant communities seldom remain temporary" (1979, 52).

In the 1950s, state-sanctioned migration in the construction industry involved workers doing very short stints in destinations that were closer to home. In those days, migrants were purely temporary. Today, however, migrants in the construction industry who are hired under the mediated mode of employment are not temporary in Piore's sense of the term. Rather, they are temporary with respect to the nature of their status (as either temporary migrants or as workers without legal status) and with respect to their lack of integration into the cities in which they work. This temporariness exists despite the fact that they are long-term migrants; they spend about eleven months of the year in the city, year after year, often under the same employer. Under this system, Piore's prediction that migrants "seldom remain temporary" has been replaced with the reality that migrants become permanently temporary.

Conclusion

While migrant workers have always been an important segment of the workforce in the Chinese construction industry, reforms to the migratory system and the construction industry, coupled with increased demand for construction workers and the increased supply of migrant workers, have developed a largely informal labor market in construction. Estimates suggest that more than 60 percent of migrant workers in the construction industry work informally. On the worksites in my sample, 100 percent of the workers were working informally. Repeated attempts to regulate this industry (in terms of employment conditions) have failed. Hence, I have very little reason to expect that the new Labor Contract Law enacted in 2008 will have a significant impact in limiting informal employment in the construction industry. My expectation is that that it will drive more formal construction jobs into the informal sector as contractors try to save on labor costs and social insurance payments.

This analysis is based on a study of only a small part of the Chinese construction industry, and I do not claim that my results are generalizable to the rest of the industry. In addition, my sample consisted of unregistered temporary migrant workers who were in informal employment; I am not sure whether the pattern of permanent temporariness that I find extends to registered temporary migrants working in other sectors.

Part III

Unions, Nongovernmental Organizations, and Workers

Chapter 8

"Where There Are Workers, There Should Be Trade Unions"

Union Organizing in the Era of Growing Informal Employment

Mingwei Liu

The growing informalization of the Chinese labor market (Mary Gallagher, Ching Kwan Lee, and Sarosh Kuruvilla, chap. 1 in this volume) has not only deeply affected workers but also seriously challenged the All-China Federation of Trade Unions (ACFTU), the single official workers' organization in China. The extreme difficulty of organizing informal workers had resulted in a significant decline in union density in the 1990s. According to Mingwei Liu (2009), Chinese union density declined from 39.60 percent in 1990 to 26.27 percent in 1999; and in the privately owned enterprises (POEs) and township and village enterprises (TVEs), where there were a large number of informal workers, union density was merely 3.43 and 1.96 percent, respectively, in 1999.

To respond to the changing labor market and to revitalize its role in the workplace, the ACFTU launched a nationwide organizing campaign in 2000 with the principle, "Where there are workers, there should be trade unions" (All-China Federation of Trade Unions [ACFTU] 2001). By the end of 2009, unions had been set up in 92 percent of the Fortune 500 companies operating in China, even in such notoriously anti-union companies as Wal-Mart, and 80.15 million migrant workers, many of whom were employed informally, had become union members (ACFTU 2010). This apparent success occurred against a backdrop of steadily increasing Chinese union membership, which went from 87 million members in 1999 to 226 million members in 2009, reversing the marked decline in the 1980s and 1990s. The Labor Contract Law that went into effect on January 1, 2008, further reaffirms and strengthens a union role in the workplace. Moreover, based on recent union and labor legislation changes in

Guangzhou and Shenzhen, even the *China Labor Bulletin,* the mouthpiece of a Hong Kong based labor nongovernmental agency (NGO) that used to be the biggest critic of the ACFTU, claimed that "a crucial turning point in the history of China's trade union movement" had been reached (*China Labor Bulletin* [CLB] 2008). Nevertheless, in general, observers are still skeptical about the ability of the ACFTU to carry out reforms and to organize successfully.

Indeed, given that independent trade unions are banned in China, union organizing there actually means setting up ACFTU branches bureaucratically at various levels, with the fundamental goal of not so much protecting workers' rights as strengthening the social control of Chinese Communist Party (CCP). Two widely reported recent labor-management conflicts—the strike at a Honda parts factory in Foshan and a series of worker suicides in Foxconn in Shenzhen—reflect the marginalization of management-controlled workplace unions in China (Barboza 2010; Bradsher and Barboza 2010).

Despite this, organizing official unions does have a significant impact on the future of the Chinese labor movement in general and on the survival of the ACFTU in particular. More important, there are growing local variations in organizing within the ACFTU that may indicate the beginnings of a gradual and bottom-up transformation of Chinese trade unionism under the still stable communist authoritarian regime.

Clearly union organizing in China is increasing. Yet not all the recent increases in union density can be ascribed to the national policies of the ACFTU. In my research,[1] I found that the organizing strategies of regional unions (*difang gonghui;* see fig. 8.1 for a diagram of the simplified structure of the ACFTU)[2] have been critical to the recent organizing successes noted in the media. However, not all the organizing successes reported are real successes because the actual organizing and bargaining outcomes differ based on both the strategy of the regional union and the nature of the employer response. A key implication of my findings is that it is important in today's Chinese context to focus on changes in organizing approaches at the lower echelons of the ACFTU rather than treating it as a monolithic top-down organization with a unified strategy.

Three Patterns of Union Organizing and Bargaining in China

How can we best understand recent union organizing in China? How do the newly established trade unions perform? Have they made progress in improving working conditions, or is the recent organizing campaign just a bureaucratic and ineffective response of the ACFTU to the new environment? In my research, I found three patterns of union organizing and bargaining in China,

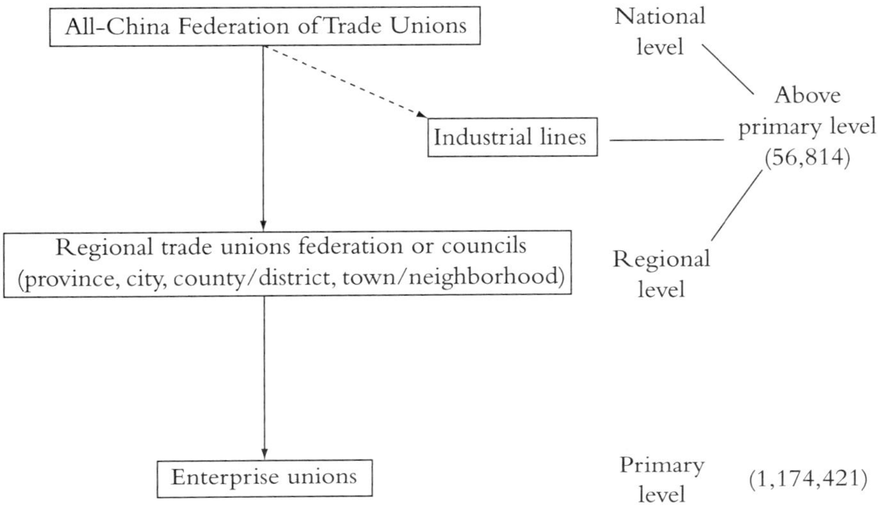

Figure 8.1 Simplified structure of the All-China Federation of Trade Unions. The numbers of unions are in parentheses.
Source: All-China Federation of Trade Unions ([ACFTU] 2007).

each having vastly different consequences for trade unions and collective bargaining: (1) the traditional organizing pattern, (2) the union association pattern (*gonghui lianhehui,* a new form of union organization covering multiple workplaces) pattern,[3] and (3) the regional industry-based bargaining pattern.

The traditional pattern of union organizing still dominates in China today. In this pattern, the national ACFTU assigns organizing quotas to regional unions, which set up enterprise unions (*qiye gonghui,* ACFTU branches at the enterprise level; see fig. 8.1) by gaining the approval of employers/management rather than by mobilizing and organizing workers per se. Because all enterprises with more than twenty-five employees are legally required to establish trade unions, regional unions typically view each individual enterprise (especially mid-size and large ones) as a basic organizing unit. When regional unions attempt to establish unions under this pattern, employers typically respond in one of two ways if avoiding unions is not possible. One employer strategy is to agree to the establishment of the union (it is the law) but to suppress it completely, so that the union exists only on paper. This strategy is very common among POEs and small foreign-invested enterprises (FIEs). The second strategy is cooptation—employers/managers dominate union activities and make the union an integral part of their management system. This strategy can be seen in some POEs, some large FIEs, Sino-foreign joint ventures (SFJVs), and state-owned enterprises (SOEs). Typically, the company human resources manager functions as the union leader.

Clearly, to ensure that unions are established in different enterprises, regional unions, under the traditional organizing pattern, have been content to sacrifice many of the rights that unions enjoy (e.g., they guarantee no collective action, allow employers to appoint union leaders and determine union functions, and reduce mandated union dues). Thus, although the employer responses of suppression and cooptation may have small yet differing impacts on union roles and some workplace outcomes, in general this method of union organizing makes enterprise unions weak, subordinate to management, and largely irrelevant to workers.

The union association pattern and the regional industry-based bargaining pattern are different and constitute more innovative responses by regional unions to the changing Chinese labor market, especially in trying to unionize small POEs and individually owned businesses (IOBs; *getihu*), where informal employment prevails.[4]

In the union association pattern, the typical approach is for regional unions in areas with high concentrations of small enterprises or IOBs to set up various forms of union associations to cover multiple workplaces, such as community unions (*shequ gonghui*), market unions (*shichang gonghui*), office building unions (*bangonglou gonghui*), and union associations of FIEs or POEs (*waiqi* or *siqi gonghui lianhehui*). Essentially, these are associations, not enterprise unions and employers have relatively little ability to oppose their formation. They cover multiple workplaces and businesses and are established by the regional unions, which appoint their own staff members as union chairmen. Thus, these union associations are relatively independent from employers, but are highly dependent on regional unions and the regional state. The support of the regional union gives these union associations the potential to confront employers during organizing and bargaining processes. Nevertheless, they seldom bargain substantively with employers, given the diverse economic and employment conditions in the individual enterprises, the usual lack of adequate training of union officials, and the sometimes insufficient government support for bargaining. Although these union associations do not really bargain collectively, they do serve other functions, such as taking charge of welfare and entertainment, and mediating labor disputes. As a result, these union associations still have a certain relevance for workers. More important, the relative independence of these unions from employers and their enhanced capacity for enforcing the administrative power of official unions in the workplace make them significantly different from the employer-dominated enterprise unions. In that sense, these unions have the potential to play a more independent labor representation role in the future.

Regional unions that follow the regional industry-based bargaining pattern choose to organize union associations by trade (*hangye gonghui lianhehui*) and engage in local industry-based negotiations of wages and other employment conditions.[5] Having the same organizing form and process as the unions established through the union association pattern, the union associations organized by trade are relatively independent from employers and highly dependent on the state. My research suggests, however, that four preconditions enable them to be more active in collective bargaining and give them more bargaining power. First, regional union leaders are typically motivated and innovative, able to transform the administrative power of the official unions into substantial bargaining power. Second, the similarities in working and employment conditions across enterprises in the same industry within the region make it much easier for these unions to conclude meaningful industry-collective contracts. Third, the local labor markets in these regions are relatively tight; thus, employers (especially large ones) can be more easily persuaded to accept unions and collective bargaining because the better working conditions promoted by unions and collective bargaining may help to attract and retain skilled labor. Finally, local governments often strongly support union bargaining activities because they are helpful for social stability. Thus, this pattern of industry-based unions has elements of the more genuine trade unions found in other countries, and their activities can be viewed as a more positive and radical adaptation of the regional unions than the other two patterns. This pattern, although the most positive, is the least common.

In both the union association pattern and the regional industry-based bargaining pattern, employer strategies or responses play a very limited role in shaping the development of the newly established unions. Although some employers welcome unions with the view that unions can help them motivate workers, reduce labor-management conflicts, or maintain a good relationship with local governments, most employers have a negative attitude and are forced by the regional unions or local governments to accept unions. More important, in these two patterns employers lose their dominance over the unions and lack ways to intervene in union activities. Next I present four cases illustrating these patterns in more detail.

Cases of Union Organizing in China

Union Organizing in NCW

NCW was a Taiwanese-owned enterprise in Shilou Town, Guangdong Province, which produced watches and clock accessories for export and employed 550 (primarily) migrant workers. Working conditions in NCW corresponded to the typical exploitative model associated with low-cost, labor-intensive production systems. Furthermore, when I conducted my field research in 2005–2006, these workers were employed informally (i.e., they were not given labor contracts). Often their wages were reduced arbitrarily, and they were frequently fired without any severance pay. As a result, the amount of labor-management conflict was high, and work stoppages and wildcat strikes were very common, albeit unsuccessful in redressing conditions because of the workers' lack of organization and lack of awareness of their legal rights.

Given the relatively large size of NCW, the regional union (the Shilou Town Trade Union Council, STTUC) had urged NCW several times before 2003 to set up an enterprise union. The employer resisted but finally relented under the pressure of the local party committee. In June 2003, the NCW union was established on paper, but the workers were completely ignorant of its existence.

With the bureaucratic requirement of establishing a union fulfilled, the STTUC had finished its "job" and did not have any incentive to check whether the union was actually effective. Thus, the union was completely under the control of the employer, a "paper union" without any substantive function. And the company did not even take the trouble to elect or appoint a union chairperson.

Nevertheless, this "paper union" was challenged by NCW workers led by Mr. W, a migrant worker who had some knowledge of unions and had confronted the management about its illegal labor practices several times. With the belief that a trade union could help workers improve their working conditions, Mr. W and his fellow workers requested that the employer recognize a union that could play a more representative role. After the employer rejected their request, Mr. W went to the STTUC for help, but was told that an NCW trade union already existed and that there could be only one union per enterprise under the Trade Union Law. Simultaneously, because of the pressure from workers, the employer immediately required all managers to sign up for the "paper union" and appointed the human resources manager to the position of union chairperson. According to Mr. W, "This is a secret 'boss union' without any workers in it."[6]

The NCW case is a typical example of the traditional ACFTU organizing model, coupled with a hostile response from the employer, that is very common among POEs and FIEs in China (Chan 1998). The complete lack of independence and bargaining power of the NCW union is a function of the way it was established, and this case exemplifies why the traditional model provides the least potential for Chinese workers. Such "paper unions" do not serve the interests of workers, and their existence means that no genuine trade union can form because the law allows only one union per enterprise. This form of union organization may result in the complete alienation of Chinese trade unions from the rank-and-file workers.

Union Organizing in DHP

DHP was an enterprise located in Humen Town, Guangdong Province, owned by a locally renowned businessman, Mr. C. DHP mainly produced packaging products, such as cigarette packs and albums, and its customers included both national companies and some large multinationals. According to the officials of the regional union (the Humen Town Trade Union Council, HTTUC), DHP was well known locally for its good working conditions and, as of 2005, had gained many honors for its responsible corporate conduct.

Given the relatively large size of DHP (more than nine hundred employees), the HTTUC followed the traditional organizing model, requesting DHP to set up an enterprise union. Unlike most other employers, Mr. C was quite active and cooperative in establishing a union and maintaining harmonious labor-management relations. He felt that these actions were necessary for his positive public image and consistent with his business philosophy of mutual gains. Thus, an enterprise union was established smoothly in 1997. Mr. C went further by allowing the workers to elect their union chairperson directly. Nonetheless, although any employee who had worked for DHP for more than one year was eligible to run for chairperson, between 1997 and 2006 none of the shop floor workers ran for this position.[7] This situation is not surprising given that most POEs in China are characterized by a paternalistic management style that makes workers afraid to challenge their employers. Indeed, all the workers could do was simply vote for the candidate who was nicest to them or most distant from the employer.[8] Because by 2006 the union chairperson had always been a middle manager, Mr. C did not need to worry about the independence of the union. In fact, the union had to report everything to him and got his permission for any activity,[9] which indicated that it had little bargaining power and was highly subordinate to Mr. C.

The HTTUC was satisfied with what Mr. C had done and left the functioning of the union almost entirely to his discretion. The extremely weak linkages between the HTTUC and the union further increased the dependence of the union on Mr. C and decreased its power. Mr. C, however, adopted the cooptation strategy; he viewed the union as his tool for communicating with the workers and promoting production. In practice, he chose just one of the official enterprise union functions designated by the ACFTU—dealing with welfare and entertainment issues to motivate employees, also in DHP interests. As a result, the union was merely a welfare department of DHP and had done quite well in promoting worker welfare under the support of Mr. C, for example, setting up special funds for workers in financial difficulty; providing workers with free physical examinations once a year; and organizing such activities as sports, travel, and collective weddings. Moreover, acting as a conduit, the union sometimes passed worker demands on to Mr. C. For example, it communicated with Mr. C about worker demands to reduce working hours from 42.5 to 40 hours per week (as required by the Labor Law) and to have a half-day leave for female workers on March 8, International Women's Day (also a legal requirement in China). Fortunately, he approved both demands.[10]

Note that the union actually did not bargain with Mr. C; it simply played the role of messenger between the workers and the boss and left the final decisions completely up to the boss's discretion. As the current DHP union chairperson admitted, the union played a very trivial role in improving the welfare of workers. The relatively improved employment conditions at DHP actually were partly a consequence of maintaining a "good" employer image and partly due to strict factory inspections by some foreign customers of DHP.[11] More important, all the workers I interviewed viewed the union as a weak managerial department rather than an organization in which they took ownership. According to these workers, their having good working conditions was not because of having a union but because of being "lucky to have a good boss."[12]

The DHP case is one of the better examples of the traditional organizing model. Compared to NCW, which adopted a union-suppression strategy and was more exploitative, DHP took a cooptation strategy toward the union and treated the workers relatively better due to the good public image of Mr. C. The DHP union functioned as the DHP welfare department and worker-management relations were quite cordial, whereas at NCW the union was a "paper union" without any substantive function and labor-management relations were riddled with conflict. Despite these differences, neither of the two unions had autonomy or significant bargaining power. Under this organizing pattern, enterprise unions can at best act as a managerial tool to provide welfare to and communicate with workers; they can seldom challenge employers as genuine representatives of the workers.

Union Organizing in Small Privately Owned Enterprises and Individually Owned Businesses in Guanlan Town, Guangdong Province

Located in Guangdong Province, Guanlan was a small town with a high concentration of FIEs as well as small POEs and IOBs. In 2005, the majority of the workers (more than 200,000) in Guanlan were migrant workers who had often been maltreated in various enterprises. Although, as of 2005, enterprise unions had been established in most of the FIEs following the traditional organizing model, it was impractical to do so in small POEs and IOBs.

To maintain social stability as demanded by the local government and to achieve organizing quotas, the regional union, the Guanlan Town Trade Union

Federation (GTTUF), decided to organize the workers in small POEs and IOBs in a new way through the Guanlan Union Association of POEs and IOBs (GUAPI). Under the direct leadership of the GTTUF, GUAPI was relatively independent from employers. It was also supported by and embedded in the local government. After repeated requests by the GTTUF chairperson, who was highly respected locally (he had worked in the town for many years, first as a government official and then as the union chairperson), the local government not only called on all the government departments to assist in establishing GUAPI but also granted it 100,000 yuan ($12,500) in start-up funding. In addition, to enhance the authority of GUAPI vis-à-vis employers, the GTTUF intentionally appointed the vice director of the local industry and commerce bureau (a government department in charge of the registration and management of various enterprises) and the vice president of the Association of IOBs (Getihu Xiehui, a quasi-government department responsible for the management of IOBs) as the GUAPI chairperson and executive vice chairperson, respectively. These arrangements, on the one hand, increased the independence of GUAPI from employers; on the other hand, they made it highly dependent on the government, serving government interests in maintaining social stability.

Centered on maintaining industrial peace, the major functions of GUAPI included organizing, welfare and entertainment, and mediating labor disputes. By June 2005, GUAPI had established 31 branches, covering all 12 communities in the town, and had organized more than 7,500 workers and self-employed individuals in 80 POEs and more than 1,700 IOBs, mainly by adopting the bureaucratic organizing method—the staff of GUAPI visited the enterprises one by one and negotiated with the employers regarding the formation of unions. In addition, during the organizing process GUAPI provided training for union cadres and activists and widely publicized trade unions and labor laws to mobilize the workers in the POEs and IOBs.[13] GUAPI also organized a series of welfare and entertainment activities, such as birthday parties for union activists, sports for workers, and support on holidays to workers in financial difficulty. The key function of GUAPI, however, was mediating labor disputes in the POEs and IOBs. In particular, GUAPI had actively intervened in wage-arrears disputes and conflicts, which were very common in the private sector and had become the major cause of social unrest in Guanlan. In 2004, for example, more than 160 workers in a POE (afraid of losing their unpaid wages) had a violent clash with the court police who had come to seal up this POE due to its illegal business activities. GUAPI immediately went to the enterprise, appeased the workers, and helped them get their unpaid wages from the local government the next day. These activities, although somewhat limited, popularized trade unions among the workers. In fact, all twelve workers whom I interviewed knew about GUAPI. Although five of them did not think GUAPI was helpful for them, three said that "it has a little use sometimes" (*youshi youdian yong*) and one worker even received his unpaid wages from his employer through GUAPI (the other three workers did not evaluate GUAPI).

Because GUAPI was established by the GTTUF, was under its direct leadership, and was supported by the government, employers did not have any means to prevent the establishment of the union, nor were they able to intervene in union activities. In fact, although a few employers did welcome GUAPI with the idea of working with it to maintain a good relationship with the local government, most of them at first did not agree to become union shops because they would have to pay union dues. Later they were forced to accept the union because of pressure from the local industry and commerce bureau, the vice director of which was also the chairperson of GUAPI.[14]

Despite the strong "government color" of GUAPI, it was not able to effectively bargain with employers for several reasons. First, the POEs and IOBs had diverse working and employment conditions. They were different types of businesses, including both large manufacturing and small grocery shops; had different modes of operation; and employed different types of workers, both local residents and migrants. These differences made it very difficult for GUAPI to conduct common negotiations with all the myriad employers that employed these members. Second, given its priority of economic growth, the local government did not want the union to do too much to make capital flow out of town, a view shared by the leaders of GUAPI and the GTTUF.[15] Therefore, although GUAPI had concluded three collective contracts involving 120 IOBs by 2005, the articles in these contracts merely repeated the Labor Law, failing to add any benefits for the workers. Nonetheless, GUAPI did play an educational role in that most of the employers and workers did not even have a rudimentary knowledge of the Chinese labor laws.

Several conditions explain the growth of GUAPI. The small size, dense concentration, and diverse working and employment conditions of the POEs and IOBs made it possible to organize an association of unions in diverse enterprises. The moderate support of local government (supporting union organizing but not bargaining) was instrumental as well. GUAPI thus organized as a union association, and focused on welfare and mediation rather than union representation. Hence, its bargaining power was weak, and it was highly dependent on the state, although reasonably independent of the employers. The goals of GUAPI centered on maintaining social stability rather than representing workers, and workers' voice was not apparent in any of its activities. That said, GUAPI did manage to organize a significant number of workers and self-employed individuals who otherwise would not have had access to union membership under the traditional organizing model. Added by-products were that GUAPI educated workers about their rights and carried out a reasonably useful dispute mediation function.

Union Organizing in the Water Pump Industry in Zeguo Town, Zhejiang Province

Zeguo was a small town in Zhejiang Province, where POEs dominated the local economy. The water pump industry, with 22 POEs employing more than 3,800 workers in 2006, was one of the central industries in the town. After 2000, the industry experienced several labor and employment problems.[16] First, the relatively tight local labor market resulted in certain labor shortages in this industry by 2004, especially during peak seasons. In addition, due to wage differences among enterprises, workers frequently switched jobs for higher pay, leading to high turnover. Second, employers often reduced workers' wages at will, making many workers' wages lower than the local minimum wage of 560 yuan ($70), and they sometimes delayed paying wages, which resulted in labor disputes and strikes. Third, unreasonable wage-rate differences among the different types of work within the enterprises also led to frequent conflicts between labor and management. Although there were enterprise unions established through the traditional organizing pattern in all twenty-two POEs, they were under the control of the employers and thus of little use to workers.

Given the small size and high concentration (in one industry) of the enterprises, the leaders of the Zeguo Town Trade Union Council (ZTTUC), under some pressure by workers, decided to organize union associations by trade and to collectively negotiate wages with employers. In July 2004, the Zeguo Water Pump Industry Union Association (ZWPIU) had been established, with all twenty-two enterprise unions as its branches. Because the ZWPIU was an industrywide union organized under ZTTUC leadership, it was relatively independent from employers. More important, it was able to overcome the weakness of the enterprise unions by confronting employers directly as the industry representative. In addition, the ZWPIU had gained great support from the local party-state, to which the union role of reducing labor conflicts was attractive. Moreover, its union leaders were relatively more skilled at labor-management relations and were able to transform the union administrative power and government support into substantive bargaining power. In addition, the tight local labor market (there was a growing shortage of skilled workers) made it easier for ZWPIU to influence employers and gain meaningful bargaining outcomes.

The major function of the ZWPIU was collective bargaining, which could not be performed effectively by the employer-controlled enterprise unions. The ZWPIU first went to the industry employers' association asking for the existing wage rates for all 236 types of work in the 22 POEs.[17] Thereafter, the

ZWPIU invited specialists in industrial engineering from the local labor bureau to help determine standard wage rates, which were further discussed with workers (the number of workers consulted in each enterprise ranged from six to more than forty, depending on the size of the enterprise). Then, the ZWPIU and the employers' association began to bargain based on the negotiated wage rates. Finally, after several rounds of bargaining, worker representatives signed and approved an industry wage agreement in November 2004.[18] This agreement detailed the minimum pay scales for jobs covering the entire production process, established a minimum monthly salary (which could not be less than the local minimum wage, an achievement given that many workers did not earn minimum wage before the wage agreement was signed), and specified that salaries must be paid on time every month unless enterprises were experiencing particular cash-flow difficulties.[19] As a result of the agreement, the workers' monthly wages increased by 5–8 percent, turnover and labor shortages lessened, the number of labor disputes decreased, and the strikes stopped. In late 2005, the second industry wage agreement was reached, giving workers an average increase of 3 percent.[20]

Because the negotiated wage rates were publicly posted within the enterprises, as required by the ZWPIU, all ten workers I interviewed knew about them and received the same wages. Even so, although three of them thought that ZWPIU had played an important role in the wage negotiations, four workers did not know about ZWPIU at all. This perception is not surprising because ZWPIU was established without significant input from the rank-and-file workers and it did not make significant efforts at grassroots mobilization, instead depending on the authority of the ZTTUC and the local government to increase its bargaining power (it did, however, consult with some workers on wage rates).

At the beginning of wage negotiations, several large employers welcomed ZWPIU because they had already given workers higher wages and thought that ZWPIU might help them stabilize their workforce and reduce labor disputes. By contrast, smaller employers were strongly against wage bargaining. Many small employers refused to bargain with ZWPIU, but later they were forced by the local government to accept and institute the negotiated wage rates.[21]

Given the characteristics of the enterprises (small size and high degrees of regional and industry concentration), the relatively tight local labor market, the capability of the union leaders, and the strong support of the local government, the ZTTUC made two strategic choices: to organize a union association in the water pump industry and to engage in collective bargaining. As a result of these strategic choices, the ZWPIU was independent from employers and gained relatively high bargaining power. It not only ensured wage increases, but also improved labor force stability and reduced labor disputes in the industry, both outcomes that were in the interests of employers and the local government.

Given that independent trade unions are not allowed by the law, this pattern of union organizing can be viewed as the next best alternative.

The Three Patterns of Union Organizing and Bargaining Revisited

The four cases outlined here clearly show that the strategies of regional unions with regard to organizing forms, processes, and union functions play a key role in shaping union organizing and bargaining outcomes. When regional unions choose the traditional organizing pattern, the newly established enterprise unions are invariably dominated by employers/management and lack independence and bargaining power. Although this pattern of union organizing has rapidly increased ACFTU membership, the resulting enterprise unions completely lose independence from employers and become increasingly irrelevant to Chinese workers. We should note that unions established via the traditional organizing pattern have had some limited role in some large profit-making SOEs. Although these unions are not independent from management, they have acted as channels for workers to exert some pressure on management. In a few such SOEs, thanks to various firm-level factors such as the strategic importance of the firm, the socialist legacy, strong union leaders, and CCP support, the unions may even have a limited voice in policies related to worker interests. In addition, as Anita Chan (1995) and Xin Tong (2005) have noted, enterprise unions in some SFJVs have experienced, due to Chinese management and party support, some degree of independence from foreign management and have managed to represent workers to a limited extent. An unusual variation in the traditional organizing pattern is the grassroots mobilization by some regional unions in setting up branches in the first batch of Wal-Mart stores (Chan 2007). Nevertheless, after this first batch of unions was established, the establishment of unions in the other Wal-Mart stores conformed to the traditional pattern described in this chapter. Despite these marginal successes, I am skeptical that the traditional organizing pattern can provide a platform for the development of more independent trade unionism in China unless there is a radical change in the independence of workplace unions from management. Such a radical change could be brought about by genuine direct elections of workplace union leaders (this was a key demand in the June 2010 Honda parts strike) or if workers with strategic positions in the labor market (such as those with highly developed skills) engage in developing informal bargaining (similar to the Hungarian experience).

The union association pattern represents an organizing innovation. Because union functions here are formally designated as organizing, welfare, and mediation, the unions are able to organize a large number of workers, especially informal workers outside the traditional organizing model; provide a certain degree of welfare for them; and even represent their interests in labor-dispute mediation. Moreover, the relative independence of these unions from employers and their potential to enforce the administrative power of the unions in the workplace may contribute to the development of more independent labor representation in the future. Arguably, these union associations are still not as much representatives of workers as they are a tool of the regional state for maintaining social stability. They do not (as yet) engage in meaningful bargaining. Yet they are growing in China. In the Luwan District of Shanghai, for example, members of various union associations accounted for roughly 90 percent of the membership of the district union federation in 2008.[22]

The regional industry-based bargaining pattern is the most promising because unions organized on this basis can replace employer-controlled enterprise unions as workers' bargaining representatives and can make use of regional government support to gain substantive bargaining power. Therefore, this organizing pattern, although regional in the way it is initiated, provides a pragmatic way to not only represent workers better but also help the ACFTU to extend its authority and influence in the workplace more nationally, if it can institute this model across the country. Although unions organized in this way are still not common, this organizing pattern is increasingly seen in east and south China, where there are dense concentration of industries producing similar products. The Labor Contract Law enacted in 2008 explicitly recognizes and encourages regional and regional industry-based collective contracts, and it may help to further expand this pattern. The weak enforcement of labor laws in China and the poor quality of Chinese union officials (Liu 2009), however, make the large-scale expansion of this pattern very difficult in the short term.

What makes regional unions depart from the traditional ACFTU organizing pattern? The cases presented here provide a tentative list of factors that are important. Clearly, the degree to which regional union leaders are embedded in the party-state apparatus is a key motivating factor because they take on the responsibility of organizing union associations as an instrument of social control. Of late, some regional union leaders have grown increasingly protective of workers' interests, spurred no doubt by state concerns manifested in the enactment of the more protective Labor Contract Law in 2008. In addition, where regional leaders are more capable and well trained, the scope for the formation of union associations is better.

The ability of regional union leaders to organize union associations is also shaped by characteristics of the enterprises and local labor market, to be sure, but local government and party support are, in my opinion, the more important variable. Where the support of the party-state is strong, the ability of employers to follow strategies that suppress unions is weaker. The role of the employer in the union association pattern is weak, and the employer is a reluctantly willing partner in the industrywide negotiations in this bargaining pattern.

Thus, in all the cases presented here, the support of the local government was a key variable. Nevertheless, even though the support of local governments may help smooth the organizing and bargaining process, it cannot make the unions genuinely representative. In the NCW case, the local party branch forced the employer to set up a union but was not able to prevent it from becoming a "paper" union. In the GUAPI case, although the local government forced many employers to accept the union, it could not (or did not want to) help GUAPI become a genuine representative for the workers. In the ZWPIU case, the choice by ZTTUC to pursue wage negotiations that increased the workers' wages made ZWPIU more representative; the support of the local government helped only to smooth the bargaining process. Thus, local governments support is a necessary condition but not a sufficient one.

Conclusion

The growth of informalization in China can only be reversed if trade unions are able to organize and bargain to ensure the better implementation of protective labor legislation. This chapter has examined some recent innovations by Chinese unions. There are five lessons from these case studies of the three organizing and bargaining patterns for the future of Chinese trade unions and industrial relations.

First, there may be two ways to revitalize enterprise unions within the traditional organizing pattern. One strategy requires reforming ACFTU structure and the principle of geographical jurisdiction so that mid-size and large enterprises can be organized into unions based on trade, especially across regions. A second strategy calls for regional unions to engage in grassroots mobilization and bottom-up organizing. By these means, enterprise unions may become more independent from employers/management and may thus be better able to act as a voice for workers.

Second, for the union associations that are already quite independent from employers, having motivated and capable leaders who can engage in more genuine collective bargaining and who can transform the administrative power of unions into substantive bargaining power is important to their success. Even if their bargaining power is still not very effective, given constraints such as unfavorable labor market conditions and insufficient government support, as long as they can truly represent workers, they may be able to find ways to protect worker interests or gradually improve working conditions.

Third, for unions that follow the regional industry-based bargaining pattern, regional unions should increase the sustainability of industry collective bargaining. Otherwise, reversal is a distinct possibility. To avoid such a reversal, the unions should increase their bargaining power substantially by engaging in grassroots mobilization rather than merely depending on their administrative power or government support.

Fourth, given the existing situation of weak labor and strong capital in China, it is often necessary for unions to gain support from the party-state—an even stronger actor in Chinese society—to smooth the organizing process. At least at present, the close CCP-union relationship may be in the interests of the ACFTU when employers' resistance to union organizing and bargaining is strong. Still, the support of the party-state is a double-edged sword. It may increase further the dependence of Chinese unions on the authority of the party-state rather than on the power of organized labor and, thus, negatively influence the development of genuinely independent trade unionism in the long run.

Finally, one of the biggest challenges for Chinese unions at all levels is local mobilization and making more efforts to organize unions completely from the bottom up. Given that the national ACFTU is still conservative and under the tight control of the CCP (see Liu, Li, and Kim 2011) and that enterprise unions in general are under the control of employers/management, meeting this challenge will require considerable efforts by regional unions that have more operational autonomy. As the cases here show, some regional unions have already adopted organizing patterns different from the traditional model. Although the local initiatives by regional unions are still very limited, especially regarding grassroots mobilization and bottom-up organizing, they do indicate the key role of regional unions in shaping organizing outcomes and possible changes in the future. More important, some local initiatives, such as the various forms of union associations, have spread to many Chinese cities and towns and have even influenced the decision making of the national ACFTU, showing a bottom-up movement. Thus, although the national union still has a significant impact on the development of the Chinese trade union movement (Liu, Li, and Kim 2011), the organizing initiatives of the regional unions may hold the best promise for adequately protecting Chinese workers and reversing the trend of informalization.

Chapter 9

The Anti-Solidarity Machine?

Labor Nongovernmental Organizations in China

Ching Kwan Lee and Yuan Shen

The increase in insecurity and informalization of the Chinese workforce described in this volume has not happened without opposition from workers acting independently (see the May 2010 wildcat strikes in Honda plants), unions (as Mingwei Liu, chap. 8 in this volume, demonstrates), and other civil society agents such as labor friendly organizations. Labor-related nongovernmental organizations (NGOs) in China are growing in number and visibility, despite formidable challenges to their existence. In this chapter, we provide a preliminary analysis of their organizational cultures and practices. Although these organizations all claim to pursue and protect workers' rights, in actual practice many have become more keen on developing their roles as government liaisons and on building patronage, on the one hand, and market opportunities, on the other. We trace these characteristics to the political and economic circumstances under which these organizations have emerged and survived. We also examine two activities commonly undertaken by Chinese labor NGOs: labor law education and the collection of unpaid wages for workers. We find that, rather than cultivating workers' collective power, many labor NGOs have an anti-solidarity tendency.

China has the largest workforce in the world, reaching almost 800 million in 2005, but the government allows only one union, the All-China Federation of Trade Unions (ACFTU), to represent worker interests. As part of the mass organization apparatus of the Chinese Communist Party (CCP), the ACFTU has been and still is hamstrung by its political subordination to the CCP and by its financial dependence on employers, who contribute 2 percent of their payrolls to the union fund. For three decades, the Chinese export-oriented, labor-intensive, industrialization strategy has subjected Chinese workers to one of the most exploitative labor regimes of the modern world. Egregious labor violations, now well documented in academic and journalist accounts, have spawned the emergence and growth of Chinese labor NGOs since the 1990s. The sorely felt need for the protection of labor and advocacy of workers' rights beyond the framework of the ACFTU is palpable, especially among aggrieved and injured workers and concerned academics, journalists, and legal workers.

To put this Chinese development into perspective, we must note that the growth of non-union worker organization and mobilization is not unique to China. In the United States, for instance, the increase in immigrant workers, the process of de-industrialization, the restructuring of the economy toward low-paid service work, and the casualization of employment have led to the growth of some 150 worker centers (Fine 2006; Gordon 2007a). These community-based (rather than workplace-based) organizations target workers, such as women, immigrants, and casual labor, traditionally shunned by unions as "un-organizable." Social movement unionism is another tendency observed in many parts of the world, including Brazil, South Africa, South Korea, and Japan (Seidman 1994; Chun 2005, 2008; Gottfried 2008). Here, union activists join hands with a variety of community organizations to address worker issues as community and citizenship issues.

The distinctive political economy of China is shaping the rise of a unique kind of labor NGO. Let us begin with a sketch of the landscape of labor NGOs in China: their leadership, organizational features, and financial support.

The Nongovernmental Organizational Landscape in China: A Preliminary Overview

We use the term *labor NGOs* in a broad sense to refer to those nonprofit organizations whose primary or secondary objectives relate to workers or certain segments thereof (e.g., women workers or migrant workers) and labor issues (e.g., industrial injuries and occupational health, litigation, or skill training). There is no accurate or official count of the number of labor NGOs operating in China. Some of these NGOs are registered as *minban feiqiye danwei* ("non-government nonprofit units"), but most are registered as commercial entities or have no formal registration at all. For example, since 2006 the Panyu Secretarial Support Center has operated without a license. Based on information gathered at several national workshops that we have organized for labor NGOs in the past two years, we are aware of the existence of some thirty labor NGOs in the major cities, with Beijing (eleven), Shenzhen (six), and Guangzhou (three) having the largest numbers. Others are found in secondary cities such as Wuhan and Qingdao and in the centrally administered city of Chongqing. Several labor NGOs have developed branches outside the headquarters city from which they originated. Little Flowers, for instance, was formed in Beijing in 1999, set up branches in Shenyang and Shenzhen in 2006, and planned to expand to Nanning and Guangzhou by 2010. The Migrant Worker Legal Assistance Station was also established in Beijing and, as of 2010, boasts a network extending to twenty provinces.

The leadership of these organizations falls into two major categories: former workers and concerned professionals (see table 9.1 for a summary of NGO characteristics). Among the leaders who are former workers, some were victims of industrial accidents or have been involved in labor disputes and litigations. These transformative personal experiences made them realize the lack of support for aggrieved workers and gave them firsthand knowledge about the legal system and the labor bureaucracy. The process of seeking redress apparently empowered some and spurred others to do something to protect other workers. For instance, a Sichuan labor NGO was formed by a group of women workers injured in the infamous 1993 toy factory fire in Shenzhen, which killed eighty-seven young migrant workers (Tan et al. 2001). The founder of another NGO in Shenzhen that focuses on occupational health lost his hand and arm in an industrial accident. Also in Shenzhen, Huang Qingnan, who co-founded the Shenzhen Worker Health Center, was a victim of a gruesome physical assault by a co-worker in a factory dormitory; his face was disfigured by the corrosive chemical used by the assailant. There are other former workers turned NGO leaders who did not sustain injuries but who were motivated by a sense of civic

TABLE 9.1
Summary of key characteristics of Chinese NGOs

Year of establishment	1992–2005
Staff size (full and part time)	2–10
Membership size	50–1,300
Service recipients	Several thousand to ten thousand
Sources of funding	Foreign foundations (e.g., Ford Foundation), international development agencies (e.g., Oxfam, in Hong Kong), foreign embassies, World Bank
Locations	Beijing, Shenzhen, Guangzhou, Nanjing, Panyu, Haikou, Dongguang, Wuhan, Chongqing, Qingdao, Shenyang, Shanghai
Activities/projects	Hotlines, labor law classes, visits to injured workers, consultation for labor arbitration and litigation, schools for migrants' children, community performances, small group activities, public lectures
Occupations of founders	Lawyers, media workers, workers, academics, cadres, managerial staff

Note: NGOs, nongovernmental organizations.

righteousness to create some kind of social protection for the millions of migrant workers. Quite a few are former managerial or technical staff (e.g., Yang Fei of the Workers' Services Center in Panyu and Zhu Hang of the Beijing Center for Workers). They are the more educated, rural-born, migrant workers with postsecondary technical or junior college qualifications.

In addition to former workers, NGO activists have hailed from several major professions: journalism, academia, and the law. One of the most established NGOs in Shenzhen was founded by a former *Legal Daily* journalist who holds a doctoral degree in Chinese literature. Before Liu Kaiming established the Institute for Contemporary Observation in 2001, he had written many investigative reports on explosive labor problems ranging from deaths from overwork, industrial injuries, and unpaid wages to labor arbitration and protests. The Xiao Li Hotline in Qingdao, which has grown from a one-man hotline into a full-fledged labor NGO, was the brainchild of Xiao Li, a local media worker with a self-taught legal worker qualification. In Beijing, the Cultural Center for Workers was founded by a husband and wife team, both of whom were journalists at *Women's Daily.*

Several migrant worker NGOs are offshoots of academic departments. The sociology and law faculties at the Sun Yat Sen University in Guangzhou run a Zhongshan University Labor Studies and Service Center. The Women Studies Center at the same university provides assistance to female migrant workers on health and legal issues. Likewise, a group of former Women's Federation officials formed a breakaway NGO called the Peking University Women and Law Research Center. (Note that these centers attached to universities do more than legal aid and academic research, although their names convey a narrower focus.) Pun Ngai, a Hong Kong–based anthropologist, and several other Hong Kong academics have been collaborating with a local women's federation branch to run a women workers' network in Shenzhen.

The legal profession is the third main source of NGO founders. Lawyers usually become concerned about labor issues after taking up cases involving young workers or migrant workers. The centrality of the law and legal procedures in labor conflict resolution in China prompts some of these concerned lawyers to offer legal education and aid to these vulnerable workers. We know of labor NGOs in Shenzhen (e.g., the Chun Feng Labor Dispute Arbitration Counseling and Service Center) and legal aid centers in Wuhan and Shanghai that have been founded explicitly to help workers with litigation, to resolve labor disputes, and to promote legal reform (e.g., expanding the coverage of labor laws to domestic workers in private homes).

Funding for these NGOs comes mainly from the international community. Oxfam (Hong Kong) plays a pivotal role, as does the Ford Foundation, the Asia Foundation, the International Labour Organization (ILO), the European

Union Human Rights Committee, development agencies attached to foreign embassies, and foreign Christian foundations. These organizations provide project-based funding to achieve specific goals, such as providing "ten cases of legal representation each year"; "publish[ing] 2,000 copies of an illustrated, abridged version of the Labor Contract Law"; and "set[ting] up legal aid workstations in 20 provinces." Any moneys left over after these objectives have been achieved can then be used to support other activities (e.g., membership recruitment, recreational activities, and English classes) deemed important by the NGOs themselves. Some labor NGOs also supplement their incomes by serving as contracted monitors for international auditing organizations or as internal auditors for multinationals, such as Nike and Adidas. Both Liu Kaiming of the Institute for Contemporary Observations and Xiao Li of the Xiao Li Hotline in Qingdao have worked as monitors in addition to offering human resource training classes to foreign companies to create revenue streams.

Between Cooptation and Commercialization

A survey of the mission statements of Chinese labor NGOs reveals that they share a similar set of self-professed organizational goals: "solidarity," "cooperation," "rights protection," and the "integration of migrant workers" appear most frequently in NGO publicity materials. We do not doubt the seriousness of purpose of these organizations and their leaders, but we have also found that they confront two dominant forces—the state and the market—that have already distracted some from their missions. NGOs that have so far avoided the twin traps of cooptation and commercialization are struggling with finding the political space and the financial wherewithal to survive.

Given the authoritarian nature of the Chinese state, we might expect suppression to be the most fatal threat for these NGOs. Yet what we have found is that Chinese state power is often exercised more adroitly and productively through subtle means rather than through outright repression. Through cooptation and state patronage, some labor NGOs have grown in size and reputation, providing services needed and endorsed by the state. Accepting state patronage shields NGOs from potential crackdowns and provides legitimacy to these organizations in the eyes of the general public, which often looks at voluntary organizations with suspicion. Yet, in doing so, leaders of these organizations become ever more careful to toe the official line in order to not upset their cozy relationship with the state. What they sacrifice, intentionally or inadvertently, is the nurturing of worker solidarity and their collective capability for self-protection.

The development of a one-man hotline operation into a full-blown, widely recognized, labor NGO illustrates this state strategy of cooptation. Around

2002, when Xiao Li started his hotline offering advice to migrant workers in Qingdao, his "organization" was a pager he carried around wherever he went. At that time, a party leader in one of the Qingdao districts began to realize the urgency and necessity of launching what he called "stability work" among the increasing number of migrant workers. As Xiao Li's hotline became more popular, the party leader decided to use this hotline as the base to carry out this stability project. The CCP official related, "The Youth League wanted to extend its work to organize the numerous migrant youngsters roaming the city. We want stability, right? The organization form is not important; the task is to create a cohesive group. You can see for yourself that no one takes Party organization life seriously these days. So why not try reading groups, making friends, studying together? These are more effective ways to pull people together."[1]

Local party leaders' interest in Xiao Li's hotline intensified in 2004, after Premier Wen Jiabao's high-profile personal intervention in collecting back wages for a migrant worker in Chongqing. The incident created a national media sensation and a competitive frenzy among local officials to show their efforts in this arena. The Qingdao party leaders decided to push Xiao Li's organization as their model achievement to help migrant workers. They not only helped him find a large office in a prime location but also nominated him for city, provincial, and national awards. In 2005, he was recognized as one of the "Ten Most Outstanding Migrant Workers in China," an honor that took him around the country to attend local CCP congresses to report his work. The Qingdao leadership made the best use of this honor, which they felt was theirs as well, and further facilitated Chen's work by organizing six to seven 8-department joint meetings to help expand the Xiao Li Hotline into two well-funded and well-equipped organizations in different parts of Qingdao, both of which are called Home for the New Citizens. Most impressively, these organizations obtained registration with the Ministry of Civil Affairs as legal social organizations, a rare feat among NGOs in China.

In addition to Xiao Li, Zhu Hang and Tong Lihua have very visible government connections. Little Flowers cooperated with a local Judiciary Bureau in one of the Beijing Neighborhood Committees to form the Little Flowers People's Mediation Committee. Zhu Hang was accorded the Beijing "Entrepreneurial Youth Contribution" Gold Award in 2004, followed by recognition as one of the "Ten Most Outstanding Migrant Workers in China" in 2005. Tong Lihua, the lawyer who founded the Migrant Worker Legal Assistance Station, has also been selected as a model lawyer for his work on juvenile protection and now migrant workers' legal rights.

The leaders of these organizations claims that state patronage makes it easier for them to implement their work because state power is widely recognized in society. For instance, when the staff and lawyer volunteers of Little Flowers confront employers who refuse to pay their workers, they can always show their semi-official identity card as members of a Beijing judiciary bureau mediation committee. The founder of Little Flowers was very explicit about the need for Chinese NGOs to stay close to the state: "It is very unwise for Chinese NGOs to stay away from the government. If you cannot function effectively, you cannot survive. Because we serve weak and disadvantaged social groups, we cannot ignore this [structural] reality [the power of the state]. We can only try to find the best position to realize our goals."[2]

The downside of becoming part of the state or its mass organizational offshoots is that organizations become ever more cautious of not overstepping the boundaries of acceptable behavior. Promoting workers' organizing and collective mobilization capabilities is considered anathema. Whenever we brought up the issue of organizing workers to take action by means of petitions or strikes, the people we interviewed immediately associated organizing with disturbance and illegality. "We are law-abiding and will only operate within the limit of the law" was a common bottom line adhered to by most labor NGOs. There apparently is no reflection about the nature of the law or of its limits and relations to worker interests. The goal of building worker solidarity is not taken seriously because it raises the specter of an organized force outside the state. This is obviously the concern of the Xiao Li Hotline. Even though he propounds a sophisticated view of worker rights as including the right to livelihood and the right to participate in decision making, "to be the masters of the country," Xiao Li sees the role of his organization as one of channeling and educating workers, not organizing them.[3]

Another peril that we have observed is the commercialization of some labor NGOs. At their beginnings, labor NGOs are often modest makeshift organizations manned by one or two founders and supported by an unstable supply of volunteers. Once they manage to survive, establish a presence and a reputation as a labor NGO, and harness multiple sources of foreign funding, many of these organizations can support a full-time staff or launch more activities. Thanks to their "independent" status, there is a market for NGO-conducted labor rights research, commissioned by the European Union, international trade union movements, the ILO, the United Nations, foreign governmental bodies, and even leading brand-name companies such as Nike and Nokia. In China, as in many developing countries, the peril of commercialization is ever present for these groups, and some NGOs have become an industry. Such displacement of their original goals is never clear-cut, but it can be detected from the core activities of the organizations.

For example, the Institute of Contemporary Observation (ICO) in Guangdong is one of the pioneers in the field of labor NGOs and has flourished since its establishment in 2002. Whereas in its early years ICO had direct contact with workers, running a hotline and offering legal advice whenever labor conflicts arose, it has since morphed into something like a consultant firm or research company specializing in conducting labor-related surveys and producing consultancy reports for the consumption of international donors. Liu Kaiming, its executive director, also serves as legal counsel for big corporations as well as a monitor of factories for auditing firms. His organization has also grown from a one-man operation to an increasingly professionalized staff of five full-time employees. They now list on their website a full-time staff of 20 and a volunteer staff of 120. Elsewhere, the facilitator in Beijing is "franchising" the organization name to another independent NGO, newly established in Nanjing. We do not know much about how and why this is done, but it smacks of the familiar corporate practice of "branding."

In several NGOs where we conducted fieldwork, an abiding concern emerging in everyday conversations is the organizational bottom line: tight project budgets, keen competition among labor NGOs for the limited pool of foreign sponsors, and the lack of trust by some of the sponsors about how funding was spent. Fighting for financial survival has become the focal concern for many organizations, and the founders are often so preoccupied with finding projects that the actual operations of these projects are delegated to their staff. Also, competition among labor NGOs is so intense that solidarity among them is very difficult to develop. People are extremely reluctant to share information about funding or their organization.

We are not suggesting that it is wrong or worthless for labor NGOs to change their organizational priority. And commercialization is happening to only a small minority of Chinese NGOs. Yet this is a tendency that is palpable and likely to grow. Labor NGOs in China struggle to survive between these two pressures of cooptation and commercialization. Jobs in civil society or the third sector are low-paying and bring little occupational prestige to the employees, who often have to endure extremely long hours of work. It is a very difficult terrain even for the most committed activists. The evolution of the Chun Feng Labor Dispute Arbitration Counseling and Service Center in Shenzhen starkly illustrates these twin pressures from the market and the state. After the success of the center in gathering more than 10,000 signatures in Shenzhen in 2006 demanding the removal of a labor dispute arbitration fee, the government cracked down and closed one of its offices. The organizers, still committed to helping workers in labor arbitration but trying to avoid official harassment, began offering legal services for a fee. As Jiang Ru, the founder of this NGO, said,

> We can only survive by taking up labor cases. This way, we do not give the government any pressure. If we did this for free, the officials would become very nervous. If you become commercial, they leave you alone. Now, they see that we

> charge a fee for our service, they thought our organization has changed....We do not have any project income, no sponsorship, and so there is no fund for any activity. We can only survive by attaching ourselves to a law firm. We operate under the Baoan branch of this law firm. (Lu 2008, 102)

By contrast, the Panyu NGO has experienced ups and downs as an organization without either state patronage or the commercialization prospects that other labor NGOs enjoy.

Nongovernmental Organizations in Action: Collecting Unpaid Wages and Running Labor Law Classes

To date, our ethnographic fieldwork at selected NGOs has focused on understanding their organizational culture and strategies. We have focused on two common activities undertaken by most of the labor NGOs: collecting unpaid wages and conducting labor law classes. Looking at how they interact with and help workers, as well as workers' responses to these activities, we find that NGOs fall short of the goals of protecting workers' legal rights, enhancing workers' rights consciousness, and building labor solidarity. NGOs may succeed in collecting some unpaid wages, but their strategy and reasoning cast workers as the subjects of charity and compassion rather than as rights bearers. Moreover, the labor law seminars are routinely run as requirements for obtaining foreign funding. These classes are mostly clause-by-clause reiterations of the National Labor Law. Many workers find these labor law classes useless, boring, and irrelevant. In some NGOs, attendance was embarrassingly low. What these classes reveal is the highly circumscribed conception of labor rights held by NGOs as those stipulated by the central government and not other extralegal rights necessary for realizing the rights on the books. Inadvertently, labor NGOs are promoting the state-defined, legalistic boundaries of rights, whereas the workers' concrete experiences in the city lead them to be critical and cynical about this narrow conception of labor rights.

Wage Collection

The following example of wage collection by Little Flowers highlights the role of the NGO as a bargain hunter, getting the best deal for the worker through negotiations with the employer and appealing to employer compassion. The law is used as a threat, but the goal is to obtain as high a payment as possible from the employer, who is not expected to agree to full payment of the owed amount. The rationale of the NGO is that many employers do not have legal registration and that their workers do not have legal contracts; consequently, the law cannot cover this large segment of the informal workforce. Getting some of the unpaid wages back is better than nothing. The NGO strategy of asserting workers' right will not lead to rights consciousness on either side, just the perpetuation of powerlessness and indignation on the part of the worker. Finally, even as the NGO staff members recognize the futility of relying on the Labor Law to protect workers, they continue to focus on the literal contents of the Labor Law, without reflecting on its contexts. That is, workers need power and rights in order to realize the provisions of the Labor Law, especially in a country where there is a serious imbalance of political power between officials and citizens, and where legal employment contracts are not the norm for migrant workers.

In January 2007, a staff member from Little Flowers, Mr. Man, went to Daxing District in Beijing, a suburb known for its many unregistered garment factories employing more than 10,000 workers, to collect 2,600 yuan for a worker. He was accompanied by a volunteer lawyer, Mr. Li. The factory was a dilapidated courtyard house, and dirty water on the ground had frozen into treacherous ice. It was hard to imagine that this small and run-down location housed four factories. The aggrieved worker and his friends came out to show Mr. Man and Mr. Li the way to the boss. The worker's wife was tending their newborn baby in the living room, which also served as their bedroom and kitchen. Mr. Man very quickly introduced himself as a mediator for the Judiciary Bureau of the Beijing Neighborhood Committee to bolster his status. Mr. Man then asked to see the license of this factory, even though he already knew that this is an unregistered factory. When the boss borrowed a license from another factory owner in the next room, Mr. Man challenged the employer and started the negotiation, saying, "How about 2,000 yuan?" The boss insisted that the worker was not a good employee, lazy and unruly. The lawyer, Mr. Li, intervened at this point and asked for a copy of the worker's labor contract that should have been signed according to the law, again knowing full well that boss had not signed labor contracts with his employees. The boss reluctantly produced a small and dirty piece of paper containing a few handwritten sentences (rather like a message slip), without any job description or signatures. When the boss and his wife began listing the various forms of misbehavior of the worker—including smoking on the shop floor, absenteeism, and tardiness—Mr. Man started to lower the amount of wages he demanded, from 2,000 to 1,800 yuan, and then the boss responded with his bottom line: 1,000 yuan. Mr. Man discussed this offer with the worker, who refused it and demanded 1,500 yuan. The employer immediately rejected this sum. After a few moments of embarrassing silence, Mr. Man and the boss began to chat like friends and talked about how difficult it was running a family workshop. Mr. Man and Mr. Li showed their sympathy and understanding while they also tried to sway the owner to buy peace with money. But the boss would not budge. Then Mr. Man and Mr. Li went outside to talk to the worker, saying "You should take his offer, then leave for a better job. 1,000 yuan is better than nothing. And you see how difficult it is for us to come a long way to here." As this was going on, the boss suddenly took back his offer and said he was not going to pay the worker a penny. Then Mr. Li reacted by taking his camera out and took a picture of the "contract," threatening to use it as evidence in court. Mr. Man and Mr. Li angrily walked out of the courtyard house. But before long, someone came up behind them and asked them to return to the house. The boss was willing to pay 1,100 yuan and to supply a train ticket to send the worker home.

In addition to the tendency among some NGOs to focus on the practical outcome of getting some money for workers, rather than insisting on the full legal payment, there are others who endorse only a strictly legalistic means of rights protection. Many lawyers we have talked to emphasize the legal boundary set by the state. Tong Lihua, the lawyer who founded the Beijing Migrant Workers' Legal Assistance Station, explicitly stated that protecting workers' legal rights means protecting only the rights stated by the labor law. He condemned workers who acted collectively and showed their power in petition or protest as illegal and "excessively radical behavior." The annual report of his organization states that:

> Whenever a few dozens or a hundred workers are owed wages, they feel the strength of numbers. The group psychology easily leads to radical behavior that legal aid lawyers and government departments find difficult to handle. In one instance, 15 workers from the same village worked in the construction site of a shopping mall in Beijing. The project was completed but they were not paid. The fifteen workers mobilized another 40 co-workers to sit down in front of the Beijing shopping mall, resulting in violent clashes with the mall security guards. The incident ended only with police intervention. In addition, labor subcontractors who were themselves owed money by the construction company provoked workers to attack the company. In another case, 151 workers gathered to attack the Labor Bureau and the Ministry of Construction, and they only obtained partial payment. Their subcontractor ordered some of the workers to climb up some huge billboards and threaten to commit suicide so as to attract the attention of the media to put pressure on the construction company. (Beijing Migrant Workers' Legal Assistance Station (006)

In short, we find two orientations among some labor NGOs, neither of which is conducive to the development of worker solidarity and capacity for collective action. On the one hand, some NGOs use the strategy and mentality of compromise and compassion, found in the way Little Flowers collects unpaid wages, at best leaving workers at the mercy of good employers rather than cultivating consciousness of their rights. On the other hand, some NGOs adopt the position of the state and consider worker collective action and protests illegal. In our view, labor rights include those defined by the labor law and also much more. The strictly legalistic definition of labor rights, the position adopted by most labor NGOs, not only is not conducive to the development of worker solidarity but indeed stifles it.

Labor Law Education

Collecting unpaid wages may not be a regular concern of some labor NGOs, but labor law training workshops are. These workshops have become standard requirements imposed on NGOs by international donors in many parts of the world. Almost all Chinese labor NGOs have done something to educate workers about the labor law, either by printing booklets summarizing the major terms of the National Labor Law or by running labor law classes for their members. For instance, Little Flowers has received funding from the World Bank to conduct regular labor law classes. Many of these are dry and uninspiring, consisting of sessions in which lawyers merely read aloud the terms of the National Labor Law. To motivate workers to come, Little Flowers makes attendance a condition for those whom they have helped to collect wages, and it sometimes pays 20 yuan to those who attend. During our fieldwork, several part-time domestic workers came because the 20 yuan per session was better than the hourly rate they earned as maids. It was also a good way to fill up some downtime, they reasoned. The recruiter of these women had received help from Little Flowers earlier, and she felt recruiting fellow workers to come to these seminars helped both parties. Most of these classes did not involve much discussion, but the occasional exchanges that did occur are telling. For instance, in one session, a woman worker recounted her experience of being "kicked around like a football" from district to district when she approached the Labor Bureau and asked the legal expert for advice:

> My factory was located in Dongcheng District, but registered in Chaoyang. When my boss refused to pay me, I went to the Labor Bureau in Dongcheng. Then they told me to go to Chaoyang because the factory was registered there. I went there and they asked me to return to Dongcheng. I was kicked around like a football. Nobody cared about my case. I thought about suing them for administrative negligence but really did not have the time or energy. In the end, I resolved the problem by my own little tricks. My boss agreed to a deal with me. But I really had no alternative. I want to ask you what I should have done if I wanted the Labor Bureau to work on this case?

The lawyer gave a most uninspiring response, urging her to go step by step up the bureaucracy and follow the legal procedure, which obviously had not worked: "According to the law, you should approach the Dongcheng Labor Bureau. You should have the tenacious spirit to persist. If a junior officer ignored you, you should approach the section chief; if the section chief still ignored you, go to the department head; still no response, go to the bureau chief. If you have this spirit, you will succeed in anything!"

This exchange is representative of the legalistic and bureaucratic approach of NGOs when it comes to law education. The workers attending these sessions respond with cynicism because their actual experience runs against the preaching of the legal experts. Listening to a lecture on the labor law, one attending worker snapped, "to talk about labor rights, let's talk first about human rights." Another worker said that there was no need to go through the terms of the labor law one section after another: "just give us a copy of the Law." What he wanted was to understand his basic constitutional rights as a person in coming to Beijing, such as how to protect his personal safety "if someone hits you on the street." Obviously migrant workers have to deal with much more mundane issues before they can enjoy or fight for their labor rights.[4]

Also missing in these legal education sessions are discussions about the underlying power structure that shapes the nature and working of the legal system. Who made the law? Why is the law not implemented? Are workers' interests and rights protected by the existing laws? What rights are not covered by the law? These are critical issues that are emphatically not open for discussion.

Other Programs

Collecting back wages and teaching labor law do not exhaust the action repertoire of Chinese labor NGOs. Some organizations pursue alternative kinds of power and emphasize "empowerment through art." They organize workers to express themselves through songs, music, drama, and writing. Performances are staged on construction sites, at universities, and in community venues, aimed at linking migrant workers and local residents. Rather than promoting their rights, these labor NGOs try to enhance integration of migrants into and acceptance of migrants by their host communities.

Servicing workers' needs, not advocacy of rights, define some labor NGOs. Zhu Hang's Beijing Center for Workers runs a primary school for migrant workers and a second-hand store for migrant workers. Almost all organize recreational activities and provide a gathering spot for workers. Playing table tennis or listening to music together may be conducive to the development of community and solidarity, but we have not seen any conscious nurturing of this potential for the enhancement of collective action. Once labor conflicts arise, workers are directed to resolve their conflict in individualistic and legalistic ways; whether these are effective is secondary.

Conclusion

As labor sociologists who work with and support these labor NGOs, we find ourselves in a difficult and ambivalent position when we write critically about their work. We want to avoid both the romanticization and the dismissal of their work and impact. This analysis does not exhaust the activities of all labor NGOs in China; it only detects the most prevailing institutionally induced tendencies. We offer these initial observations, all subject to revision in light of further research, in the spirit of engaging reflection and soliciting debate. We also note that there are exceptions to this anti-solidarity tendency of Chinese labor NGOs. For instance, a Shenzhen-based NGO focusing on women workers has consciously tried to instill the consciousness of and capability for solidarity among their members by advising them on strategies of collective action (Friedman 2007). More recently, a group of Peking University social work faculty and students has experimented with a social enterprise model of promoting worker rights and community. We will have to see if the goal of forging solidarity in the community where workers live bears fruit.

The global currency of rule of law and universal human rights is associated with the ascendance of neoliberalism as an ideology. In China, the rhetoric of law and rights sweeps under the carpet fundamental issues of state authoritarianism, unaccountable governance, and overall worker powerlessness. The professed commitment of labor NGOs to these state goals may have allowed them the political space to grow and prompted them to deliver valuable services to the working class. Nevertheless, alternatives may have been buried in the process. Especially as China confronts the challenge of the widespread casualization or informalization of employment, many workers work without legal contracts and are therefore outside the purview of the law. If labor rights are narrowly defined as simply the legal right to a labor contract, it will perpetuate workers' powerlessness and vulnerability. What is needed is a conception of citizenship rights that treats laborers not as individual parties to a contract in a marketplace but as members of a political community with rights to association, a decent livelihood, and the capability of deciding what that decent livelihood entails. In short, workers need rights outside the current labor law to secure the rights stipulated in the labor law.

At a more general level, our findings suggest that having NGOs as organizational forms is no guarantee that civil society or citizen power is developing. NGOs can nurture the micro-foundations of the self-organizing capacity and democratic citizenship of a society. Yet whether these potentials are realized depends on what is happening *inside* these NGOs—their organizational cultures and practices. Research must focus on these grounded processes and relationships between NGOs and workers to gauge what the NGO as a mode of organization is doing for the society in which NGOs are found and, specifically, the extent to which labor NGOS can help mitigate the growth of informalization.

In the 1990s, when China scholars debated intensely the rise of civil society in China, the focus was almost always on the number of NGOs or on the regulations that have given rise to government-organized NGOs. Civil society and citizenship politics are alive and well; however, we must understand the everyday internal cultures, practices, and dynamics of these organizations before we can determine whether they bring about civil society or merely reproduce state domination or market-driven inequality.

Chapter 10

Conclusion

Mary E. Gallagher, Sarosh Kuruvilla, and Ching Kwan Lee

This volume elucidates the evolving tensions among three forces: the market (exemplified by the strategies of state-owned enterprises and private employers), the state (the central government and the party as well as local governments), and the Chinese working class (including workers, labor unions, and civil society). The future of informalization in China depends on the continuing interplay among these forces. And, from the evidence presented here, we do not see prospects for a significant reduction in informalization in the near term, despite the aggressive efforts of the central Chinese state to curb the practice through the introduction of new labor laws beginning in 2008.

Each of the chapters in this volume contributes to this argument in different ways. Part I focuses on the differential interests and strategies within the Chinese state. Albert Park and Cai Fang (chap. 2) have carefully and comprehensively mined existing government databases to provide an estimate of the degree of informalization in China. They show that between 36 and 39 percent of urban employment is informal. Mary Gallagher and Baohua Dong (chap. 3) highlight the differing interests within the Chinese state. Focusing on the legislative process that produced the labor contract law of 2008, they demonstrate that intragovernmental disagreement about how much protection to afford workers led to divergent draft laws and that the final version of the law reflects these internal disagreements. Further, they conclude that, despite the curbs on informalization offered by the law, its lack of implementation and enforcement is substantially weakening its impact, highlighting the differential interests of the central government and local governments. Many local governments have enacted regulatory measures to dilute the impact of the law, especially because the law was enacted during a global economic slowdown. There is some evidence that the use of informal labor has actually increased since the passage of the law. Mark Frazier (chap. 4) contributes to the argument by highlighting the gaps between the central government policy on pensions and local government countermeasures, also drawing attention to the societal pressure from below to close these gaps. Specifically, he argues that in the wake of decreasing employment security Chinese workers, now highly cognizant of their pension rights, place the burden of social insurance on the state as a fundamental right of citizenship. And, despite some variation, local governments tend to be increasingly responsive to the rising expectations of urban citizens.

The chapters in part II examine the interests and strategies of Chinese employers. Kun-Chin Lin (chap. 5) shows how market pressures led to a restructuring of the state-owned oil industry into a smaller core of permanent employees and a larger periphery of informal labor, suggesting that even state-owned companies are adopting practices that increase informalization, despite the new labor laws. Lu Zhang (chap. 6) shows how management policy in the automobile industry of restructuring and "flexibilization" resulted in the large growth of both temporary and subcontracted workers, echoing the core-periphery distinction highlighted by Lin. Zhang's research also uncovers a "movement from below," highlighting forms of resistance by informal workers such as sabotage, slowdowns, absenteeism and wildcat strikes. Sarah Swider (chap. 7) outlines the transition in the highly regulated the construction industry from secure employment to a market-based industry characterized by informal employment. She draws special attention to the peculiar plight of informal migrant workers, who are not able to integrate as citizens into the cities in which they work even as their long absence at urban work sites weakens their ties to their home and family.

Part III examines how the agents of workers (trade unions and NGOs) respond to the growing informalization of the Chinese labor market. Mingwei Liu (chap. 8) outlines the variation in strategies within the trade union movement in China and the innovative strategies of community unions and regional unions, which, with local government support, have organized using strategies quite different from those followed by the central trade union, the ACFTU. Ching Kwan Lee and Yuan Shen (chap. 9) highlight the tensions between the central and local governments in their study of NGOs. Whereas the Chinese government has an interest in controlling and suppressing these organizations, local governments tend to encourage them because they like the services that these NGOs provide. Lee and Shen demonstrate the structural pressures that NGOS face from both the state (which seeks to control them) and the market (their sources of funding) and argue that this causes tension between the

NGO goals of promoting worker solidarity, on the one hand, and surviving as organizations, on the other. They are thus pessimistic about the ability of NGOs to promote worker solidarity.

The evidence collected here, showing the conflicting interests and strategies of the central and local governments, employers, and agents of workers, leads us to be pessimistic about a reversal in the near term of the trend toward informalization. Although the central government is clear about providing workers with more protection, government-owned enterprises and private employers continue to pursue informalization strategies, with the acquiescence of local governments. NGOs and unions, while experimenting with different strategies, do not demonstrate the capacity to ensure that the new laws will be implemented. Hence, it is not surprising that more recent studies indicate an increase in informalization after the passage of the new Labor Contract Law. More recent studies (Chung, 2011) also indicate that compliance has increased among large foreign-owned enterprises but that both government-owned companies and smaller and medium-size firms seek to evade the legislation. Hence our pessimism that informalization will be quickly curtailed or reversed is confirmed so far.

Yet, as these dynamics continue to unfold, there are also reasons for cautious optimism. As this volume goes to press in summer 2010, a wave of coordinated strikes at foreign-owned firms in China hint at the possibility of working-class mobilization. Mary Gallagher (2010) argues that this new-found militancy is the product of a confluence of demographic, social, and political trends that will increase the bargaining power of Chinese workers. The demographic change focuses on the shortage of workers. Labor shortages are now evident in several parts of China, notably the Pearl River Delta, the Yangtze River Delta around Shanghai, and even in central China. These shortages are a function of a decline in the working population as a consequence of the one-child policy; policy changes in agriculture that have made migration to industrial jobs less attractive to rural residents; and, finally, institutional discrimination against migrants as a result of the *hukou* system, which remains a barrier to the permanent migration and urbanization of many rural citizens. There are those who argue that the present labor shortage is temporary, given underemployment in agriculture and the possible eventual removal of the barriers to permanent migration. On the other hand, there are those, like Fang Cai, who suggest that China may be at the Lewisian turning point when labor scarcity begins to shift the economy away from labor-intensive input-driven growth to enhanced productivity, declining inequality, and greater domestic consumption. If the latter is true, then this will indubitably increase the bargaining power of Chinese workers.

Social changes also matter. Younger Chinese migrant workers are different from their parents. They are more demanding, more rights conscious, and more attuned to the inequalities in treatment and opportunity they face as second-class citizens. They tend to be better educated, with a greater exposure to the mass media and technology, and more acclimated to city life. Their expectations for the future are different from the previous generation, and they are not likely to return to the farms. These workers, as Zhang (chap. 6) demonstrates, are more likely to mobilize and engage in wildcat strikes and protests, emboldened by the knowledge that jobs are not scarce.

Third, and finally, is the response of the central Chinese state and the central trade union federation. Apart from the enactment of new labor laws, the Chinese government is permitting a greater degree of media openness (as witnessed in the case of the strikes in summer 2010), while directing the ACFTU to expand the presence of ACFTU-affiliated unions in foreign-invested enterprises. Although these efforts have done relatively little to expand the confidence of workers in the union, the strikes in spring and summer 2010 have led both the central and local governments to call for new measures to empower unions and "worker representative committees" at the firm level. Local regulations are currently being drafted in Guangdong and Shanghai that stipulate collective wage bargaining between employers and workers through these institutions. These efforts may serve to further increase the bargaining power of workers.

China will remain an important location for production, given its comparative advantages of lower wages, good infrastructure, and a variety of investment incentives. The important changes mentioned here as a cause for optimism must be tempered by the differential interests and conflicts highlighted throughout the volume. The implementation and enforcement of new protective and empowering legislation continue to be the responsibility of the local governments. Central government support for better legal protections and trade union empowerment will be mitigated by local government competition for investment and by its own overarching concern for political stability.

Notes

Chapter 2

1. According to Maitra et al. (2005), base employer contribution rates as a share of wages were 22 percent for pension insurance, 12 percent for medical insurance, 2 percent for unemployment insurance, and 0.5 percent for maternity and industrial injury insurance. For migrants, the total employer contribution rate is 12.5 percent. Many enterprises do not fully comply with contribution requirements, even for registered workers, even though they are subject to audits and fines as well as informal sanctions by government officials.

2. This could be an underestimate of the size of the private sector, given that it excludes employment in wholly foreign-owned firms or in mixed ownership forms with majority private ownership (including TVEs).

3. Although the *China Labor Statistical Yearbook* does not provide a source for these numbers, they are probably from the CLSRS because breakdowns are provided by sector and official employment data by sector are from the CLSRS.

4. Since 2003, migrants have been included in the urban household survey sample, but migrants account for less than 1.5 percent of the sample, which is much below the 17 percent of the urban nonagricultural labor force reported in table 2.2.

5. The NBS 2004 short form survey sample, like the NBS urban household survey sample in the same year, includes very few migrants (less than 4 percent of sampled workers).

6. The MOLSS surveyed thirteen large cities with populations above 2 million, eight cities with populations between 1 and 2 million, ten cities with populations between 500,000 and 1 million, nineteen cities with populations between 200,000 and 500,000, and sixteen cities with populations less than 200,000. The number of households surveyed in each group was 3,000, 2,500, 2,000, 1,500, and 800, respectively, with 20 households surveyed in any given neighborhood.

7. The following types of workers were categorized as informal: (1) hired workers without formal contract not listed as formal employees; (2) domestic workers, temporary agency workers, and casual laborers; (3) community service workers without formal contracts; (4) workers hired on the basis of hourly pay, daily pay, weekly pay, and uncertain pay (in terms of time and/or account); (5) paid helpers in family and self-employed businesses; (6) workers hired by individual entrepreneurs (*getihu*); (7) individual business owners (*getihu*). Note that the ILO recommends

that small business with fewer than ten workers be considered informal but that in China individual businesses are those with seven or fewer workers. Workers in the agricultural sector are excluded from the analysis.

8. The five large cities are Shanghai, Fuzhou, Xian, Wuhan, and Shenyang; the five small cities located in the same regions are Wuxi, Zhuhai, Baoji, Yichan, and Benxi.

9. In each city, one hundred households were surveyed, ten households in each of ten neighborhoods, which were selected as being regionally representative of each city. In one-half of the neighborhoods, local residents were randomly sampled, and in the other half, migrants were randomly sampled, yielding a sample of fifty local resident households and fifty migrant households in each city. Information was collected for all adults living in each of the sample households, yielding a sample of approximately 400 individuals, with slightly more local residents than migrants (220 vs. 180).

10. These percentages could overstate the informal employment rate if they include workers who have not signed contracts but who effectively enjoy permanent employment.

Chapter 3

1. The NPC passed a new law on labor dispute resolution on December 29, 2007. This new law, the Labor Dispute Mediation and Arbitration Law addresses some of these problems and went into effect on May 1, 2008.

2. Some of the largest labor protests in the history of the PRC occurred in the years following the massive layoffs in the state sector. For a detailed report on these protests, see Human Rights Watch (2002).

3. The MOLSS was merged with the Ministry of Personnel in 2008 to form the Ministry of Human Resources and Social Security (MOHRSS).

4. There were calls by academics and businesspeople to repeal or revise the Labor Contract Law after the economic crisis led to a steep drop in exports. The NPC, however, stated that revision or repeal was out of the question ("Economist Zhang Weiying" 2009; "China Won't Revise Labor Contract Law" 2009).

5. Interview with CEDA staff member, Beijing, July 2006.

6. Domestic press articles did summarize the comments. Many of these articles are cited throughout this chapter ("Collection of the Masses' Opinions" 2006; "The Draft Labor Contract Law" 2006; "Ten Focal Points" 2006).

7. See, for example, Buckley (2006); Shi (2006, 8); Shih (2006, 18); Dyer (2007, 11); Batson (2007, 8).

8. This concern is addressed partially in the final version of the law, which caps the economic compensation for highly paid employees at three times the average wage of the locality.

9. See, for example, Cremer 2007, 2); Cody (2007, 5); Schafer (2007).

10. See also Costello, Smith, and Brecher (2007); Smith, Brecher, and Costello (2007, 82)

11. The Japanese Chamber of Commerce also sent written comments to the NPC. These comments were similar in content to the other business associations, but were not linked explicitly to broader reform debates. These comments also did not seem to attract the same level of public scrutiny.

12. On the changing nature of Chinese legislation, see Cho (2002, 2006).

13. Interviews with government officials, academics, and enterprise managers, Shanghai, July 2007. See also commentary and links at http://www.danwei.org/law/shanxi_slaves_and_the_labor_co.php.

14. Local judicial explanations of the Labor Contract Law and the Labor Dispute Resolution Law include "Jiangsu High People's Court and Jiangsu Labor Dispute Arbitration Committee Circular on the Use of the PRC Law on Mediation and Arbitration in Labor Disputes," issued October 10, 2008; "Jiangsu High People's Court Guiding Opinion on the Handling of Labor Dispute Cases in Economic Crisis," issued February 27, 2009; "Guangdong High People's Court and Guangdong Province Labor Dispute Arbitration Committee Guiding Opinion on Questions

about the Use of the Labor Dispute Mediation and Arbitration Law and the Labor Contract Law," issued June 23, 2008; "Shanghai High People's Court Circular on Questions about the Use of the Labor Contract Law," issued March 3, 2009.

15. PRC Law on Mediation and Arbitration of Labor Disputes, enacted December 29, 2007, effective May 1, 2008, articles 4–5 (on negotiation and the application for mediation and arbitration), 10 (on organizations that provide mediation).

Chapter 4

1. This is not to say that local governments successfully brought an end to all pension protests. Pension protests were reported in Anhui province in 2004 (Associated Press 2004).

2. The BAS target group is the registered urban population of residents eighteen to sixty-five years old, randomly drawn from fifty communities (*shequ, juweihui*) in eight urban districts. The BAS uses the probabilities proportional to size (PPS) sampling method. For the 2004 BAS, 1,099 individuals were contacted and 618 surveys were completed—a response rate of 56.1 percent.

3. In fact, the Chinese government and the CCP have explicit rules on a retirement age for officials, generally at ages sixty to sixty-eight. Thus this focus group participant was not technically accurate in claiming that cadres could work to age eighty.

4. The Shanghai survey was carried out in 2005, one year before the Shanghai pension scandal made national and international headlines. A new survey would probably show a considerable drop in trust of local government to administer pensions, depending on how respondents assigned responsibility for the scandal.

Chapter 5

I thank Sarosh Kuruvilla, Mary Gallagher, Ching Kwan Lee, Vivienne Shue, Dorothy Solinger, William J. Hurst, Ran Tao, and Tom Gold for their valuable feedback on ideas developed in this chapter. Research relevant to this chapter was funded by the Fulbright-IIE Scholarship, David Boren NSEP International Fellowship, Helen Kellogg Institute for International Studies Visiting Fellowship, Leverhulme Postdoctoral Fellowship in Contemporary Chinese Studies at Oxford, and National University of Singapore FASS Staff Research Support Scheme. The empirical details of the case study derive from the author's fieldwork in twelve locations across seven Chinese provinces from 2000 to 2002, combined with interviews with corporate and bureaucratic officials in Beijing and the analysis of specialized Chinese-language publications related to the Chinese petroleum industry. Shaofeng Chen, Cuifen Wen, Chen-yu Chen, and Yu Xiao earn my gratitude for their excellent research assistance.

1. For theories of centrality in networks, see Berkowitz (1998); Marsden (2002); Freeman (1979).

2. Also see Roland (2004, 109–31) on fast- and slow-moving institutions (e.g., policy vs. culture), using a similar language of incremental and discontinuous change.

3. Whether changes in labor relations in the nonstate (i.e., collective, private, and foreign-invested) sectors amount to an incremental or discontinuous transformation is outside of the scope of this chapter. See Jianjun Zhang (2008, 59–61, 106–7) on the terms of employment in township and village enterprises; Démurger et al. (2006) on the private sector; and Gallagher (2002) on foreign-invested enterprises.

4. See Lin (2008c) for a literature review. The following summary about the oil sector is taken from Lin (2006, 2008c).

5. This topic has been understudied and undocumented even within China. Telephone interview with a Chinese Academy of Sciences economist, Beijing, August 2008.

6. Note that these wage ratios did not reflect additional wages from performance bonuses and subsidies, which remained a point of uncertainty, negotiation, and contention within the firm and between the SOEs and the central government (Liu 1998). Bian and Logan (1996, 742) note that the 1985 wage regulation reduced the gap between manual and nonmanual workers.

Interestingly, the cadre wage grades (sixteen tiers) were compressed to be more comparable to the workers' grades (eight tiers) to encourage movement between the two realms.

7. This commonplace dynamic has been modeled by Huang (1990).

8. For specific analyses of income increases and their impact on social inequality, see Bian and Logan (1996); Granick (1991).

9. For details, see Lin (2008b).

10. This reform had precedents in joint ventures (Weller and Li 2000).

11. Unless stated otherwise, original data in the following sections draw from my interviews in various oil fields and refineries, 2000–2002. For details, see Lin (2003).

12. Note that these figures specify only the basic, nonfloating component of wages and not the bonuses and social wages that constituted an increasing share of the net income of workers. We might never have adequate data to estimate the true wages and disparities during this period.

13. Disturbingly, employment and wage data for Sinopec and PetroChina in the U.S. Security and Exchange Commission (SEC) reports are wildly inconsistent between documents, across years, and against company yearbook data. I have found no adequate explanation for these discrepancies. For example, I have noted consistently lower numbers of employees and worker-related outlays cited in Sinopec Listed Co. SEC documents.

14. For a book-length treatment of this topic, see Gold et al. (2009). *China Labor Watch* offers numerous anecdotes of enterprises cutting down or suspending pension payments for laid-off workers, www.chinalaborwatch.org/.

15. These approaches are by no means mutually exclusive, but their inherent inconsistencies have not been critically evaluated.

16. See, for example, Korzec (1992); Warner (1995, 1996); Cook (2000); Smyth, Zhai, and Wong (2001); Knight and Song (2005); Li and Sato (2006); Banister (2005a, 2005b); Lett and Banister (2006); Tao (2006).

17. See, for example, White (1987); Hay et al. (1994); Johnston (2002); Child (1994); Frazier (2006).

18. See, for example, O'Brien (1992); Huang (1990); Christiansen (1992); Xie and Hannum (1996); Bian and Logan (1996); Freund (1998); Ji (1998); Sargeson (1999, chap. 7); Frasier (2006).

19. See, for example, Huang (1990); Granick (1991); O'Brien (1992); Xie and Hannum (1996); Bian and Logan (1996).

20. See Blecher (2002) for a critical disaggregation of this view.

21. For quantitative assessments of the importance of seniority, especially relative to other human capital factors, see Peng (1992); Hu, Li, and Shi (1988); Gustafsson et al. (2001).

22. Li and Sato (2006, 124–25) present contrary evidence and argue that the decline of in-kind and bonus payments from 1988 to 1999 in the state-owned sectors suggests effective government control of wages. But this trend may also be related to a general lack of profitability of SOEs. In any case, they emphasize that the decline does not necessarily suggest marketization.

23. See, for example, Meng (2000, 93); Bian (1994, 162–63); Howard (1991); Guthrie (1998).

24. Similarly, Child (1994, 206) notes that individual markers such as education and training account for only half of wage variations in the early 1990s.

25. The locality has received major theoretical attention in comparative studies (Palmer and Friedland 1987; Carruthers 2004).

26. Representative studies of network capitalism include Mizruchi and Schwartz (1987); Gerlach (1992); Grabher (1993); Herrigel (1996); Petit (1999); Freeland (2001); Perrow (2002); Dobbin (2004); Smelser and Swedberg (1994, 2005).

27. For a representation of the conventional view, see Bian (1994, 187).

28. In the formative years of Chinese oil discovery in the 1960s and 1970s, experienced drillers from older oil fields were often sent to new oil fields to jump-start production. They settled down and subsequently formed the core of the technical and political leadership at the oil bureau and sometimes local government. In the West, these network-entrepreneurial managers are more likely to get promoted (Smith-Doerr and Powell 2005, 383–84).

29. See influential studies by Stark (1996) and McDermott (2007).

30. Telephone interview with Chinese Academy of Sciences economist, Beijing, August 2008.

31. Due to financial difficulties from depreciating contracts, some noncore companies paid their workers only 75 percent of their salary for several months in 2002, withholding the liquidity to finance their contract with the core company. The remaining 25 percent would be paid on the condition that the year-end profitability, or additional loans from the bank, made further wage payments possible. Some noncore firms borrowed heavily to make ends meet, including to provide wage payments (Lin 2006).

32. Abbott points out that the "literature on work organization needs to more deeply consider the labor opportunity structure as a determinant of the organization of production" (2005, 323).

33. For a detailed discussion of these concepts, see Sorensen (1994).

34. Bian (1994, 197) also points out that the internal labor market was supported by internal housing market.

35. See Ji (1998) for detailed analyses of legal and regulatory loopholes that provided opportunities for managers to contest and deceive their political and regulatory principals.

36. See Lin (2008a) for case studies of the diversification strategies of the Daqing and Karamay PABs.

37. For example, in 2002 approximately two hundred out of a total of seven hundred companies in the Daqing high-tech development zone remained registered with the Daqing PAB. From 2001 to 2002, they had unloaded some 7,000–8,000 workers from the PAB, helping it to achieve the target of 15,000 layoffs per year as demanded by the CNPC (Lin 2008a).

38. Predictably, this strategy, in contrast to the earlier one, incurs high compliance costs and social-institutional instabilities on the ground level (Lin 2009).

39. This trust-building is important, especially given the concerns for cross-boundary competition or collusion (Lin 2009).

40. For contrasting views on the relative prices of labor and capital in the early reform era, see Jefferson and Rawski (1992); Putterman and Dong (2000).

41. See Csanadi (1997, 2006) for a sophisticated treatment of the complex interactions of political and organizational networks in state-owned sectors.

42. For more detailed overviews of wage reforms during this period, including sectoral examples, see Takahara (1992); Hu, Li, and Shi (1988); Zhao and Nichols (1996).

43. As in the past, wages in these monopolistic or rentier sectors remain significantly higher than the industrial average and rising, leading to popular outcries for government intervention to effect adjustments (Zhang 2007; Zheng and Chen 2007).

44. Comparative labor studies have also noted that organizational interests cut across traditional notions of class interests as defined by ownership or family background (Mizruchi and Schwartz 1987, chap. 1).

45. Sargeson (1999) and Lin (2009) have argued that fragmentation can be conducive to mobilization.

Chapter 6

1. The fieldwork on which this chapter is based was supported by a fellowship from the International Dissertation Field Research Fellowship Program of the Social Science Research Council, with funds provided by the Andrew W. Mellon Foundation. Preliminary fieldwork was funded by the Institute for Global Studies in Culture, Power and History and the Department of Sociology at Johns Hopkins University. The writing process and followup fieldwork was supported by National Science Foundation Dissertation Improvement Grant #0623349 and by the Association for Asian Studies China and Inner Asia Council (CIAC) Small Grants Awards.

2. I use the pseudonyms for the seven plants for confidentiality (Earth, Jupiter, Mars, Mercury, Neptune, Uranus, and Venus). When publicly available information is quoted, however, the real names of the companies and plants are used.

3. There are three ownership types in the Chinese automobile assembly sector: JVs of large SOEs and foreign car producers, SOEs, and privately owned enterprises (POEs). SOEs and JVs are still the predominant ownership types, but several POE automobile assemblers have grown very quickly in China in recent years. Due to lack of accessibility, I do not include POE automobile assemblers in the current study; incorporating the POEs for comparison awaits future research.

4. The interviews were conducted in a semi-structured manner, and on average, each interview lasted approximately 2–2.5 hours. Most of these interviews were conducted outside the factory at local teahouses, restaurants, or workers' homes and dormitories. The initial interviews with workers (29 out of 150 of the total sample of interviewed workers) were arranged with the help of company managers and conducted at the factories. It was not a surprise that management tended to introduce me to the "model workers" or team leaders who were most likely to present the positive side of management and the companies. To reduce the bias in my sample selection, I also pursued independent research avenues and arranged the other four-fifths of the interviews with workers through my personal connections and a snowballing strategy without the involvement of company managers.

5. The original notion of *triple alliance* comes from Peter Evans's (1979) classic work on the alliance of multinational, state, and local capital in Brazil. Eric Thun (2004, 455) applies this term to describe the relationship among the central state, foreign capital, and domestic capital in the Chinese automobile industry. I use this term similarly but emphasizing that it is a state-led triple alliance—the central state plays the dominant role in forging the alliances between FDI and large Chinese auto groups. See Zhang (2010a, chap. 2) for a more detailed discussion.

6. The American Motor Corporation/Chrysler and Volkswagen were the pioneers in JVs in 1984 and 1985, respectively, followed by major new investments by, among others, Peugeot, Citroen, General Motors, Honda, Toyota, Ford, and Hyundai throughout the 1990s and early 2000s.

7. In China, lean production system is also known as the Toyota Production System (TPS).

8. The auto industry was designated as one of the seven "pillar industries" of China and to be of strategic importance by the State Council in the Seventh, Eighth, and Ninth Five-Year Plans (1986–1990, 1991–1995, and 1996–2000). It has been redeclared a "leading industry" under the Tenth and Eleventh Five-Year Plans (2001–2005 and 2006–2010).

9. The only exception was Guangzhou Honda, in which Honda had a 50 percent share. That was primarily because Honda promised to export its Chinese JV-assembled models to the Honda European markets.

10. It was widely held among government officials and management that only SOEs that entered JVs with foreign firms or private national capital were expected to survive the intense competition in the post-WTO world, according to a speech by Ma Xiaohe (2004), the director of the National Development and Reform Committee, Industry Research Institute.

11. Interview no. 31, Shanghai, March 2007.

12. China is different from other cases of fast expansion of automobile industry such as Brazil, South Africa, and South Korea in the late 1970s and 1980s. In those cases, the fast expansion of automobile industry went hand in hand with a rapid expansion in the number of workers employed in both the automobile industry and manufacturing more generally. See Humphrey (1982); Seidman (1994); Koo (2001); Silver (2003).

13. This description is based on interviews with workers and managers at Earth in summer 2004.

14. Certainly, as my observations in June 2004 indicated, there were other measures contributing to the improvement of productivity, such as automation, speedup, and a performance-based wage and bonus system.

15. Interview with F15, Changchun, October 2006.

16. Interview with S13, Shanghai, November 2006.

17. The crucial yardstick to determine an individual's status as staff or worker is his or her educational credentials. Most newly recruited staff members have a minimum of a bachelor's degree, and they usually sign two- to five-year labor contracts initially. Staff members have different pay schemes, career tracks, and status from blue-collar workers in the factory hierarchy. This

chapter focuses on the labor force dualism among production workers, but it is important to note that the sharp division between staff and workers within the formal contract workforce is another main source of workers' discontent.

18. Interview with M1, Shanghai, January 2005.

19. Interview with F2, Changchun, August 2004.

20. The use of temporary workers by SOEs can be traced back to the pre-reform era when urban enterprises hired peasants as temporaries to adjust for seasonal fluctuations of production (Blecher 1983). In the 1980s, the hiring of peasant labor in SOEs became a legitimate employment practice because the state recognized that it was necessary to have a cheap and flexible source of workers in certain urban sectors (Li and Hu 1991, 340). Thus, the scale of using temporary workers in the reform era became far larger and the procedures were more regularized than in the pre-reform era (Solinger 1995).

21. There are different terms used for labor dispatch, such as *agency employment, labor subcontracting, co-employment, triangular employment*. This chapter uses *labor dispatch* and *agency employment* to refer to this type of irregular employment.

22. This estimate is based on piecemeal data I collected from the four automobile factories currently using temporary workers. No official statistics on temporary workers in the automobile industry are available so far. By definition, student apprentices are trainees rather than full-time workers—although they indeed work as full-time production workers. There is a chance that student apprentices may be hired as formal contract workers by the factories upon graduation. But auto employers tended to use student apprentices as temps on a yearly basis rather than offering them formal contract employment.

23. Many of the vocational schools in China today run labor dispatch services. They introduce their students to work at client firms and charge 25–30 percent of student workers' monthly wages as commission fees. Student agency workers differ from student apprentices in that the former have labor contracts with their schools and are hired as full-time agency workers. There is little chance for student agency workers to become formal contract employees at client firms.

24. For example, at one of the largest iron and steel complexes in China, more than half the production workers were temporary agency workers in 2006. Agency workers had three-month service contracts and their wages were only one-fourth of those of formal workers, as I observed in factory visits in March 2007.

25. As I observed in Tianjin, January 2008.

26. *Production pace* refers to the amount of time (in seconds) needed to assemble a sedan unit based on a certain line speed.

27. The sixteen workers were transferred to a newly built assembly plant of Jupiter. Interview with F17, Changchun, October 2006.

28. Interviews with F6 and F7, Changchun, August 2004.

29. Interview with C16, Wuhu, March 2007.

30. For instance, in Brazil and South Korea, prior to large-scale autoworker protests, autoworker wages were significantly high. Yet workers also experienced strong feelings of relative deprivation because the rapid expansion of the auto industry in these two countries had been achieved largely at their expense, with rising productivity and profitability accompanied by stagnant or declining wages. For the struggles of South Korean autoworkers in the 1980s, see Koo (2001); for the Brazilian autoworker struggles in the 1970s, see Humphrey (1982).

31. Interview with Q11, Qingdao, June, 2004.

32. On this point, John Price (1997) provides detailed comparisons on the different labor-management relations in the sectors of strategic ascent or decline in postwar Japan.

33. Interview with S19, Shanghai, November 2006.

34. Interview with M14, Shanghai, November 2006.

35. Field notes, June 2004–July 2007.

36. Interview with F14, Changchun, October, 2006.

37. Among the seventy-three temporary workers I interviewed, two had become group leaders heading small production work groups of ten and fifteen line operators, respectively.

38. Interview with S20, Shanghai, November 2006.

39. According to a survey conducted by the Shanghai Federal Trade Union in 2004, the average educational level of agency workers in Shanghai was less than nine years formal schooling, whereas the average education level of agency workers in the auto sector was nine to twelve years (Tu 2007, 14–22). My interviews with managers at Neptune and Jupiter in 2006 found that the leading automobile assemblers had strict recruitment requirements for agency workers, including youth (under twenty-three years old), a minimum of nine years of education, good health, and physical strength.

40. At most of the automobile factories I studied, temporary agency workers had no chance to become formal contract workers. Only Neptune granted 65 (out of 5,000) agency workers the status of formal contract workers for the first time on January 1, 2005. But later that year, due to the dramatic market downturn, Neptune laid off 2,000 agency workers and closed the door for temporary workers to become formal contract workers.

41. Formal workers and temporary workers lived in separate dormitory residences. Formal workers had better living conditions than temporary workers. The unequal living condition of temporary workers was another big complaint.

42. Interviews with district LDMAC officials and arbitrators, Guangzhou September 2006; Shanghai, February 2007. So far, there are no nationwide systematic statistics on the number of labor dispute cases related to agency employment available in China.

43. Interview with F19, Changchun, October 2006.

44. As table 6.3 indicates, even though temporary workers earned much less than formal workers, their average wages were still comparable to or higher than the local average wages.

45. My field research suggests that although labor force dualism has kept formal workers from actively supporting temporary workers, the relationship between formal and temporary workers was less adverse than the conventional characterizations of the "split labor market" (Bonacich 1972, 1976) would otherwise suggest. For example, more than two-thirds of the formal workers I interviewed said they did not look down on agency workers and that they did not see much difference between them and agency workers when they all worked side by side on assembly lines. But another one-third of the formal workers mentioned that agency workers had less education and bad manners and that they had nothing in common. Due to space limits, I do not examine here the intergroup relationship between formal and temporary workers in detail. Nevertheless, it is a very important factor in understanding the shop floor labor politics under labor force dualism (see Zhang 2010a, chap. 5).

46. Interview with S26, Shanghai, April 2007.

47. Interview with F15, Changchun, October 2006.

48. See Labor Contract Law, Chapter 5, Section 2, Articles 57–67 (in Chinese) for details. According to my interviews with Chinese labor law scholars, the initial legislative objective in implementing the law was to reduce the number of agency employees by half. Interviews no. 16 and 18, Qingdao, September 2006; interviews 27 and 28, Beijing, January 2007.

49. A survey conducted by Shanghai Federal Trade Union found that over 25 percent of agency workers had been converted from formal contract workers with direct labor contracts with their former employers (Tu 2007).

50. For example, one labor dispute case filed by an agency employee of a KFC chain store in Beijing lasted for two years and received wide media coverage and public attention focusing on the legality of agency employment. See, for example, Chen and Chang (2006); Chen and Dong (2007).

51. As Gallagher and Dong note (chap. 3 in this volume), the ACFTU had far more influence and voice in the legislative drafting process than any other nongovernmental and business/employer organizations, given the high bureaucratic position of the ACFTU chairman in the CCP political hierarchy and its close ties to Hu Jingtao, the CCP top leader.

52. The speech of Zhang Shicheng, vice director of the Administrative Law Department Legal Affairs Committee in NCP, recording of "the 16th China and Foreign Country Management Symposium for Officials, Industries and Academics." Cited from Dong (2008).

53. On the waves of labor unrest and disputes by both laid-off state workers and the new migrant working-class-in-formation in China since the mid-1990s, see Lee (2000, 2002, 2007); Eckholm (2001); Feng (2002); Pan (2002); China Labour Bulletin ([CLB] 2005, 2009a, 2009b); Pun (2005); Solinger (2005); White (2007); Hurst (2009); Silver and Zhang (2009).

54. On the different phases of the Chinese economic reform, see Naughton (2007, chap. 4).

55. Interview with B3, Beijing, January 2008.

56. Email correspondence with F1, October 2009.

57. Follow-up phone interview with F13, October 2009.

58. Follow-up phone interview with S1, September 2009.

59. Email correspondence and phone interviews with F1, F13, F17, F20, S1, S2, S13, S19, Q1, Q9, C3, and C12, November 2008 and May and October 2009.

60. The detailed benefits vary by individual companies. In general, temporary agency workers received 20–25 percent of the benefits that formal contract workers received at the automobile factories I studied. Although the new Labor Contract Law states that temporary workers should have the right of equal pay for equal work because they do the same work as formal contract workers at the client firms, in reality, employers can always make the case to deny that temporary workers do work equal to formal workers based on the workers' skills and qualifications. See more discussion in Lin (chap. 5 in this volume).

61. Interview no. 23, Shanghai, January 2007.

62. Informal discussion meeting organized by Ministry of Labor and Social Security (MLSS) on revising the second draft law, Qingdao, September 2006.

63. A classic case of this state boundary-drawing strategy is the effect of the state-enforced household registration (*hukou*) system between rural and urban residents. As many have noted, the *hukou* system has long relegated rural residents to second-class citizenship and limited their access to good jobs in the urban areas (see, e.g., Solinger 1999).

64. See ChinaNet *Zhong Guo Wang* (China.com.cn). 2010.

65. This emphasis on the centrality of building regime legitimacy in relation to promoting economic development in post-reform China parallels to Castells's (1992, 33–70) analysis of the development states in East Asia.

66. To what extent that the Chinese economy today is a capitalist economy is a different issue that cannot be addressed here.

67. The concept of masses originated in the Chinese Communist Revolution and the Maoist mass line. The masses consisted of workers, peasantry, intellectuals, and national bourgeoisie. The masses' interests were concordant with one another and with those of the state (Townsend 1967).

68. According to Ministry of Human Resources and Social Security (2009), in 2008, 1.2 million workers filed over 693,000 labor dispute cases with Chinese authorities, a 98 percent increase over 2007. There were 22,000 collective labor dispute cases accepted by the committees, a 71 percent increase over 2007. The doubling of both arbitration cases and labor-related lawsuits had partly to do with the sharp increase in factory closures and wage defaults in the 2008 global economic downturn. But it also reflected workers' growing awareness of their rights and confidence in the Chinese legal systems of public redress (China Labor Bulletin 2009a).

69. Such related lines include autoworkers' community lives, the impacts of the new regulation on labor dispatch, localism in labor politics with the expansion of automobile production into different localities in China, and patriotism involved with the development of automobile industry in China on labor activism.

Chapter 7

1. There are two exceptions: Guang (2005) and Yuan and Wong (1999). Yuan and Wong (1999) give us an overview of changes in the industry but do not detail industrial labor relations, whereas Guang (2005) deals with industrial labor relations but only within a specific small segment of the industry (those workers in renovations).

2. In 2002, it was estimated that there were 94 million migrant workers, of which 31.4 percent were working in the construction industry (Guojia jianshebu jianan hangye zhigong laodong he shehui baozhang yanjiu ketizu, 2004).

3. The "Three-Anti" Campaign focused on getting rid of corruption, waste, and excessive bureaucracy; the "Five-Anti" Campaign against capitalists targeted bribery, theft of state assets, cheating in labor, tax evasion, and theft of state secrets.

4. This upward trend of permanent employment increased the size of firms in the construction industry. By 1956, the average number of employees per enterprise was 2,500, significantly larger than the range of 2 to 40 people per enterprise in Western countries (Chao 1968).

5. For example, a construction enterprise under the Construction Engineering Ministry would be directed to do a project in a province in the northeast. The enterprise would move all necessary equipment, staff, workers, and their families hundreds of miles to do the project. Once the project was completed, the enterprise might be assigned to a project in the southeast. This transfer required that all equipment, staff, employees, and their families be moved to the new location. In contrast, in most countries, construction companies are geographically based units that draw from the local workforce rather than moving people from place to place.

6. A *danwei* is a work unit that manages many aspects of an employee's life, such as retirement, entertainment, and education for the employee's children.

7. The local workforce was from within the province and often from nearby towns and villages. In comparison, full-time employees were moved from location to location (sometimes across the country), meaning they were often from other provinces or cities.

8. Compared with other countries, the proportion of permanent to temporary employees was quite high.

9. Draft laborers were not included in the official labor statistics but were estimated to represent 3.5 million worker-days of construction work in 1958 (Chao 1968).

10. The system was not completely effective in stopping migration, especially in the face of catastrophe (Thaxton 2008).

11. The 1985 decree, Provisional Regulations on the Management of Temporary Residents in the Urban Areas, created this new status.

12. The general contracting companies are construction companies that provide project management and some technical expertise on the jobsite. Specialists companies are those that provide highly skilled workers, like architects and engineers, and the labor-only companies provide the manual labor that will actually build the building.

13. SOEs were ordered to reduce the size of their fixed, or permanent, workforce and were not allowed to hire any more workers other than the skilled professionals necessary to keep the companies operating. All new construction jobs in the field were to be filled by contract (migrant) workers.

14. There were also reforms changing the industrial organization targeting SOEs in the mid-1990s. As a result, some became shareholding companies, joint ventures, partnerships, and private enterprises, and others went bankrupt. By 2001, SOEs represented only 35 percent of the enterprises and 20 percent of the total industry employment (Qian and Hui 2004).

15. Unfortunately, despite the shift to informalization, there are no statistics or data that give us a clear picture of how much of the industry is operating in the formal versus the informal sector.

16. Again, there are no good statistics on how many of the migrants are unregistered/illegal. Wu (2005), however, estimates that 12 percent of the urban population is made up of unregistered migrants, and Wang (2005) notes that in some cities, such as Beijing and Chongqing, more than half the migrants are not registered.

17. I find the concept "labor markets" to be unsatisfactory for this analysis because it focuses only on how people get connected to a job. As Ortiz (2003) suggests in a review of the literature on labor markets, labor processes, and labor market segmentation, there is a need to make connections across these different areas of study to answer pressing questions in the literature. Along these lines, I have developed the concept "modes of employment" to capture the connections and relationships among these concepts.

18. In this study I focus only on unregistered temporary migrants. There may or may not be additional modes of employment operating among registered migrants.

19. Social networks still play a role in people getting jobs under the mediated mode of employment, but they do not define or organize the labor market.

20. This arrangement is an institutionalized but informal contract, meaning that the practice and use of the contract is widespread and standardized but that the form is verbal, not written.

21. Each mode of employment highlights different issues and trends among migrant workers in informal work. The configurations of the different modes of employment among informal workers may vary across cities and in other industries.

22. The contractor usually deems the lump sum to be the amount that the migrant worker will make for the year's work, but workers calculate it based on a per-day rate multiplied by the expected number of working days minus costs.

23. Contractors who provide food and shelter for "free" tend to compensate for this by paying lower wages. In this sense, food and shelter are not really free.

24. There is variability in (1) the amount and types of upfront costs that workers face for different contractors (and from place to place) and (2) which costs are covered upfront by the contractor and which are recovered by the contractor. Also, the monthly stipend is not usually more than 100 yuan ($12), with some special exceptions made in the form of "loans."

25. In some cases, workers are housed off site, but contractors usually provide the housing and transport to the job site. In both cases, contractors limit the mobility of workers, demanding that they request permission to leave the job site or the housing area.

26. These workers do have a relationship with their direct supervisor. But they do not usually develop relationships with other supervisors across the job site or develop relationships with supervisors above their direct boss.

27. There are a few cases in which women are hired to do construction work, but they are a small number of the overall workforce in this industry. Contractors from the south are more likely to hire women.

28. There are other more general reasons (not specific to mediated employment) why migrants are hesitant to bring their families to the cities. Perhaps the most serious deterrent is that raising children is much more expensive in the cities because migrants do not have access to public goods, such as health care and education. Also, many workers do not think the city is a good environment in which to raise children.

29. In this study, there were some cases in which husbands and wives had found work in the same city, but in more cases than not, they ended up in different cities. Even when men had relatives working in the same city, the long hours and arduous nature of construction jobs made it difficult for visits to occur.

30. Interview with Zengzeng (a migrant worker), Beijing, November 26, 2004.

Chapter 8

1. This chapter is based on more than four hundred open-ended interviews conducted from 2005 to 2008 (including both formal interviews and informal talks) with union officials, managers, and workers in fourteen geographically dispersed Chinese cities.

2. ACFTU has a top-down bureaucratic structure with three levels: national, regional, and primary. The national and regional unions are set up both along industrial lines and within geographical boundaries (with a parallel structure to that of the CCP and government). Unions at the primary level are organized according to the principle of enterprise unionism.

3. As a new organizational form, the status of union associations has not been clearly defined in China. In some cases, these associations are much like grassroots unions directly communicating and representing workers; in other cases, the associations act as intermediaries between regional unions and enterprise unions.

4. In China, the difference between an IOB and a POE lies in the number of employees. The former has fewer than eight workers, whereas the latter employs more than eight workers.

5. Union associations by trade are different from the ten national level industrial unions, which have very ambiguous and weak roles in the ACFTU system.

6. Interview with Mr. W, Guangzhou, July 29, 2005.

7. Interview with DHP union chair, Dongguan, June 5, 2006.

8. Interviews with DHP workers, Dongguan, June 5, 2006.

9. Interviews with DHP union cadres, Dongguan, June 5, 2006.

10. Interviews with DHP union cadres.

11. According to the DHP union chairperson, most of the achievements of the union, such as obtaining fewer working hours and better welfare, were gained during the preparation by DHP for factory inspections.

12. Interview with DHP worker, Dongguan, June 5, 2006.

13. GUAPI put up posters on the streets and handed out leaflets to workers, describing both basic labor standards (e.g., minimum wages and working hours) and the benefits of joining a union. Rather than informing workers what a genuine trade union should do, the education focused on the dual-function role of Chinese unions: (1) representing both the national collective good and worker interests and (2) mediating welfare and labor disputes.

14. Interviews with GTTUF chairperson and several employers, Guanlan, Shenzhen, August 9, 2005.

15. Interviews with GTTUF and GUAPI officials, Guanlan, Shenzhen, August 9, 2005.

16. Interview with Zeguo Town Trade Union Council (ZTTUC) chairperson, Zeguo, Wenling, July 15, 2006.

17. The employers' association was also established in July 2004 with the coordination of the local government to meet the needs of trade-level collective bargaining.

18. Each enterprise union assigned three to five worker representatives to attend the industry workers' meeting.

19. Under these conditions, enterprises had to guarantee the minimum monthly allowance for basic living to their employees.

20. The consumer price index (CPI) of Zhejiang Province was 103.9 in 2004 and 101.3 in 2005 (in 2003, the CPI was 100) (National Bureau of Statistics [NBS] of China 2005, 2006). Thus, the two contracts still gave workers slight wage increases after adjusting for inflation (the average inflation-adjusted wage increase was 1.1–4.1 percent and 1.7 percent, respectively). More important, without this wage negotiation mechanism, such increases would not have been guaranteed.

21. Interviews with ZTTUC chairperson and some employers, Zeguo, Wenling, July 15, 2006.

22. Interviews with Luwan District union officials, Shanghai, July 3, 2008.

Chapter 9

1. Interview with party official, Qingdao, August 15, 2007.

2. Interview with the founder of Little Flowers NGO, Beijing, April 5, 2007.

3. Interview with Xiao Li, Qingdao, August 15, 2007.

4. Interview with worker, Beijing, April 15, 2007.

References

Abbott, Andrew. 2005. "Sociology of Work and Occupations." In *The Handbook of Economic Sociology,* 2nd ed., edited by Neil J. Smelser and Richard Swedberg. Princeton: Princeton University Press and the Russell Sage Foundation.

All-China Federation of Trade Unions (ACFTU). 2001. Opinions on Strengthening Union Organizing in New Enterprises. Internal Document, ACFTU, February 7.

——. 2002. *Zhongguo gonghui tongji nianjian 2001* (China Trade Union statistical yearbook, 2001). Beijing: Zhongguo tongji chubanshe.

——. 2007. *Zhongguo gonghui tongji nianjian 2006* (China Trade Union statistical yearbook, 2006). Beijing: Zhongguo tongji chubanshe.

——. 2010. "Review of the Work of the Grassroots Organizing Department of the ACFTU 2009." www.acftu.org/template/10004/file.jsp?cid=233&aid=83287.

American Chamber of Commerce, People's Republic of China. 2011. www.amchamchina.org/article/10.

Arrighi, Giovanni. 2007. *Adam Smith in Beijing: Lineages of the Twenty-First Century.* London: Verso.

Associated Press. 2004. "East China Factory Workers Protest Rising Prices, Low Pensions." www.chinalaborwatch.org/en/web/article/.php?article_id=50200 (accessed October 29, 2007).

Banister, Judith. 2005a. "Manufacturing Earnings and Compensation in China." *Monthly Labor Review* 128(8): 22–40.

——. 2005b. "Manufacturing Employment in China." *Monthly Labor Review* 128(7): 11–29.

Barboza, David. 2006. "China Drafts Law to Empower Unions and End Labor Abuse." *New York Times,* October 13.

——. 2010. "Electronics Maker Promises Review after Suicides." *New York Times,* May 26. www.nytimes.com/2010/05/27/technology/27suicide.html.

Bärninghausen, Till M., Yuenli Liu, Zhiping Zhang, and Rainer Sauerborn. 2007. "Willingness to Pay for Social Health Insurance among Informal Sector Workers in Wuhan, China: A Contingent Valuation Study." *BMC Health Services Research* 7(114).

Barley, Stephen, and Gideon Kunda. 2004. *Gurus, Hired Guns, and Warm Bodies: Itinerant Experts in a Knowledge Economy.* Princeton: Princeton University Press.

Batson, Andrew. 2007. "China Toils over New Labor Law." *Wall Street Journal,* May 7.

Beijing Migrant Workers' Legal Assistance Station. 2006. "Annual Report: Working Station of Legal Aid for Migrant Workers." Beijing.

Bian, Yanjie. 1994. *Work and Inequality in Urban China.* Albany: SUNY Press.

Bian, Yanjie, and John R. Logan. 1996. "Market Transition and the Persistence of Power: The Changing Stratification System in Urban China." *American Sociological Review* 61(5): 739–58.

Berkowitz, Stephen D. 1988. "Markets and Market-Areas: Some Preliminary Formulations." In *Social Structures: A Network Approach,* edited by Barry Wellman and Stephen D. Berkowitz. Cambridge, UK: Cambridge University Press.

Blecher, Marc J. 1983. "Peasant Labor for Urban Industry: Temporary Contract Labor, Urban-Rural Balance and Class Relations in a Chinese County." *World Development* 11(8): 731–45.

——. 2002. "Hegemony and Workers' Politics in China." *China Quarterly* 170: 283–303.

Bonacich, Edna. 1972. "A Theory of Ethnic Antagonism: The Split Labor Market." *American Sociological Review* 37(5): 547–59.

Bradsher, Keith, and David Barboza. 2010. "Strike in China Highlights Gap in Workers Pay." *New York Times,* May 28. www.nytimes.com/2010/05/29/business/global/29honda.html?pagewanted=all.

Brandt, Loren, and Thomas Rawski. 2008. *China's Great Economic Transformation.* Cambridge, UK: Cambridge University Press.

Buckley, Christine. 2006. "Foreign Investors May Quit If China Tightens Up Labor Law." Times Online, June 19. www.business.timesonline.co.uk/tol/print.do?articleid=676240.

Burt, Ronald S. 2004. "From Structural Holes: The Social Structure of Competition." In *The New Economic Sociology: A Reader,* edited by Frank Dobbin. Princeton: Princeton University Press.

Cai, Fang, Du Yang, and Wang Meiyan. 2008. *Employment and Inequality Outcomes in China.* Institute of Population and Labour Economics, Chinese Academy of Social Sciences. www.oecd.org/dataoecd/54/52/42546043.pdf.

Cai, Yongshun. 2006. *State and Laid-Off Workers in Reform China: The Silence and Collective Action of the Retrenched.* London: Routledge.

Carruthers, Bruce G. 2004. "From City of Capital: Politics and Markets in the English Financial Revolution." In *The New Economic Sociology: A Reader,* edited by Frank Dobbin. Princeton: Princeton University Press.

"Cases Soar as Workers Seek Redress." 2009. *China Daily* (online), April 22.

Castells, Manuel. 1992. "Four Asian Tigers with a Dragon Head: A Comparative Analysis of the State, Economy, and Society in the Asian Pacific Rim." In *States and Development in the Asian Pacific Rim,* edited by Richard P. Appelbaum and Jeffrey Henderson, 33–70. London: Sage.

Chalmers, Norma J. 1989. *Industrial Relations in Japan: The Peripheral Workforce.* London: Routledge.

Chan, Anita. 1995. "The Emerging Patterns of Industrial Relations in China and the Rise of Two New Labor Movements." *China Information* 9(4): 36–59.

——. 1998. "Labor Relations in Foreign-Funded Ventures, Chinese Trade Unions and the Prospects for Collective Bargaining." In *Adjusting to Capitalism: Chinese Workers and the State,* edited by Greg O'Leary. Armonk, N.Y.: M. E. Sharpe.

——. 2001. *China's Workers under Assault: The Exploitation of Labor in a Globalizing Economy.* Armonk, N.Y.: M. E. Sharpe.

——. 2007. "Organizing Wal-Mart in China: Two Steps Forward, One Step Back for China's Unions." *New Labor Forum* 16(2): 87–96.

——. 2008. "Made in China: Walmart Unions." *YaleGlobal Online.* http://yaleglobal.yale.edu/display.article?id=8283.

Chan, Kam Wing, and Li Zhang. 1999. "The *Hukou* System and Rural-Urban Migration in China: Processes and Changes." *China Quarterly* 160: 818–55.

"Chang Kai Explains the Policy of the Draft Labor Contract Law" (Chang Kai jieshi laodong hetongfa caoan zhengce). 2007. January 13. www.9ask.cn/blog/user/wr666/archives/2007/14953.html#top.

Chang, Kai, and Kungang Li. 2006. "bixu yange guizhi laodongzhe paiqian" (Labor dispatch must be strictly regulated and restrained). *China Labor* (March): 9–12.

Chang, Kuei-min. 2007. "State, Migration, and Body: Migrant Reproduction Politics in Chinese Cities." MA thesis, National Tsing Hua University, Taiwan.

Change to Win. 2007. "The Question Isn't Why We Went to China—It's Why Wouldn't We?" www.changetowin.org/connect/2007/06/th_question_isnt_why_we_went.html.

Chao, Kang. 1968. *The Construction Industry in Communist China.* Chicago: Aldine.

Chen, Chen, and Jun Dong. 2007. "kendeji laowu paiqian'an yinfa de faxue sikao" (Legal reflection from the KFC labor dispatch case). Labor Law Network. www.shlaodong.com/lswz/20070404/152622.htm (Accessed March 7, 2008).

Chen, Lin, and Liang Chang. 2006. "Laodong paiqianzhong de falv wenti" (Some legal issues in labor dispatch). *Beijing Daily* (online), July 27. www.beijingdaily.com.cn/.

Child, John. 1994. *Management in China during the Age of Reform.* Cambridge, UK: Cambridge University Press.

Chin, Gregory T. 2003. "Building 'Capitalism with China's Characteristics': The Political Economy of Model Joint Ventures in the Automotive Industry." PhD diss., York University.

China Association of Automobile Manufacturers (CAAM). 2005. "Qiche zhizaye zhiye jishu jiaoyu diaoyan baogao" (Survey report on vocational education in automobile manufacturing sector). http://caam.org.cn/caam/caam.web/Detail.asp?id=193.

China Automotive Technology Research Center (CATRC). 1983–2006 [published annually]. *Zhongguo qiche gongye nianjian* (China automotive industry yearbook). Tianjin: China Automotive Technology Research Center Press.

China Labor Bulletin. 2009a. "Chinese Government Says Labor Disputes Doubled in 2008." May 11. www.china-labour.org.hk/en/node/100461.

——. 2009b. "Going It Alone: The Workers' Movement in China (2007–2008)." July 9. www.clb.org.hk/en/files/share/File/research_reports/workers_movement_07-08.pdf.

China Labor News. 2008. "Migrant Workers Leaving Shenzhen Queue All Night to Cash in Their Pensions." www.clntranslations.org/article. Translated from *Nanfang dushibao* (Southern Metropolitan Daily), January 15, 2008. News.sina.com.cn/c/2008-01-15/030113258863s.shtml (accessed September 20, 2008).

——. 2005. "High Cost of Wage Recovery Deepens Sense of Futility in Legal Route, Stirs Up Social Unrest." November 10. www.china-labour.org.hk/public/contents/article?revision%5fid=18842&item%5fid=18840.

——. 2008. "A Turning Point for China's Trade Unions." August 21. www.clb.org.hk/en/node/100294.

China National Petroleum Corporation (CNPC). 1998. "Zhongguo shiyou gongye guanli tizhi gaige yanjiu" (A study of the reform of the governance structure of the Chinese oil industry). Unpublished corporate research report, Beijing.

ChinaNet (Zhong Guo Wang). 2010. "ACFTU: Labor Dispatch Should only Be Used at Substitutive, Short-Term and Temporary Posts." March 9. www.china.com.cn/gonghui/2010-03/09/content_19566933.htm (Accessed March 18, 2010).

"China Won't Revise Labor Contract Law amid Financial Crisis: Lawmaker." 2009. *Xinhua* (online), March 9.

Cho, Young Nam. 2002. "From 'Rubber Stamps' to 'Iron Stamps': The Emergence of Chinese Local People's Congresses as Supervisory Powerhouses." *China Quarterly* 171: 724–40.

——. 2006. "The Politics of Lawmaking in Chinese Local People's Congresses." *China Quarterly* 187: 592–609.

Christiansen, Flemming. 1992. "Market Transition in China: The Case of the Jiangsu Labor Market, 1978–1990." *Modern China* 18(1): 79–80.

Chun, Jennifer Jihye. 2005. "Public Dramas and the Politics of Justice: Comparison of Janitors' Union Struggles in South Korea and the United States." *Work and Occupations* 32(4): 486–503.

——. 2008. "The Contested Politics of Gender and Irregular Employment: The Revitalization of the South Korean Democratic Labour Movement." In *Labour and the Challenges of Globalization: What Prospects for Transnational Solidarity?* edited by Andreas Bieler, Ingemar Lindberg, and Devan Pillay. London: Pluto Press.

Chung, Sun Wook. 2011. "A Variety of Labor Law Enforcement and Compliance in China." MS thesis, Cornell University, Ithaca, NY.

Cody, Dan. 2007. "New Rules to Protect Workers." *South China Morning Post,* February 6.

"Collection of the Masses' Opinions on the Labor Contract Law." 2006. Xinhuanet (online), April 6. http://news.xinhuanet.com/newscenter/2006–04/06/content_4392500.htm.

Congressional-Executive Commission on China (CECC). Annual Report, 2009. Washington D.C.: U.S. Government Printing Office.

Cook, Maria. 2007. *The Politics of Labor Reform in Latin America: Between Flexibility and Rights.* University Park: Pennsylvania State University Press.

Cook, Sarah. 2000. "Readjusting Labour: Enterprise Restructuring, Social Consequences and Policy Responses in Urban China." In *Changing Workplace Relations in the Chinese Economy,* edited by Malcolm Warner. Basingstoke, UK: Macmillan.

——. 2008. "The Challenge of Informality: Perspectives on China's Changing Labour Market." *IDS Bulletin* 39(2): 48–56.

Cooke, Fang Lee. 2008. "Labour Market Regulation and Informal Employment in China: To What Extent Are workers Protected?" Paper presented at the third China Task Force annual meeting, 25th–26th June 2008. University of Manchester, UK.

Cooper, Rae, and Bradon Ellem. 2008. "The Neoliberal State, Trade Unions and Collective Bargaining in Australia." *British Journal of Industrial Relations* 46(3): 532–54.

Costello, Tim, Brendan Smith, and Jeremy Brecher. 2007. "Labor Rights in China." Foreign Policy in Focus. www.fpif.org.

Cremer, John. 2007. "New Clauses Worry Multinationals." *South China Morning Post,* June 8.

Csanadi, Maria. 1997. *Party-States and Their Legacies in Post-Communist Transformation.* Cheltenham, UK: Edward Elgar.

——. 2006. *Self-Consuming Evolutions.* Budapest: Akademiai Kiado.

Dan, Chungang. 2009. "Xinmi, Henan Province Peasant Worker's 'Thoracic Lung Exam Surgery' Attracts the Attention of Many." *Xinhua* (online), July 23.

Démurger, Sylvie, Martin Fournier, Li Shi, and Wei Zhong. 2006. "Economic Liberalization with Rising Segmentation on China's Urban Labor Market." ECINEQ Working Papers no. 46. Society for the Study of Economic Inequality, www.ecineq.org.

Dobbin, Frank, ed. 2004. *The New Economic Sociology: A Reader.* Princeton: Princeton University Press.

Dong, Baohua. 2007. "Reflections on Harmonious Labor Relations." *Journal of Shanghai Normal University* (Philosophy and Social Science Ed.) 36(2).

——. 2008. "From the Labor Law to the Labor Contract Law." Paper presented at the conference on Breaking Down Chinese Walls?: The Changing Faces of Labor and Employment in China, Cornell University, September 26–28.

"The Draft Labor Contract Law Public Solicitation for Opinions Yields 191,849." 2006. Xinhuanet (online), April 21.

Du, Yang, Fang Cai, and Meiyan Wang. 2007. "Marketization and/or Informalization?: New Trends of China's Employment in Transition." Photocopy. Institute of Population and Labor Economics, Chinese Academy of Social Sciences.

Dyer, Geoff. 2005. "Carmakers Feel Pain in Chinese Market." *Financial Times,* April 23.

——. 2007. "China's Labor Debate Spurs War of Words for U.S. Interests." *Financial Times,* May 3.

Eckholm, Erik. 2001. "Chinese Warn of Civil Unrest across the Country: Communist Party Document Paints Picture of Discontent." *International Herald Tribune,* June 2–3.

"Economist Zhang Weiying Calls for a Decisive Halt in the Implementation of the Labor Contract Law, Says It Hurts the Interests of Workers." 2009. *Caijing* (online), February 8.

Erickson, Christopher L., and Sarosh Kuruvilla. 1998. "Industrial Relations System Transformation." *Industrial and Labor Relations Review* 52(1): 3–21.

European Union Chamber of Commerce. 2006. "Background." Euro-Cham. www.europeanchamber.com.cn/show/details.php?id=768.

Evans, Peter. 1979. *Dependent Development: The Alliance of Multinational, State, and Local Capital in Brazil.* Princeton, NJ: Princeton University Press.

"Explosion in Disputes." 2009. *Beijing Review* (online) January 22.

Feng, Tongqing. 2002. *Zhongguo Gongren de Mingyun: Gaige Yilai Zhongguo Gongren de Shehui xingdong* (The Destiny of Chinese Workers: Social Action of Workers since the Reform). Beijing: Social Sciences Academic Press.

Fine, Janice. 2006. *Worker Centers: Organizing Communities at the Edge of the Dream.* Ithaca: Cornell University Press.

Frazier, Mark W. 2006. "Commanding Heights Industrialization and Wage Determination in the Chinese Factory, 1950–1957." In *How China Works: Perspectives on the Twentieth-Century Industrial Workplace,* edited by Jacob Eyferth. London: Routledge.

——. 2010. *Socialist Insecurity: Pensions and the Politics of Uneven Development in China* (Ithaca: Cornell University Press).

Freeland, Robert F. 2001. *The Struggle for Control of the Modern Corporation: Organizational Change at General Motors, 1924–1970.* Cambridge, UK: Cambridge University Press.

Freeman, Linton. 1979. "Centrality in Social Networks: Conceptual Clarification." *Social Networks* 1: 215–39.

Friedman, Eli and Ching Kwan Lee. 2010. "Remaking the World of Chinese Labour: a 30-Year Retrospective." *British Journal of Industrial Relations,* 48(3): 507–34.

Freund, Elizabeth M. 1998. "Downsizing China's State Industrial Enterprises: The Case of Baoshan Steel Works." In *Adjusting to Capitalism: Chinese Workers and the State,* edited by Greg O'Leary. Armonk, N.Y.: M.E. Sharpe.

Friedman, Edward, Paul Pickowicz, and Mark Selden. 2005. *Revolution, Resistance, and Reform in Village China.* New Haven: Yale University Press.

Friedman, Eli. 2007. "External Pressure and Local Mobilization: Transnational Activism and the Emergence of the Chinese Labor Movement." MA thesis, University of California, Berkeley.

Gallagher, Mary Elizabeth. 2002. "Reform and Openness: Why Chinese Economic Reforms Have Delayed Democracy." *World Politics* 54(3): 338–72.

——. 2005a. *Contagious Capitalism: Globalization and the Politics of Labor in China.* Princeton: Princeton University Press.

——. 2005b. "China in 2004: Stability Above All." *Asian Survey,* 45(1): 21–32.

——. 2009. "China's Older Workers: Between Law and Policy, between Laid-Off and Unemployed." In *Laid-Off Workers in a Workers' State: Unemployment with Chinese Characteristics,* edited by Thomas B. Gold, William J. Hurst, Jaeyoun Won, and Li Qiang. New York: Palgrave Macmillan.

——. 2010. "What do China's Workers Want?: The Government's Ad Hoc Response." *New York Times,* June 13, 2010. http://roomfordebate.blogs.nytimes.com/2010/06/13/what-do-chinas-workers-want.

Gallagher, Mary Elizabeth, and Junlu Jiang. 2002. "China's Labor Legislation: The 1995 Labor Law and the 2001 Trade Union Law, Introduction and Analysis." *Chinese Law and Government* 35(6).

Gao, Paul. 2002. "A Tune-up for China's Auto Industry." *McKinsey Quarterly* 1: 144—55.

Gerlach, Michael L. 1992. "The Japanese Corporate Network: A Blockmodel Analysis." *Administrative Science Quarterly* 37(1): 105–39.

Giles, John, Albert Park, and Fang Cai. 2006. "How Has Economic Restructuring Affected China's Urban Workers?" *China Quarterly* 185: 61–95.

Global Labor Strategies. 2007. "Behind the Great Wall of China: U.S. Corporations Opposing New Rights for Chinese Workers." Global Labor Strategies (online). http://laborstrategies.blogs.com.

Gold, Thomas B., William J. Hurst, Jaeyoun Won, and Li Qiang, eds. 2009. *Laid-Off Workers in a Workers' State: Unemployment with Chinese Characteristics.* New York: Palgrave Macmillan.

Gordon, Jennifer. 2007. *Suburban Sweatshops: The Fight for Immigrants Rights.* Cambridge, Mass.: Belknap Press

Gottfried, Heidi. 2008. "Social Contracts in Transition?: Precarious Employment in Comparative Perspective." Paper presented at the Multiple Flexibilities Workshop, SSRC Inter-Asian Connections Conference, Dubai, UAE, February 21–23.

Grabher, Gernot, ed. 1993. *The Embedded Firm: On the Socioeconomics of Industrial Networks.* London: Routledge.

Granick, David. 1991. "Multiple Labour Markets in the Industrial State Enterprise Sector." *China Quarterly* 126: 269–89.

Granovetter, Mark S. 1974. *Getting a Job: A Study of Contacts and Careers.* Cambridge, Mass.: Harvard University Press.

——. 1994. "Business Groups." In *The Handbook of Economic Sociology,* edited by Neil J. Smelser and Richard Swedberg. Princeton: Princeton University Press and the Russell Sage Foundation.

Guang, Lei. 2005. "Guerrilla Workfare: Migrant Renovators, State Power, and Informal Work in Urban China." *Politics and Society* 33(3): 481–506.

Guo, Aiping. 2006. "Reflection of Labor Relationship in the Construction of Harmonious Society." *Qiu Shi,* August.

Guojia jianshebu jiananzhuang hangye zhigong laodong he shehui baozhang yanjiu ketizu (National Ministry of Construction, Building and Installation Industry Employee, Labor, and Social Insurance Research Group). 2004. "Jianzhu anzhuang hangye gongren de shengchan shenghuo zhuangkuang kaocha baogao" (A research report on the living and working conditions of workers in the construction and installation industry). Guojia jianshebu (National Ministry of Construction), Beijing.

Gustafsson, Björn, Li Shi, Ludmila Nivorozhkina, and Katarina Katz. 2001. "Rubles and Yuan: Wage Functions for Urban Russia and China at the End of the 1980s." *Economic Development and Cultural Change* 50(1): 1–17.

Guthrie, Doug. 1998. "Organizational Uncertainty and Labor Contracts in China's Economic Transition." *Sociological Forum* 13(3): 457–94.

Hairong, Yan. 2006. "Rurality and Labor Process Autonomy." *Cultural Dynamics* 18: 5–31.

Hall, Richard. 2006. "Australian Industrial Relations in 2005—The Work Choices Revolution." *Journal of Industrial Relations* 48(3): 291–303.

Hanser, Amy. 2006. "A Tale of Two Sales Floors: Changing Service Work Regimes in China." In *Working in China: Ethnographies of Labor and Workplace Transformation,* edited by Ching Kwan Lee. London: Routledge.

Harper-Ho, Virginia. 2005. *Labor Dispute Resolution in China: Implications for Labor Rights and Legal Reform.* Berkeley: University of California Press.

Harwit, Eric. 1995. *China's Automobile Industry.* New York, NY: M.E. Sharpe.

Hay, Donald A., Derek J. Morris, Guy Liu, and Shujie Yao. 1994. *Economic Reform and State-Owned Enterprises in China, 1979–1987.* Oxford: Clarendon Press.

Herrigel, Gary. 1996. *Industrial Constructions: The Sources of German Industrial Power.* Cambridge, UK: Cambridge University Press.

Hoffman, Charles. 1968. *Work Incentives: Practices and Policies in the PRC, 1953–1965.* Albany: SUNY Press.

Houseman, Susan. 2001. "Why Employers Use Flexible Staffing Arrangements: Evidence from an Establishment Survey." *Industrial and Labor Relations Review* 55(1): 149–70.

Howard, Pat. 1991. "Rice Bowls and Job Security: The Urban Contract Labour System." *Australian Journal of Chinese Affairs* 25: 93–114.

Howell, Chris. 2009. "The Transformation of French Industrial Relations: Labor Representation and the State in a Post-*Dirigiste* Era." *Politics and Society* 37(2): 229–56.

Howell, Jude. 1998. "Trade Unions in China: The Challenge of Foreign Capital." In *Adjusting to Capitalism: Chinese Workers and the State,* edited by Greg O'Leary. Armonk, N.Y.: M. E. Sharpe.

Hu, Teh-wei, Ming Li, and Shuzhong Shi. 1988. "Analysis of Wages and Bonus Payments among Tianjin Urban Workers." *China Quarterly* 113: 77–93.

Hu, Xiaoyi. 1999. "Yanglao baoxian, '98 pandian" (Overview of pension insurance in 1998). *Zhongguo Shehui baozhang* (China Social Security magazine) 55: 14–15.

"Hu: China to Promote Sustainable Development, Protect Workers' Rights and Interests." 2008. Xinhua (Online). January 7.

Huang, Yasheng. 1990. "Web of Interests and Patterns of Behaviour of Chinese Local Economic Bureaucracies and Enterprises during Reforms." *China Quarterly* 123: 431–58.

Human Rights Watch. 2002. *Paying the Price: Worker Unrest in Northeast China.* New York: Human Rights Watch.

Humphrey, John. 1982. *Capitalist Control and Workers' Struggles in the Brazilian Auto Industry.* Princeton: Princeton University Press.

Hurst, William. 2004. "Understanding Contentious Collective Action by Chinese Laid-Off Workers: The Importance of Regional Political Economy." *Studies in Comparative International Development* 39(2): 94–120.

——. 2009. *The Chinese Workers after Socialism.* New York, NY: Cambridge University Press.

Hurst, William, and Kevin J. O'Brien. 2002. "China's Contentious Pensioners." *China Quarterly* 170: 344–60.

Institute of Population and Labor Economics Project Group. 2007. Chinese Academy of Sciences. http://iple.cass.cn/e/e.htm.

Ishida, Mitsuo. 1997. "Japan: Beyond the Model for Lean Production." In *After Lean Production: Evolving Employment Practices in the World Auto Industry,* edited by Thomas A. Kochan, Russell D. Lansbury, and John Paul MacDuffie. Ithaca, NY: Cornell University Press.

Jacka, Tamara. 2006. *Rural Women in Urban China.* Armonk, N.Y.: M. E. Sharpe.

Janky, Bela, and Robert Gal. 2007. "Public Opinion on Pension Systems in Europe." ENEPRI Research Report no. 36. http://shop.ceps.eu/BookDetail.php?item_id=1519 (accessed August 19, 2008.).

Jefferson, Gary H., and Thomas G. Rawski. 1992. "Unemployment, Underemployment, and Employment Policy in China's Cities." *Modern China* 18(1): 42–71.

Ji, You. 1998. *China's Enterprise Reform: Changing State/Society Relations after Mao.* London: Routledge.

Jin, Dejun. 2003. "Zhongguo jianzhuye gaige yu fazhan yanjiu baogao" (Reform and development in China's construction industry). Ministry of Construction Policy Research Center, Beijing.

Johnston, M. Francis. 2002. "Elites and Agencies: Forging Labor Policy at China's Central Level." *Modern China* 28(2): 147–76.

Kalleberg, Arne. 2000. "Nonstandard Employment Relations: Part-Time, Temporary and Contract Work." *Annual Review of Sociology* 26: 341–65.

——. 2001. "Organizing Flexibility; The Flexible Firm in a New Century." *British Journal of Industrial Relations* 39(4): 479–504.

——. 2003. "Flexible Firms and Labor Market Segmentation." *Work and Occupations* 30(2): 154–75.

Ke, Ping. 2009. "Can the 'Open-Chest Lung Exam' Expedite Reform of Worker Protections?" *Shanxi Daily* (online), August 18.

Knight, John, and Lina Song. 2005. *Towards a Labour Market in China.* Oxford: Oxford University Press.

Koo, Hagen. 2001. *Korean Workers: The Culture and Politics of Class Formation.* Ithaca: Cornell University Press.
Kornai, Janos. 1992. *The Socialist System: The Political Economy of Communism.* Oxford: Clarendon Press.
Korzec, Michael. 1992. *Labour and the Failure of Reform in China.* New York: St. Martin's Press.
Kroeber, R. Arthur. 2011. "Developmental Dreams: Policy and Reality in China's Economic Reforms." In *Beyond the Middle Kingdom: Comparative Perspectives on China's Capitalist Transformation,* edited by Scott Kennedy. Stanford, CA: Stanford University Press.
Kuruvilla, Sarosh. 1996. "Linkages between Industrialization Strategies and Industrial Relations/Human Resource Policies: Singapore, Malaysia, the Philippines, and India." *Industrial and Labor Relations Review* 49(4): 635–57.
Kuruvilla, Sarosh, and Christopher Erickson. 2002. "Change and Transformation in Asian Industrial Relations." *Industrial Relations* 41(2): 171–228.
"Labor Dispute Cases Suddenly Erupt in the First Half of 2009." 2009. *Caijing* (online), July 13.
"Last Year Provincial Courts' Labor Disputes Increase 157.43%" [Quansheng fayuan qunian laodongzhengyi anjian tongbi zengzhang 157.43%]. 2009. *Nanfang News Network* (online). February 15.
Lautsch, Brenda. 2002. "Uncovering and Explaining Variance in the Features and Outcomes of Contingent Work." *Industrial and Labor Relations Review* 56(1): 23–43.
Lee, Ching Kwan. 1998a. *Gender and the South China Miracle: Two Worlds of Factory Women.* Berkeley: University of California Press.
———. 1999. "From Organized Dependence to Disorganized Despotism: Changing Labour Regime in Chinese Factories." *China Quarterly* 157: 44–71.
———. 2007. *Against the Law: Labor Protests in China's Rustbelt and Sunbelt.* Berkeley: University of California Press.
Lee, Ching Kwan. 2000. "Pathways of Labor Insurgency." In *Chinese Society: Changes, Conflict and Resistance,* edited by Elizabeth Perry and Mark Selden. London: Routledge.
———. 2002. "From the Specter of Mao to the Spirit of the Law: Labor Insurgency in China." *Theory and Society* 31: 189–228.
Lee, Ching Kwan, and Mark Selden. 2008. "Inequality and Its Enemies in Revolutionary and Reform China." *Economic and Political Weekly,* December 27.
Lett, Erin, and Judith Banister. 2006. "Labor Costs of Manufacturing Employees in China: An Update to 2003–04." *Monthly Labor Review* 129(11): 40–45.
Lian, Yingting, and Hongwei Chen. 2007. "laodong zhengyi anjian jingpen shier nian: shuliang zengjia 13.5 bei" (Labor dispute cases exploded over the past twelve tears: The number increased by 13.5 times). *Legal Daily,* August 19. http://news.xinhuanet.com/employment/2007-08/19/content_6563586_3.htm (Accessed January 22, 2008).
Lin, Kun-Chin. 2007. "With Strings Attached? Improving the Administration of Central State-Financed Investment Projects in the PRC." *Asian Journal of Political Science* 15(3): 319–43.
Li, Mengbai, and Hu Xin, eds. 1991. *Liudong renkou dui da chengshi fazhan de yingxiang ji duice* (The influence of the floating population on the development of big cities and policy response). Beijing: Jingji ribao chubanshe.
Li, Minqi. 2004. "Workers' Participation in Management and Firm Performance: Evidence from Large and Medium-Sized Chinese Industrial Enterprises." *Review of Radical Political Economics* 36(3): 358–80.

Li, Shi, and Hiroshi Sato. 2006. *Unemployment, Inequality and Poverty in Urban China.* London: Routledge.

Liang, Zai, and Zhongdong Ma. 2004. "China's Floating Population: New Evidence from the 2000 Census." *Population and Development Review* 30: 467–88.

Lin, Kun-Chin. 2003. "Corporatizing China: Reinventing State Control for the Market." PhD diss., University of California, Berkeley.

——. 2006. "Disembedding Socialist Firms as a Statist Project: Restructuring the Chinese Oil Industry, 1997–2002." *Enterprise & Society: The International Journal of Business History* 7(1): 59–97.

——. 2007. With Strings Attached? Improving the Administration of Central State-Financed Investment Projects in the PRC." *Asian Journal of Political Science* 15(3): 319–43.

——. 2008a. "Local Governmental Effect on Oil and Petrochemical Enterprise Reform in China." Oil, Gas & Energy Law Intelligence (OGEL) 6(1). www.ogel.org/about-author-a-z-profile.asp?key+1461.

——. 2008b. "Macroeconomic Disequilibria and Enterprise Reform: Restructuring the Chinese Oil and Petrochemical Industries in the 1990s." *China Journal* 60: 49–79.

——. 2008c. "Pricing Labor in Reforming State-Owned Enterprises in China." Paper presented at workshop on Inter-Asian Connections Conference, Dubai School of Government, Dubai, UAE, February 21–23.

——. 2009. "Class Formation or Fragmentation?: Allegiances and Divisions among Managers and Workers in State-Owned Enterprises." In *Laid-Off Workers in a Workers' State: Unemployment with Chinese Characteristics,* edited by Thomas B. Gold, William J. Hurst, Jaeyoun Won, and Li Qiang. New York: Palgrave Macmillan.

Liu, Cheng. 2006. "Research on Several Problems of the Draft Labor Contract Law." Paper presented at the Conference on the Draft Labor Contract Law, Shanghai, China, April.

——. 2007. "Towards the Guiding Principles for Labor Contract Legislation with Comments upon Labor Contract Law (Draft) and Relevant Remarks." *Journal of Shanghai Normal University (Philosophy and Social Science Ed.)* 36(2).

Liu, Mingwei. 2009. "Chinese Employment Relations and Trade Unions in Transition." PhD diss., Cornell University.

Liu, Mingwei, Chunyun Li, and Sunghoon Kim. 2011. "The Changing Chinese Trade Unions: A Three Level Analysis." In *China's Changing Workplace,* edited by P. Sheldon, S. Kim, Y. Li, and M. Warner. London: Routledge.

Liu, Mingwei, Sarosh Kuruvilla, and Sun-wook Chung. 2010. "Selective Law Enforcement in China: Evidence from the Implementation of the Labor Contract Law." Unpublished paper to be submitted to *Industrial Relations.*

Liu, Zhenjun. 1998. *Youtian qiye gongzi fenpei and guanli* (Wage distribution and management in oil fields). Shandong: Shiyou daxue chubanshe.

Lu, Jialing. 2008. "Manufacturing Solidarity?: The Paradox of Chinese Labor NGOs." PhD diss. Tsinghua University, Beijing.

Lu, Xiaobo, and Elizabeth J. Perry, eds. 1997. *Danwei: The Changing Chinese Workplace in Historical and Comparative Perspective.* Armonk, N.Y.: M. E. Sharpe.

Lu, You-Jie, and Paul W. Fox. 2001. "The Construction Industry in China: Its Image, Employment Prospects, and Skill Requirements." Sectoral Activities Programme, Working Paper no. 180. International Labour Office, Geneva.

Ma, J. C. Laurence, and Biao Xiang. 1998. "Native Place, Migration, and the Emergence of Peasant Enclaves in Beijing." *China Quarterly* 155: 546–81.

Ma, Xiaohe. 2004. Speech given at the Forum of Chinese Auto General Managers, June 7. *Sina Financial Report.* www.sina.com (accessed August 12, 2004).

Maitra, Pushkar, Russell Smyth, Ingrid Nielsen, Chris Nyland, and Cherrie Zhu. 2005. "Firm Compliance with Social Insurance Obligations Where There Is a Weak Surveillance and Enforcement Mechanism: Empirical Evidence from Shanghai." *Pacific Economic Review* 12(5): 577–96.

Mangan, John. 2000. *Workers without Traditional Employment: An International Study of Non-standard Work.* Cheltenham, UK: Edward Elgar.

Marsden, Peter V. 2002. "Egocentric and Sociocentric Measures of Network Centrality." *Social Networks* 24: 407–22.

Meng, Xin. 2000. *Labour Market Reform in China.* Cambridge, UK: Cambridge University Press.

Meyer, Rachel. 2008. "Perpetual Struggle: Sources of Working-Class Identity and Activism in Collective Action." PhD diss., University of Michigan.

Migdal, Joel S., Atul Kohli, and Vivienne Shue, eds. 1994. *State Power and Social Forces: Domination and Transformation in the Third World.* Cambridge, UK: Cambridge University Press.

Milkman, Ruth. 2006. *L.A. Story: Immigrant Workers and the Future of the U.S. Labor Movement.* New York: Russell Sage Foundation.

Ministry of Human Resources and Social Security (MOHRSS). 2007. "2007nian laodong he shehui baozhang shiye fazhan tongji gongbao" (2007 report on labor and social security developments). http://w1.mohrss.gov.cn/gb/zwxx/2008–06/05/content_240415.htm (accessed August 9, 2008).

Ministry of Human Resources and Social Security of P. R. China. 2009. "Laodong zhengyi tiaojie zhongcai fa shishi yi zhounian zuotanhui zhaokai" (Annual forum held for labor dispute mediation and arbitration law). www.gov.cn/gzdt/2009-05/09/content_1309305.htm.

"Ministry of Human Resources and Social Security Will Develop Specific Measures to Regulate the Labor Dispatch." 2008. Xinhua (Online). http://news.xinhuanet.com/legal/2008-09/27/content_10121294.htm (Accessed March 18, 2010).

Ministry of Labor and Social Security (MOLSS). 2000. *Zhongguo laodong tongji nianjian 2000* (China labor statistics yearbook, 2000). Beijing: Zhongguo laodong shehui baozhang chubanshe.

——. 2005. *Zhongguo laodong tongji nianjian 2005* (China labor statistics yearbook, 2005). Beijing: Zhongguo laodong shehui baozhang chubanshe.

Ministry of Labor and Social Security and National Statistical Bureau. 2007. "Statistical Report on Developments in Labor and Social Security Undertakings." www.molss.gov.cn/gb/news/2007-05/18/content_178167.htm.

Ministry of Labor, Social Insurance Bureau, ed. 1997. *Zhongguo shehui baoxian nianjian 1997* (China social insurance yearbook, 1997). Beijing: Zhongguo renshichubanshe.

Mizruchi, Mark S., and Michael Schwartz, eds. 1987. *Intercorporate Relations: The Structural Analysis of Business.* Cambridge, UK: Cambridge University Press.

National Bureau of Statistics of China (NBS). 2001. *China Statistical Yearbook.* Beijing: Chinese Statistics Press.

——. 2002. *China Statistical Yearbook.* Beijing: China Statistics Press.

——. 2005. *China Statistical Yearbook.* Beijing: China Statistics Press.

——. 2006. *China Statistical Yearbook.* Beijing: China Statistics Press.

——. 2008. *China Statistical Yearbook.* Beijing: China Statistics Press.

National People's Congress (NPC). 2009. "Guanyu shehui baoxianfa caoan zhengqiu yijian de qingkuang" (On the solicitation of comments on the draft social insurance law). February 23. www.npc.gov.cn (accessed February 27, 2009).

Naughton, Barry. 2007. *The Chinese Economy: Transitions and Growth.* Cambridge, Mass.: MIT Press.

"New Characteristics of Labor Disputes during the Financial Crisis." 2009. *Dongfang Fayan* (online), May 6.

Ngai, Pun. 1999. "Becoming *Dagongmei* (Working Girls): The Politics of Identity and Difference in Reform China." *China Journal* 42: 1–18.

——. 2005. *Made in China: Women Factory Workers in a Global Workplace.* Durham: Duke University Press.

Nova, Scott. 2007. "China Labor Law Reform." Memo to primary contacts, WRC affiliate universities and colleges, Workers Rights Consortium, March 1.

"NPC Standing Committee Strongly Criticizes the Brick Kiln Incident." 2007. Caijing (online), June 24. www.caijing.com.cn/ajax/print.html.

O'Brien, Kevin J. 1992. "Bargaining Success of Chinese Factories." *China Quarterly* 132: 1086–1100.

O'Leary, Greg. ed. 1998. *Adjusting to Capitalism: Chinese Workers and the State.* Armonk, N.Y.: M. E. Sharpe.

Ortiz, Sutti. 2002. "Laboring in the Factories and in the Fields." *Annual review of Anthropology* 31: 395–417.

Otis, Eileen M. 2007. "Beyond the Industrial Paradigm: Market-Embedded Labor and the Gender Organization of Global Service Work in China." *American Sociological Review* 73: 15–36.

Palmer, Donald A., and Roger Friedland. 1987. "Corporation, Class, and City System." In *Intercorporate Relations: The Structural Analysis of Business,* edited by Mark Mizruchi and Michael Schwartz. Cambridge, UK: Cambridge University Press.

Pan, Philip P. 2002. "'High Tide' of Labor Unrest in China." *Washington Post,* January 21.

Parker, Mike, and Jane Slaughter. 1995. "Unions and Management by Stress." In *Lean Work, Employment and Exploitation in the Global Auto Industry,* edited by Steve Babson. Detroit, MI: Wayne State University Press.

Peng, Yusheng. 1992. "Wage Determination in Rural and Urban China: A Comparison of Public and Private Industrial Sectors." *American Sociological Review* 57(2): 198–213.

Perrow, Charles. 2002. *Organizing America: Wealth, Power and the Origins of American Capitalism.* Princeton: Princeton University Press.

——. 1994. "Shanghai's Strike Wave of 1957." *China Quarterly* 137: 1–27.

Petit, Pascal. 1999. "Structural Forms and Growth Regimes of the Post-Fordist Era." *Review of Social Economy* 57(2): 220–43.

Piore, Michael J. 1979. *Birds of Passage: Migrant Labor and Industrial Societies.* Cambridge, UK: Cambridge University Press.

Piven, Frances. 2008. "Can Power from Below Change the World?" *American Sociological Review* 73: 1–14.

Piven, Frances, and Richard Cloward. 1977. *Poor People's Movements: Why They Succeed, How They Fail.* New York: Vintage Books.

——. 1957. *The Great Transformation: The Political and Economic Origins of Our Time.* Boston: Beacon Hill.

Price, John. 1997. *Japan Works: Power and Paradox in Postwar Industrial Relations.* Ithaca: Cornell University Press.

"Protections for agency workers' rights meet legal difficulties." 2005. Xinhua (Online). http://news.xinhuanet.com/legal/2005-06/20/content_3108717.htm (Accessed April 10, 2009).

Pun Ngai. 2005. *Made in China: Women Factory Workers in a Global Workplace.* Durham: Duke University Press.

Putterman, Louis, and Xiao-Yuan Dong. 2000. "China's State-Owned Enterprises: Their Role, Job Creation, and Efficiency in Long-Term Perspective." *Modern China* 26(4): 403–47.

Qian, Xiaoying, and Zhao Hui. 2004. "The Construction Sector in the People's Republic of China: Policy Analysis on Sectoral Development and Employment Challenges." Socio-Economic Technical Paper no. 15. Employment-Intensive Investment Branch, International Labour Office, Geneva.

"Reflection on Implementation of the Labor Contract Law." 2008. *Guangming Daily,* August 4.

Roland, Gérard. 2004. "Understanding Institutional Change: Fast-Moving and Slow-Moving Institutions." *Studies in Comparative International Development* 38(4): 109–31.

Sako, Mari, and Hiroki Sato, eds. 1997. *Japanese Labour and Management in Transition: Diversity, Flexibility and Participation.* London: Routledge.

Sargeson, Sally. 1999. *Reworking China's Proletariat.* New York: St. Martin's Press.

Schafer, Sarah. 2007. "Now They Speak Out: If U.S. Business Is a Quiet Force for Progress in China, as It Claims, Why Is It Protesting against Labor Reform?" *Newsweek International Edition,* May 28.

Schurmann, Franz. 1968. *Ideology and Organization in Communist China.* Berkeley: University of California Press.

Scott, James. 1987. *Weapons of the Weak: Everyday Forms of Peasant Resistance.* New Haven: Yale University Press.

Seidman, Gay W. 1994. *Manufacturing Militance: Workers' Movements in Brazil and South Africa, 1970–1985.* Berkeley: University of California Press.

Sheehan, Jackie. 1998. *Chinese Workers: A New History.* London: Routledge.

Shi, Jiangtao. 2006. "New Labor Law Would Bring Conflicts, European Firms Fear." *South China Morning Post,* April 22.

Shih, Toh Han. 2006. "Labor Contract Law Draws Protest from Every Side." *South China Morning Post,* November 13.

Silver, Beverly J. 2003. *Forces of Labor: Workers' Movements and Globalization since 1870.* Cambridge, UK: Cambridge University Press.

Silver, Beverly J., and Lu Zhang. 2009. "China: Emerging Epicenter of World Labor Unrest?" In *China and the Transformation of Global Capitalism,* edited by Ho-fung Hung. Baltimore: Johns Hopkins University Press.

Smelser, Neil J., and Richard Swedberg, eds. 1994. *The Handbook of Economic Sociology.* Princeton: Princeton University Press and the Russell Sage Foundation.

——. 2005. *The Handbook of Economic Sociology.* 2nd ed. Princeton: Princeton University Press and the Russell Sage Foundation.

Smith, Brendan, Jeremy Brecher, and Tim Costello. 2007. "An Emerging Chinese Labor Movement." *New Labor Forum* 16(1): 83–85.

Smith-Doerr, Laurel, and Walter W. Powell. 2005. "Networks and Economic Life." In *The Handbook of Economic Sociology,* 2nd ed., edited by Neil J. Smelser and Richard Swedberg. Princeton: Princeton University Press and the Russell Sage Foundation.

Smyth, Russell, Zhai Qingguo, and Wang Jing. 2001. "Labour Market Reform in China's State-Owned Enterprises: A Case Study of Post-Deng Fushun in Liaoning Province." *New Zealand Journal of Asian Studies* 3(2): 42–72.

Solinger, Dorothy J. 1989. "Urban Reform and Relational Contracting in Post-Mao China: An Interpretation of the Transition from Plan to Market." *Studies in Comparative Communism* 22(2–3): 171–85.

——. 1995. "The Chinese Work Unit and Transient Labor in the Transition from Socialism." *Modern China* 21(2): 155–83.

——. 1998. "Job Categories and Employment Channels among the 'Floating Population.'" In *Adjusting to Capitalism: Chinese Workers and the State,* edited by Greg O'Leary. Armonk, N.Y.: M. E. Sharpe.

——. 1999. *Contesting Citizenship in Urban China: Peasant Migrants, the State, and the Logic of the Market.* Berkeley: University of California Press.

——. 2001. "Why We Cannot Count the 'Unemployed.'" *China Quarterly* 167: 671–88.

——. 2002. "Labor Market Reform and the Plight of the Laid-Off Proletariat." *China Quarterly* 170: 304–26.

——. 2003. "Chinese Urban Jobs and the WTO." *China Journal* 49: 61–87.

——. 2005. "Beijing's Number One Worry." *South China Morning Post,* February 12.

Sorensen, Aage B. 1994. "Firms, Wages, and Incentives." In *The Handbook of Economic Sociology,* edited by Neil J. Smelser and Richard Swedberg. Princeton: Princeton University Press and the Russell Sage Foundation.

"Special Report on the Labor Contract Law." 2008. Xinhua (Online), December 30.

Stark, David. 1996. "Recombinant Property in East European Capitalism." In *Restructuring Networks in Post Socialism: Legacies, Linkages, and Localities,* edited by Gernot Grabher and David Stark. Oxford: Oxford University Press.

Steinfeld, Edward. 1998. *Forging Reform in China: The Fate of State-Owned Industry.* Cambridge, UK: Cambridge University Press.

Swider, Sarah. 2009. "Behind Great Walls: Modes of Employment among Migrant Construction Workers in China's Informal Labor Market." PhD diss., University of Wisconsin-Madison.

Sydow, Jörg, and Arnold Windeler. 1998. "Organizing and Evaluating Interfirm Networks: A Structurationist Perspective on Network Processes and Effectiveness." *Organization Science* 9(3): 265–84.

Takahara, Akio. 1992. *The Politics of Wage Policy in Post-Revolutionary China.* London: Macmillan.

Tan, Shen et al. 2001. "Following the Trail of Blood and Tears: An Investigation of the Women Migrant Victims of the 11.19 Shenzhen Toy Factory Fire." *Tianya* 3–4.

Tanner, Murray Scot. 1999. *The Politics of Lawmaking in Post-Mao China: Institutions, Processes and Democratic Prospects.* New York: Oxford University Press.

Tao, Ran. 2006. "The Labor Market in the People's Republic of China." In *Labor Markets in Asia: Issues and Perspectives,* edited by Jesus Felipe and Rana Hasan. Basingstoke, UK: Palgrave Macmillan.

Taylor, Bill, Kai Chang, and Qi Li. 2003. *Industrial Relations in China.* Cheltenham, UK: Edward Elgar.

"Ten Focal Points of the Draft Labor Contract Law in the Eyes of the Masses." 2006. Xinhuanet (online), April 21. http://news.xinhuanet.com/newscenter/2006-04/21/content_4458619.htm.

Thaxton, Ralph. 2008. *Catastrophe and Contention in Rural China: Mao's Great Leap Forward Famine and the Origins of Righteous Resistance in Da Fo Village.* Cambridge, UK: Cambridge University Press.

Theron, Jan. 2004. "Employment Is Not What It Used to Be: The Nature and Impact of the Restructuring of Work in South Africa." In *Beyond the Apartheid Work-Place: Studies in Transition,* edited by Eddie Webster and Karl von Holdt, 302–23. Pietermaritzburg: University of KwaZulu-Natal Press.

Thun, Eric. 2004. "Industrial Policy, Chinese-Style: FDI, Regulation, and Dreams of National Champions in the Auto Sector." *Journal of East Asian Studies* 4: 453–89.

Tobin, Damian. 2003. "Corporate Governance, Industrial Reform and Enterprises Performance in China: The Case of Shanghai Petrochemical Company." Paper presented at the Fourth Colloque international sur l'économie chinoise, CNRS/Université d'Auvergne, Clermont-Ferrand, France, October. www.cerdi.org/Colloque/Coll_Paper.asp?COLNUM=18.

Tomba, Luigi. 2002. *Paradoxes of Labour Reform.* London: RoutledgeCurzon.

Tong, Xin. 2005. "Labor Unions in Enterprises." *Chinese Sociology and Anthropology* 37(4): 52–71.

Townsend, James R. 1967. *Political Participation in Communist China.* Berkeley: University of California Press.

Treece, James. 1997. "China Takes Hard Road to a Market Economy." *Automotive News,* July 14, p. 1.

Tu, Guoming. 2007. "Shanghai shi qiye laowu yonggong de xianzhuang, wenti yu duice" (Agency employment at enterprises in Shanghai: current situations, problems, and countermeasures). In *The Development and Legal Regulation of Labor Dispatch,* edited by Changzheng Zhou, 14–22. Beijing: China Labor and Social Security Publishing House.

Vernon, Raymond. 1966. "International Investment and International Trade in the Product Cycle." *Quarterly Journal of Economics* 80(2): 190–207.

Vosko, Leach. 2006. *Precarious Employment: Understanding Labor Market Insecurity in Canada.* Montreal: McGill-Queen's University Press.

Walder, Andrew G. 1986. *Communist Neo-Traditionalism: Work and Authority in Chinese Industry.* Berkeley: University of California Press.

——. 1992. "Property Rights and Stratification in Socialist Redistributive Economies." *American Sociological Review* 57(4): 524–39.

Wang, Bixue. 2006. "Laowu paiqian zaoyu falv nanti" (Labor dispatching encounters legal difficulty). *People's Daily,* January 4.

Wang, Fei-Ling. 2005. *Organizing through Division and Exclusion: China's Hukou System.* Stanford: Stanford University Press.

Wang, Shaoguang. 2008. "The Great Transformation: The Double Movement in China." *Boundary 2* 35(2): 15–47.

Warner, Malcolm. 1995. *The Management of Human Resources in Chinese Industry.* New York: St Martin's Press.

——. 1996. "Beyond the Iron Rice-Bowl." In *Management Issues in China, vol. 1: Domestic Enterprises,* edited by David H. Brown and Robin Porter. London: Routledge.

——. 2000. *Changing Workplace Relations in the Chinese Economy.* Basingstoke, UK: Macmillan.

Watts, Jonathan. 2006. "Wal-Mart Backs Down and Allows Chinese Workers to Join Union." *Guardian,* August 11.

Weller, Robert, and Li Jiangshen. 2000. "From State-Owned Enterprise to Joint Venture: A Case Study of the Crisis in Urban Social Services." *China Journal* 43: 83–99.

Wellman, Barry, and Stephen D. Berkowitz, eds. 1988. *Social Structures: A Network Approach.* Cambridge, UK: Cambridge University Press.

Weng, Shiyou. 2009. "Laowu paiqian guiding congjin zhiding, da qiye yonggong chengben keneng shangsheng" (Labor dispatching regulations will become tighter, labor cost is expected to rise at large enterprises). *Economic Observations,* October 24.

White, Chris. 2007. "China's New Labour Laws: The Challenge of Regulating Employment Contracts." Evatt Foundation Papers. http://evatt.org.au/publications/papers/193.html.

White, Gordon. 1987. "The Politics of Economic Reform in Chinese Industry: The Introduction of the Labour Contract System." *China Quarterly* 111: 365–89.

Wong, Shiyou. 2009. "Labor dispatch Will Be Tightly Regulated; Labor Costs of Large Enterprises May Rise." *Economic Observer,* October 24.

Wu, Wei. 2005. "laowu paiqian chongji laodong yonggong zhidu" (Labor dispatch assaults labor and employment system). *China Labor and Social Security Report,* June 22.

Wu, Xiaogang. 2005. "Registration Status, Labor Migration, and Socioeconomic Attainment in China's Segmented Labor Markets." Population Studies Center Research Report no. 05-579. University of Michigan Institute for Social Research, Ann Arbor, July.

Wu, Yaowu, and Fang Cai. 2006. "Informal Employment in Urban China: Size and Characteristics." *China Labor Economics* 3(1): 67–84.

Xie, Yu, and Emily Hannum. 1996. "Regional Variation in Earnings Inequality in Reform-Era Urban China." *American Journal of Sociology* 101(4): 950–92.

Xu, Jie. 2007. "The Second Draft of the Labor Contract Law: Chang Kai and Dong Baohua Battle Again." *China Economic Weekly,* January 15.

Yu, Min 2007. "lun paiqian laodongzhe yu zhengshigong de daiyu chabie" (On treatment differences of dispatched workers and formal workers). *Journal of China Institute of Industrial Relations* 121(14): 28–31.

Yuan, Victor, and Xin Wong. 1999. "Migrant Construction Teams in Beijing." In *Internal and International Migration: Chinese Perspectives,* edited by Frank N. Pieke and Hein Mallee. Richmond, UK: Curzon Press.

Yusuf, Shahid, Kaoru Nabeshima, and Dwight H. Perkins. 2006. *Under New Ownership: Privatizing China's State-Owned Enterprises.* Washington, D.C.: Stanford University Press and the World Bank.

Zhang, Jianjun. 2008. *Marketization and Democracy in China.* London: Routledge.

Zhang, Li. 2001. *Strangers in the City: Reconfigurations of Space, Power, and Social Networks within China's Floating Population.* Stanford: Stanford University Press.

Zhang, Lu. 2008. "Lean Production and Labor Controls in the Chinese Automobile Industry in an Age of Globalization." *International Labor and Working-Class History* 73(1): 24–44.

——. 2010a. "From Detroit to Shanghai? Globalization, Market Reform, and Labor Politics in the Chinese Automobile Industry." PhD diss., The Johns Hopkins University, Baltimore, MD.

——. 2010b. "Do Spreading Auto Strikes Mean Hope for a Workers' Movement in China?" *Labor Notes Magazine,* no. 376. www.labornotes.org/2010/06/do-spreading-auto-strikes-mean-hope-workers-movement-china.

Zhang, Man. 2007. "Problems, Causes, and Resolutions: Investigation Report on Typical Labor Dispute Cases in Guangdong." http://yxlw.acftu.org/template/6/file.jsp?cid=15&aid=196 (Accessed May 23, 2010).

Zhang, Weijie. 2006. "laowu paiqian, ruhe burang laodongzhe chikui" (How not to disadvantage workers in labor dispatch). *Worker's Daily,* March 15, p.7.

Zhang, Weiying. 2007. "Zhang Weiying: Problems in State-Owned Companies Reform." *Peking University News,* November 18. http://ennews.pku.edu.cn/news.php?s=195376509 (accessed September 6, 2008).

Zhang, Xiaodan. 2005. "Bargaining without Union: Paternalist Labor Relations in China's Reform Era." PhD diss., Columbia University, New York, NY.

Zhang, Zhijin. 2005. "laodong paiqian jigou yingdang quid" (Labor dispatch organizations should be banned). *Economic Information Daily,* August 20.

Zhao, Lei. 2008. "The Busiest Courtroom in China." *Southern Weekend,* December 4.

Zhao, Minghua, and Theo Nichols. 1996. "Management Control of Labour in State-Owned Enterprises: Cases from the Textile Industry." *China Journal* 36: 1–21.

Zheng, Shangyuan. 2008. "budang laowu paiqian jiqi guanzhi" (Wrongful labor dispatch and regulation on it). *Jurists Review* 2: 8–13.

Zheng, Yongnian, and Minjia Chen. 2007. "China's Recent State-Owned Enterprise Reform and Its Social Consequences." China Policy Institute Briefing Series no. 23. China Policy Institute, Nottingham, UK.

Zhu, Zhe. 2007. "Legislation to Focus on Social Issues." *China Daily (online),* 12 March. www.chinadaily.com.cn/china/2007-03/12/content_824812.htm.

Zimmerman, James. 2006. Letter submitted to the Standing Committee of the National People's Congress, Law Committee, Financial and Economic Affairs Committee, Legislative Affairs Commission, The American Chamber of Commerce, People's Republic of China, April 19.

Zou, Patrick X. W., Dongping Fang, and Shou Qing Wang. 2007. "An Overview of the Chinese Construction Market and Construction Management Practice." *Journal of Technology Management in China* 2(2): 163–76.

Zweig, David. 2001. "China's Stalled 'Fifth Wave': Zhu Rongji's Reform Package of 1998–2000." *Asian Survey* 41(2): 231–47.

Notes on Contributors

Fang Cai is professor and director of the Institute of Population and Labor Economics, Chinese Academy of Social Sciences. He completed his Ph.D. at the Graduate School of the Chinese Academy of Social Sciences in 1989. He is an agricultural and labor economist whose research focuses on the Chinese economy. In recent years, he has published a coauthored book on the Chinese economy; an edited book series of China population and labor green books; and papers on population aging, migration and employment, and economic reform in China. Currently he codirects the China Urban Labor Survey. He has consulted for the World Bank on Chinese poverty assessment, the pension reform, and for the United Nations Development Programme on the "Human Development Report" of 2009.

Baohua Dong is a professor of law at East China University of Politics and Law in Shanghai, where he is also the director of the Legal Aid Service Center for Workers. Dong has published widely on the Labor Contract Law, labor and social law, and labor dispute resolution. He is the deputy head of the China Labor Law Study Association.

Mark W. Frazier is the ConocoPhillips Professor of Chinese Politics and director of the School of International and Area Studies at the University of Oklahoma. He received his Ph.D. in political science from the University of California. His recent research examines the politics of labor and social policies in China. He has published articles on pension politics in *Asia Policy, Studies in*

Comparative International Development, and the *China Journal* and has recently completed a book manuscript titled *Socialist Insecurity: Pensions and the Politics of Uneven Development in China.* He is also the author of *The Making of the Chinese Industrial Workplace* (Cambridge University Press, 2002).

MARY E. GALLAGHER is an associate professor of political science at the University of Michigan, where she is also the director of the Center for Chinese Studies; she is also a faculty associate at the Center for Comparative Political Studies at the Institute for Social Research. She received her Ph.D. in politics in 2001 from Princeton University. She has written *Contagious Capitalism: Globalization and the Politics of Labor in China* (Princeton University Press, 2005) and was a Fulbright Research Scholar from 2003 to 2004 at the East China University of Politics and Law in Shanghai, where she worked on her forthcoming book, *The Rule of Law in China: If They Build It, Who Will Come?,* examining the legal mobilization of Chinese workers. She has published articles in *World Politics, Law and Society Review, Studies in Comparative International Development,* and *Asian Survey.*

SAROSH KURUVILLA is currently professor of industrial relations, Asian studies, and public affairs at Cornell University. He obtained his Ph.D. in business administration from the University of Iowa in 1989. His research interests focus broadly on comparative Asian industrial relations and specifically on the linkages among industrial relations policies and practices, national human resource policies and practices, and economic development policies. His recent research is concerned with developing policy approaches to improve national skills development, skills upgrading, and labor policy in China and India. He serves as a consultant to many international agencies and governments and has published many articles on labor and human resource policies.

CHING KWAN LEE is professor of sociology at the University of California, Los Angeles. She received her Ph.D. in sociology from the University of California, Berkeley, in 1994. She is the author of two prize-winning books on Chinese labor, *Gender and the South China Miracle: Two Worlds of Factory Women* (University of California Press, 1998) and *Against the Law: Labor Protests in China's Rustbelt and Sunbelt* (University of California Press, 2007), and of many articles and edited volumes. She is currently working on projects on the politics of rights and changing citizenship regimes in China and on Chinese investment and labor practices in Africa.

KUN-CHIN LIN is a lecturer at King's China Institute, King's College, London. He obtained his Ph.D. in political science from the University of California,

Berkeley, and was a Leverhulme Postdoctoral Fellow in Contemporary Chinese Studies at the University of Oxford. His research focuses on the politics of market reform in developing countries, industrial organization and labor relations, federalism and public goods provision, energy policy and foreign direct investment, and political and regulatory risk analysis. He is an editorial board member of *Business & Politics* and a member of Frost & Sullivan's Board of Economic Advisers.

MINGWEI LIU is an assistant professor of labor studies and employment relations in the School of Management and Labor Relations at Rutgers University. He received his Ph.D. in industrial and labor relations from Cornell University in 2009. His research focuses on Chinese employment relations, trade unions, labor laws, and human resource issues. He has also conducted research on comparative employment relations in Asian countries and high-performance work systems in the health-care sector.

ALBERT PARK is Reader in economics at Oxford University, with a joint appointment at the School of Interdisciplinary Areas Studies at Oxford. He received his Ph.D. in economics from Stanford University in 1996. His current research interests focus on poverty, human capital (health and education), labor markets, and globalization. He currently codirects the Gansu Survey of Children and Families (GSCF), a longitudinal study of rural youth in western China, and the China Health and Retirement Longitudinal Survey (CHARLS).

YUAN SHEN is currently professor of sociology at the School of Humanities and Social Sciences, Tsinghua University, Beijing. His current research focuses on labor movements and nongovernmental organizations in China. In addition, he is the director of the Center for the Study of Contemporary China, Tsinghua University, and an editor of the *Tsinghua Sociology Review.*

SARAH SWIDER is currently an assistant professor at Wayne State University. She received her Ph.D. in sociology from the University of Wisconsin-Madison. Her research interests include labor and labor movements, gender, global inequality and immigration, political sociology, sociology of work, and Asian studies. Most of her work is interdisciplinary and focuses on understanding labor movements and labor markets from a global perspective. This includes an examination of women migrant domestic workers in Hong Kong and, most recently, work on migrant construction workers in China.

LU ZHANG is an assistant professor in the Department of Sociology at Temple University. She received her Ph.D. from Johns Hopkins University in 2010. Her primary research interests include labor and social movements, globalization, and the political economy of development in East Asia, especially China. She has published articles on the evolving state-labor-business relationships, the dynamics of labor unrest, and the development path in reform China. Zhang is currently working on the impacts of the global economic crisis and the labor law reforms (2007–2008) on the state-labor-capital relations in China and on structural change in the Chinese industrial labor force, in particular the characteristics and tendencies of the new generation of migrant workers. She also started a second, book-length project that explores the causes and impacts of capital relocation within China (from coastal to inland regions) and out of China to new low-cost countries (such as Vietnam).

Index

absenteeism, 11, 124, 182, 189
Adidas, 177
agency/dispatch workers, 2–3, 6, 107–8, 113–17, 123–27, 129–34
agricultural employment, 1, 21–22, 142, 152, 190
All-China Federation of Trade Unions (ACFTU), 7, 12–13, 41, 46–47, 50–54, 59–60, 130, 133–34, 157–59, 163, 169–74, 191
American Chamber of Commerce (Am-Cham), 47–48, 50–51, 54
Anhui, 109
apprentice workers, 54, 117, 124
arbitration, 38, 42–43, 57–58, 175–76, 180
Argentina, 6
Asia Foundation, 176
Association of IOBs, 165
"at will" employment, 52
Australia, 6
automobile industry, 11
  agency/dispatch workers, 107–8, 113–17, 123–27, 129–34
  assembly lines, 107, 111, 115, 118, 124
  bargaining power, 118–19, 124, 126
  competition, 11, 107–8, 111, 122, 128
  foreign investment, 110–12
  formal workers, 11, 107–8, 113–19, 123, 131–32
  job security, 109, 114–17, 119–23, 132
  joint ventures (JVs), 109–14, 119, 128, 134
  Labor Contract Law, 108
  labor contracts, 107, 112–16, 120–23, 132
  migrant workers, 126
  pensions, 116, 125
  production, 110–12, 114–16, 118–19, 127–28, 131
  profitability, 110–11, 122, 127–28
  restructuring, 110–13, 122
  state-owned enterprises (SOEs), 107, 109–14, 116, 128, 134
  unions, 109, 113, 126–27
  wages, 108, 111, 113–14, 116, 119–23, 126–27, 132
  workers' resistance, 11, 108, 118–27
  workforce changes, 107, 110–18, 121–22
  See also individual automobile companies

bailouts, 89
banking, 63, 87, 96, 99–102, 150
bankruptcy, 4, 57, 63
Barninghausen, Till, 2
barter, 97–99
Beijing, 66–67, 70, 71, 75–77, 79, 84–85, 88, 99, 109, 145, 174–75
Beijing Area Study (BAS), 66–70, 74, 76
Beijing Center for Workers, 176, 185–86
Beijing Construction Commission, 145
Beijing Municipality, 145
Beijing Neighborhood Committees, 178, 182
Birds of Passage, 152–53
Blecher, Marc, 62

Brazil, 174
brick kiln scandal, 56
buyouts, 113

call centers, 6
canteens, 89
capitalism, 4, 42, 61, 128, 135
casual workers, 2, 5, 11, 174, 186
census data, 18, 20, 22–24, 28–29, 34–35, 138
Chan, Anita, 169
Chang Kai, 46, 49
Chang'an automobile company, 110
Changchun, 67, 71, 73, 78, 109, 118
Change to Win consortium, 51
Chaoyang, 184
Chery automobile company, 110
child labor, 56
China Bar Association, 46
China Labor Bulletin, 158
China Labor Statistical Yearbook, 21, 24
China National Petroleum Corporation (CNPC), 89–90, 99–102
China Statistical Yearbook, 17
China Urban Labor Survey (CULS), 2, 27
Chinese Automotive Manufacturer Association, 122
Chinese Communist Party (CCP), 7–8, 41–42, 45, 51, 54, 59, 63, 79, 129–30, 134–36, 142, 158, 172–73
Chinese Enterprise Directors Association (CEDA), 46
Chinese New Year holiday, 124, 148
Chinese Political Consultative Conference, 51
Chongqing, 175, 178
Chun Feng Labor Dispute Arbitration Counseling and Service Center, 176, 180
Cloward, Richard, 137
collective sector employment, 17–19, 24–27, 29, 39
Communist Youth League, 46
Comprehensive Labor Statistics Reporting System (CLSRS), 18–19, 21–24, 26, 30
construction industry
  agency/dispatch workers, 129
  draft laborers, 142
  embedded employment, 146–48
  employment changes, 139–41, 144–45, 153
  fatalities, 141
  geographical reorganization, 142–43
  growth, 139–40
  individualized employment, 147–48
  mediated employment, 12, 146–53
  migrant workers, 12, 138, 141, 143–46, 148–54, 189
  nationalization strategy, 142
  regulations, 12, 141–42, 144–45
  restructuring, 143–45, 153–54
  rural brigades (RBs), 139, 141
  size, 139–40, 144
  state-owned enterprises (SOEs), 139–41
  temporary workers, 142–46
  urban collectives (UCs), 139, 141
Construction Law of the People's Republic of China, 141
Contract Law of the People's Republic of China, 141
Cooke, Fang Lee, 2
cooperative employment, 18–19, 79, 116
Cultural Center for Workers, 176
Cultural Revolution, 85

Daqing, 86, 104
Deng Xiaoping, 41
DHP, 163–64
Dongcheng, 184–85
Dongguan, 65
double movement paradigm, 11, 61, 78
downsizing, 113, 128
Du Yang, 2

early retirement, 62–63, 65, 113
Earth automobile company, 109, 113–14, 120–21, 124–25, 127
  employer types
  agriculture, 21–22, 142, 152, 190
  collective sector, 17–19, 24–27, 29, 39
  cooperative, 18–19, 79, 116
  foreign, 18–19, 29, 39
  government, 24–25, 29
  joint ownership, 18–19
  limited liability corporations, 17–19
  "other", 17–19, 22, 25
  private enterprise, 17–19, 21–22, 29, 44
  self-employment, 18–22, 25, 27, 29, 32–35, 165–66
  share-holding corporations, 18–19
  state-owned, 17–19, 24–26, 29, 39
  tertiary/service sector, 21, 29–31
  township and village enterprises (TVEs), 21–22, 100, 157
  See also informal employment
employment. *See* labor
employment agencies, 6
Employment Promotion Law, 8, 45
Erickson, Christopher, 84–85
Eurobarometer survey, 68–69
European Union Chamber of Commerce (EU-Cham), 47–48, 50, 56

European Union (EU), 68, 179
European Union Human Rights Committee, 176–77
exports, 38, 57–58, 87, 116, 161, 174

Fang Cai, 27, 95–96, 190
farmers, 66, 72–73, 152, 191
FAW Auto Group, 118
Five-Year Plan, 102
Ford Foundation, 176
Fordist production method, 96, 111, 118
foreign employment, 18–19, 29, 39
foreign-invested enterprises (FIEs), 5, 7, 39, 159–60, 162, 164, 191
Fortune 500 companies, 157
Foshan, 67, 70, 71, 75, 158
Foxconn, 158
France, 6, 68
Friedman, Eli, 5, 8
Fushan, 96

Gallagher, Mary, 190
Geely automobile company, 110
Germany, 109
Getihu Xiehui, 165
Giles, John, 95–96
global financial crisis (2008–2009), 3, 9, 32, 38, 43, 45, 57, 65, 131
Global Labor Strategies, 50
gross domestic product (GDP), 1, 21, 29–31, 139–40
Guangdong, 57–58, 109, 161, 163–164, 191
Guangzhou, 58, 109, 125, 132, 158, 174–75
Guanlan Town Trade Union Federation (GTTUF), 164–66
Guanlan Union Association of POEs and IOBs (GUAPI), 165–67, 171

Hannum, Emily, 96
Hay, Donald, 95
health insurance, 32, 34–35, 66
Heilongjiang, 63, 86
Home for the New Citizens, 178
Honda automobile company, 14, 135, 158, 169, 173
Hong Kong, 1, 32, 51, 158, 176
Horizon Research, 67
hospitals, 89, 99, 101
hotels, 99, 101, 138
hotlines, 175–80
Hu Jintao, 37, 45, 46, 79, 130
Huang Qingnan, 175
hukou system, 22, 116–17, 143, 145, 151, 190
Humen Town Trade Council (HTTUC), 163
Hungary, 169
Hurst, William, 96

imports, 87, 89, 99
Incoming Construction Force Administration Office, 145
individually owned businesses (IOBs), 13, 160, 164–66
Industrial and Commercial Bureau, 18
industrial dummies, 95
informal employment
  age differences, 27–28
  categories, 2
  defined, 2, 20
  education level, 27–28
  employer motivations, 20–21
  gender differences, 3
  Labor Contract Law, effect of, 3, 9, 129, 154, 188–90
  migrant workers, 2–3, 22–29, 138, 144–46, 154
  National Labor Law, effect of, 5–6
  pensions, 21, 34, 64–65
  permanence, 6, 12, 24–29
  phases, 4–7
  private sector, 21–22, 24–26
  sectoral distribution, 3, 23
  urban permanent residents, 24–29
  See also labor
Institute for Contemporary Observation (ICO), 176, 177, 179–80
International Labour Organization (ILO), 20, 176, 179
International Women's Day, 164

Japan, 39, 87, 109, 115, 139, 174
Jiang Ru, 180–81
Jiangsu, 57, 59
Jiangyang, 59
Jilin, 63, 109
joint ownership employment, 18–19
joint ventures (JVs), 4, 29, 96, 107, 109–10, 139
Jupiter automobile company, 109, 114, 119, 121, 125–27, 131–32
just-in-time (JIT) production system, 110, 116, 118–19

Karamay, 104
kidnapping, 56
Korea, 39, 174
Kuruvilla, Sarosh, 84–85

labor
  agency/dispatch workers, 2–3, 6, 107–8, 113–17, 123–27, 129–34

labor *(continued)*
agricultural, 1, 21–22, 142, 152, 190
arbitration, 38, 42–43, 57–58, 175–76, 180
casual workers, 2, 5, 11, 174, 186
contention, 57, 60, 62–64, 104, 118
contracts, 4–6, 20, 26–29, 32–33, 40, 52–55, 65, 102, 107, 112–16, 120–23, 132, 146–49
disputes, 42–43, 57–59, 65, 125, 130, 165, 176
flexibility, 39–40, 44–45, 50, 52–53, 114–15
lifetime employment, 3, 5, 37, 39–40, 61, 63
mediation, 13, 42, 57–58, 166–67, 169–70
military, 142
prison, 142
security, 4, 7, 20, 34, 37, 119–23, 132
slave, 56
statistics, 1–2, 5, 17–29, 43, 188
strikes, 7, 14, 38, 39, 124–25, 162, 179, 191
subcontracted workers, 6, 9, 51, 54–55, 96, 144
temporary workers, 2, 11, 44, 47, 49, 55, 106–8, 113–17, 123–27, 142–46
wage movements, 11, 85–96
workers' protections, 8–9, 30, 32, 55–57, 62
See also informal employment
See also unions
labor bureaus, 32, 42, 44, 46, 109, 116, 133, 142, 168, 183–85
Labor Contract Law
agency/dispatch workers, 129–34
automobile industry, 108
bottom-up mobilization, 38, 59, 130
collective bargaining, 32, 59
contracts, 32, 52–55, 65, 129
drafting process, 36–38, 45–49, 51–53, 132–33
enforcement, 9, 32–33, 48–50, 57–59
foreign business associations, 49–50, 53, 54–56, 60
implementation, 36–38, 48–49, 57–59
informal employment, effect on, 3, 9, 129, 154, 188–90
mediation, 57–58
Northern/Southern School debates, 49–50, 56
pensions, 34, 43, 65
public comment, 36–37, 45–47, 50–51, 53
social insurance programs, 32, 65–66
standards, 36, 40–41, 48–49, 57
state-owned enterprises (SOEs), 51, 55–56
subcontracted workers, 6, 9, 51, 54–55
unions, 46–47, 49–50, 53–54, 59–60, 157, 164, 170
workers' protections, 8–9, 30, 32, 55–57
Labor Dispute Mediation and Arbitration Law, 8, 45
Law on Collective Contracts, 45
Law on Mediation and Arbitration of Labor Disputes, 57–58
layoffs, 5, 21, 26, 44, 52, 55–57, 62, 90, 103, 111, 115, 123, 131
Lee, Ching Kwan, 5, 8
Legal Daily, 176
Lehman Brothers, 57
Lenin, Vladimir, 41
Liaohe, 86
Liaoning, 63, 86
liberalism, 4, 38, 135, 137, 186
lifetime employment, 3, 5, 37, 39–40, 61, 63
limited liability corporations, 17–19
Little Flowers, 175, 178–79, 181–84
Little Flowers People's Mediation Committee, 178
Liu Kaiming, 176, 177, 180
lobbying, 50–51, 56
Lu Zhang, 6
Luwan, 170

Macao, 1
Mao Zedong, 37, 41, 85, 135, 143
Mars automobile company, 109, 114, 121, 124
Marx, Karl, 41
maternity leave, 41, 43
media coverage, 9, 47, 50, 51, 56–58, 130, 178
mediation, 13, 42, 57–58, 166–67, 169–70
medical insurance, 5, 21, 43, 73
Mercury automobile company, 109, 114, 132
Mercury Training Program, 132
Migrant Worker Legal Assistance Station, 175, 178, 183
migrant workers
automobile industry, 126
construction industry, 12, 138, 141, 143–46, 148–54, 189
employment sectors, 23–24
hometown connections, 12, 150–52
informal employment, effect on, 2–3, 22–29, 138, 144–46, 154
labor contracts, 5, 28–29, 32–33, 146–49
mediated employment, 12, 146–53
"missing" workers, 23–24
nongovernmental organizations (NGOs), 13, 175–76, 178, 185
pensions, 2, 10, 64–65, 72–73, 79
population, 1, 19–20, 138, 143
social networks, 149–50
unions, 13, 157, 162
urban migration, 44, 138, 143
military labor, 142
mine workers, 6, 140

Mingwei Liu, 157
minimum wage, 6, 41, 129, 167–68
Ministry of Civil Affairs, 12, 178
Ministry of Construction, 141, 183
Ministry of Human Resources and Social Security (MOHRSS), 45, 134
Ministry of Labor, 42
Ministry of Labor and Social Security (MOLSS), 23, 27–28, 34, 45–46, 49, 52–56
Ministry of Personnel, 51, 55
"missing" workers, 17, 20–21, 23–24, 28, 30–31

Nanjing, 67, 71, 73–75, 77–78, 180
Nanning, 175
National Bureau of Statistics (NBS), 1, 18, 20–21, 24–26, 29, 138
National Labor Law
  contracts, 5, 37, 40, 52–54
  drafting process, 38, 44
  enforcement, 41, 44
  informal employment, 5–6
  labor disputes, 42–43
  labor flexibility, 39–40, 44–45
  layoffs, 44
  lifetime employment, 39–40
  motivations, 39, 43–44
  origins, 37–38
  social insurance programs, 40–41
  standards, 5–6, 40–41
  unions, 41–43
national oil corporations (NOCs), 84, 89–90, 99, 103, 105–6
National People's Congress (NPC), 9, 36, 38–39, 46–47, 51–53, 56, 65–66
natural gas industry. *See* oil industry
NCW, 161–62, 164, 171
Neptune automobile company, 114–15, 123, 127, 131–32
New York Times, 50
Nike, 177, 179
Nokia, 179
noncompete agreements, 48–49
nongovernmental organizations (NGOs)
  collection of unpaid wages, 173, 181–84
  commercialization, 7, 13, 179–81
  cooptation, 7, 13, 177–79
  financial support, 12, 174, 176–77, 179–80
  growth, 173–74, 177
  labor law education, 173, 181, 184–85
  leadership, 12, 174–76
  locations, 174–75
  migrant workers, 13, 175–76, 178, 185
Northern School of labor relations, 49–50

oil industry
  bailouts, 89
  bonuses, 86–87, 95
  core/noncore companies, 11, 84, 87, 89–90, 92–93, 96, 98–99, 101–4
  exchange relations, 97–105
  exports, 87
  extraction, 88, 90, 92
  financial centralities, 84, 96–98, 100, 102, 104
  imports, 87, 89, 99
  labor centralities, 84, 96–98, 100, 102–4
  national oil corporations (NOCs), 84, 89–90, 99, 103, 105–6
  networked organizations, 84, 96–105
  pensions, 86, 92–94
  petroleum administrative bureaus (PABs), 84, 86–87, 89, 98–100, 102–4
  processing, 88, 90, 92
  profitability, 87, 89–90, 102
  refineries, 84–85, 87, 89–90, 96, 99, 103
  restructuring, 11, 84, 87–90, 92–94, 97, 99, 102–4
  wage movements, 11, 85–96, 104–5
one-child policy, 3, 190
Organization for Economic Cooperation and Development (OECD), 40
overtime pay, 41, 59, 119, 124
Oxfam, 176

Panyu, 174, 176, 181
Panyu Secretarial Support Center, 174, 181
Park, Albert, 95–96
Pearl River Delta, 190
peasants, 66, 73, 79, 116–17, 142, 143, 151
Peking University, 176, 186
Peking University Women and Law Research Center, 176
pensions
  automobile industry, 116, 125
  delayed payments, 63–64, 68
  expenditures, 64, 66
  farmers, 73
  geographic location, 35, 63
  inequalities, 74, 79
  informal employment, 21, 34, 64–65
  Labor Contract Law, 34, 43, 65
  legal rights, 70–73
  migrant workers, 2, 10, 64–65, 72–73, 79
  oil industry, 86, 92–94
  payroll contributions, 64
  peasants, 73, 79
  protests, 63–64
  reforms, 65–66

pensions *(continued)*
state confidence, 74–75
state responsibility, 66, 68–72
state-owned enterprises (SOEs), 62–64
trust, 75–77
People's Republic of China (PRC), 38, 57
petitions, 179, 183
PetroChina, 89, 91–94, 99, 101–2
petroleum administrative bureaus (PABs), 84, 86–87, 89, 98–100, 102–4
petroleum/petrochemical industry, 84–86, 89, 100–101. *See also* oil industry
Piore, Michael, 152–53
Piven, Frances, 136–37
Polanyi, Karl, 11, 61, 78
prison labor, 142
privately owned enterprises (POEs), 17–19, 21–22, 25, 44, 71, 157, 159, 160, 162–67
Property Law, 36
Pun Ngai, 176

Qingdao, 109, 175, 177, 178

refineries (oil), 84–85, 87, 89–90, 96, 99, 103
Regulations on Labor Dispatching, 133
Renmin University, 46, 49
Research Center for Contemporary China, 66
residence permits. *See* hukou
retiree employment, 25–26
retirement benefits, 62–64, 67–77, 86
rural brigades (RBs), 139, 141

sabotage, 11, 119, 124, 189
Saturn automobile company, 109, 114, 121
Sauerborn, Rainer, 2
Scott, James, 136
self-employment, 18–22, 25, 27, 29, 32–35, 155–66
Separation of Management from Field Operations, The, 144
severance payments, 32, 40, 52, 59, 87, 93, 113, 162
Shandong, 86, 109
Shanghai, 21, 26, 32, 47, 57, 58, 68–69, 76–77, 96, 109, 125, 170, 191
Shengli, 86
Shenyang, 32–33, 175
Shenzhen, 32–33, 65, 158, 174–75, 180
Shenzhen Worker Health Center, 175
Shilou Town Trade Union Council (STTUC), 162
Sichuan, 175
Sino-foreign joint ventures (SFJVs), 159, 169
Sinopec, 89, 91–94, 100, 102
slave labor, 56
slowdowns, 11, 124, 189
social insurance agencies (SIAs), 64–66
Social Insurance Law (SIL), 45, 65–66
socialism, 4, 40, 43, 62–63, 98, 105
Solinger, Dorothy, 138
South Africa, 6, 174
Southern School of labor relations, 49–50, 56
Soviet Union, 85
spin-offs, 101, 104, 113
Standing Committee (NPC), 38, 56, 65
State Council, 39, 46, 52, 56, 60, 87, 88–89, 100–101, 106
state-owned enterprises (SOEs)
agency/dispatch workers, 129–30
automobile industry, 107, 109–14, 116, 128, 134
construction industry, 139–41
employment changes, 17, 129, 139
Labor Contract Law, 51, 55–56
layoffs, 5, 26, 57
lifetime employment, 3, 5
pensions, 62–64
restructuring, 4–5, 10, 44, 63–64, 83, 128
unions, 159, 169
wage padding, 92
welfare programs, 78
steel industry, 117, 130, 151
strikes, 7, 14, 38, 39, 124–25, 162, 179, 191
subcontracted workers, 6, 9, 51, 54–55, 96, 144
subsidies, 34, 63, 66, 86, 98, 103, 105, 127, 132
Sun Yat Sen University, 176
Supreme Court of China, 58
Supreme People's Court, 57
sweatshops, 36, 50
Swider, Sarah, 142

Taiwan, 1, 51, 161
Tangxia, 58
Tanner, Murray Scot, 38–39, 51
taxation, 8, 20–21, 64, 79, 87, 106, 144
Taylorist production method, 110–11
telecommunications industry, 23, 78, 130
Temporary Regulations on the Labor Contract System, 39, 42
temporary workers, 2, 11, 44, 47, 49, 55, 106–8, 113–17, 123–27, 142–46
Tendering Law of the People's Republic of China, 141
Tentative Provisions for Construction Industry and Capital Investment Administration System Reform, 144

Tong Lihua, 178, 183
township and village enterprises (TVEs), 21–22, 100, 157
Trade Union Law, 41, 54, 59, 162
trade unions. *See* unions

unemployment insurance, 21, 34–35, 43, 104
unions
  All-China Federation of Trade Unions (ACFTU), 7, 12–13, 41, 46–47, 50–54, 59–60, 130, 133–34, 157–59, 163, 169–74, 191
  automobile industry, 109, 113, 126–27
  bargaining power, 13, 161–64, 166–72
  community, 13, 160
  cooptation, 159–60, 163–64
  density, 157–58
  dues, 160, 166
  enterprise, 13, 41–42, 159–60, 162–63, 167–68, 170–72
  grassroot, 7, 11–14, 47, 169, 171–72
  Labor Contract Law, 46–47, 49–50, 53–54, 59–60, 157, 164, 170
  market, 13, 160
  membership statistics, 157, 170
  migrant workers, 13, 157, 162
  National Labor Law, 41–43
  office building, 13, 160
  regional, 7, 13–14, 158–61, 169–72
  regional industry-based bargaining organizing pattern, 159–61, 167–70, 172
  state-owned enterprises (SOEs), 159, 169
  Trade Union Law, 41, 54, 59, 162
  traditional organizing pattern, 159–64, 167, 169
  union association organizing pattern, 159–61, 164–67
United Kingdom, 68
United States, 12, 50–51, 57, 109, 126, 139, 174, 179
Uranus automobile company, 109, 114, 121
urban collectives (UCs), 139, 141
urban permanent residents, 24–29
urban units, 21–22, 24
US-China Business Council, 47, 51

Venus automobile company, 109, 114, 116, 121, 123
Volkswagen automobile company, 118

Walder, Andrew, 104
Wal-Mart, 54, 157, 169
Wang Meiyan, 2
Washington, D.C., 50
water pump industry, 13, 167–69
Weapons of the Weak, 136
welfare, 2, 61–65, 68–70, 79, 93, 104, 160, 163–64
Wen Jiabao, 37, 45, 47, 130, 178
Women's Daily, 176
work stoppages, 38, 142, 162
Workers Rights Consortium, 50
Workers' Services Center, 176
workplace injuries, 4, 21, 41, 43, 62, 174–76
World Bank, 175, 184
World Trade Organization (WTO), 89, 111
Wuhan, 175

Xiao Li, 176–81
Xin Tong, 169

Yang Fei, 176
Yangtze River Delta, 190
Yantai, 109
Yaowu Wu, 27–28
Yu Xie, 96
Yuenli Liu, 2

Zeguo Town Trade Union Council (ZTTUC), 167–68, 171
Zeguo Water Pump Industry Association (ZWPIU), 13, 167–68, 171
Zhejiang, 13, 57, 167
Zhiping Zhang, 2
Zhongshan University Labor Studies and Service Center, 176
Zhu Hang, 176, 178, 185–86